JOE MADDON

We're Gonna Party Like It's 1908

by
Rich Wolfe

DEDICATION

TO:

JOE HUTCHISON IN GLENDALE, ARIZONA,
MIKE PRUYN OF NAPERVILLE
AND GOODYEAR, ARIZONA,
DICKIE WALTERS IN DAVENPORT, IOWA,
JON HOFER IN LAWRENCE, KANSAS,
TIM BROZOVICH OF ROCK ISLAND
AND SCOTTSDALE

AND CUBS FANS JUST LIKE
THEM EVERYWHERE.

YOU DESERVE A WORLD CHAMPIONSHIP!!

ACKNOWLEDGMENTS

This book would not be possible without the help of super people like Dale Ratermann in Carmel, Ind., Dave Reed of Lebanon, Ind., and Wendy Ledger hiding out in the beautiful mountain country of Northern California.

Let's not forget Mike Swanson of the Kansas City Royals, Scott Trible and Stacy Wilkinson of the Montgomery Biscuits and the wonderful people at Lafayette College like Kathleen Parrish, Phil Labella and particularly the talented Geoff Gehman of the Class of 1980 whose wonderful words translated into the Foreword for this book. Leapin' Leopard Paul Reinhard of Sports Talk blog was a great help. Everything about Lafayette was first class.

A special tip of the Hatlo Hat to Paul Tash and the terrific Tim Rozgonyi, the honchos at the Tampa Bay Times and TBO.com and their fabulous writers Michelle Bearden and Ben Montgomery. Also, The Boston Globe and the talented Gordon Edes. Credit to Tim Salmon and Boss Mitch Rogatz at Triumph Publishing. Handsome Jim Manon, the king of Rochelle, Illinois, was terrific. And the closer, MaryKay Hruskocy Scott, came in with a great save at the end.

I'll never forget the help of Cal Ripken, Jr., Bill Ripken and especially Steve Salem at the Ripken Foundation. I'll never forget the incredible hospitality of the dynamic Greg Werner and Rick Mason in Michigan for letting me work unencumbered in their gorgeous vacation home. It was a perfect place to get much accomplished. They were a blast, and it is much appreciated.

We'd better not forget John Hansen and Rex Hudler at the Kansas City Royals' flagship station 610 Sports-KCSP in K.C. Speaking of Hansens, we better mention Eric, the bard of South Bend. Also, the always smilin' Bob Sierk from Clinton, Iowa City and Scottsdale.

But the biggest thank you goes to my Media Partner, the CBS Radio Group Chicago... Their Big Boss is the ole' Dayton Flyer hoopster Tim Pohlman, Megan Jones is their marketing guru and Mitch Rosen calls the shots over at The Score-WSCR where he has built the sports giant of the Midwest.

Thank you all!!

PREFACE

You are about to be swept into the brilliant minds of Joe Maddon fans, awe-struck by their farsighted scheming, stricken dumb by their wonderful stories as they lay bare their sordid love affair with the Chicago Cubs.

My first Cubs book happened quite by accident. On October 14, 2003, I received a call from my largest distributor, the distributor for Sam's Club, Costco and Borders. He said, "We want a Cubs fan book for Christmas." I told him, "Well, I'm not a Cubs fan, I'm a Cardinals fan. My brothers are Cubs fans, many of my friends are Cubs fans, and my younger son is a Cubs fan. You have 14 months before Christmas. You can certainly find somebody to do it."

He said, "No, we want it for *this* Christmas, and we want you to do it with your format because the Cubs are going to the World Series tonight or tomorrow night." I said, "You're in California. You don't know the history of the Cubs very well." When they told me how many copies of the book they were going to order, I said, "You'll have them within a month." Literally, 28 days later, *For Cubs Fans Only* was going down the turnpike. That book sold three times the number of copies of any book in Cubs history.

There, I said it: I'm a **ST. LOUIS CARDINALS*** fan. Cue the apocalypse. You may feel that's a whole bowl of wrong, but authors are accustomed to criticism. Occasionally, some of that criticism even comes from outside our immediate families. As mentioned, three of my older brothers are Cubs fans as

---

*All six games of the 1944 World Series were played at Sportsman's Park in St. Louis. The rival mnagers—Luke Sewell of the Browns and Billy Southworth of the **CARDINALS**—shared a one-bedroom apartment… never expecting that both teams would be in town at the same time.

is my younger son. The former I attribute to some sort of 4-H experiment that went haywire, and the latter to a possible mix-up at the hospital.

Actually, I'm a Cardinals fan for the same reason many other Midwesterners are Cubs fans: Harry Caray. While I was growing up on an Iowa farm, Harry was magnetic when broadcasting games over KMOX in St. Louis. Harry was aces until he had one Busch too many in St. Louis and headed to Chicago to repay that debt to Satan.

While I was signing Cubs books at Nordstrom in Oak Brook several years ago, a yuppie was surveying pictures of other books that I've done. He said rather loudly, "Hey, this author did a book on **HARRY CARAY***. Harry was terrible his last few years." I looked up at him and replied, "Harry Caray could be drunk on his ear while suffering from Alzheimer's and still be more exciting than any announcer on the air today. Plus, he was a great, giving man who loved baseball and baseball fans to his toenails and probably signed more free autographs than anyone in baseball history, if you don't count **STAN MUSIAL**** or Ron Santo." To me, Harry had magic.

Chicago is a pain in the neck...horrible traffic, lousy parking, miserable winters. I love Chicago...because it is the best sports town in America, with the best ballpark in America, with the most beautiful spring and fall seasons in America, but most of all, it simply has the best people of any major city in this country—particularly, the sports fans. The fans

---

*In 1949, **HARRY CARAY**'s first wife Dorothy divorced him. In 1979 Harry wrote her: "Dearest Dorothy, Enclosed is my 360th allimony check. How much longer is this s - - - going to continue?" Dorothy responded: "Dearest Harry, Til death do us part. Love, Dorothy." Harry paid monthly till he passed away in Palm Springs in 1998.

Enos Stanley "Stan" Kroenke, the man who moved the Rams back to Los Angeles, is named after Cardinals greats Enos Slaughter and **STAN MUSIAL.

are knowledgeable, passionate, loyal and most of all, enjoyable. Thus, it was with great anticipation that I set off to do this book...because it means I'll get to see many good friends again in Chicago and slip down to see the Irish play in South Bend.

For some of us, baseball recalls broken glass, broken bats and broken dreams of lingering reflections of a simpler, more innocent time.

For many of us, baseball defined our youth, still overly-impacts our adulthood and is one of the few things that can make you feel young and old at the same time.

And for all of us, it is—most of all—a game of memories: the transistor under the pillow, sitting outside a small store feverishly opening newly purchased baseball cards, our first uniform, learning to keep score, the dew and mosquitoes, the sounds of the radio or our first big league game. Little did many of us know that baseball would be the best math and geography teacher we would ever have...and none of us knew the vibrant green of the field during our first Major League game would be the lushest green, the greenest green and the most memorable green that we would ever see in our entire lifetime.

There is a big problem in doing a book about a person who has one or more characteristics that really stand out. In this case, it's Joe Maddon's intelligence and kindness. Everyone dwelled on that. Since this is a book of tributes from Joe Maddon's friends, obviously there's going to be some repetition. Repetition is usually a problem. For example, in my Mike Ditka book, seven people described a run Ditka made in Pittsburgh the week of JFK's assassination as the greatest run they'd ever seen, yet only one of those made the book. The editor didn't understand that when the reader was through with the book, few would remember the importance, the singularity of that catch and run. However, if most of the seven stories had remained intact, everyone would realize that one play summarized Ditka's persona and his career. So, too, the reputation of

Joe Maddon, except many times greater. It was overwhelming. Many pages were deleted from this book because there were constant similar testimonials. Even so, many remain.

In doing more than four dozen books, I've never encountered as much repetition. It's been close several times, such as in my Jim Harbaugh and Tony Gwynn books. It's a real tribute to Maddon, but a real challenge to the editors.

I write books only on people who seem admirable from a distance. The fear, once you start a project, is the subject will turn out to be a jerk. Not true with Maddon. As you will soon find out, you would want everyone you know to possess the qualities that have made Joe Maddon a success.

Growing up on a farm in Iowa, I avidly read all of the Horatio Alger-style books of John R. Tunis, the Frank Merriwell collection, and Clair Bee's Chip Hilton series, all which preach the values of hard work, perseverance, full obedience, and sportsmanship, where sooner or later, one way or another, some forlorn, underweight underdog will succeed beyond his wildest dreams in the arena of life. Frank Merriwell, thy name is Joe Maddon. Joe Maddon was better than Frank Merriwell. He was real life...harder working than Roy Hobbs...a Rudy with talent. Maddon was manna from heaven for the Tampa Bay Rays and Chicago Cubs fans.

From the age of 10, I've been a serious collector of books, mainly sports book. During that time—for the sake of argument, let's call it 30 years—my favorite book style is the "eavesdropping" type where the subject talks in his own words. In his own words, without the "then he said" or "the air was so thick you could cut it with a butter knife" voice of verbiage that makes it hard to get to the meat of the matter...books like Lawrence Ritter's *The Glory of Their Times: The Story of the Early Days of Baseball Told by the Men Who Played It* or Donald Honig's *Baseball When the Grass Was Real.* Thus I adopted that style when I started compiling the oral histories of the Vin Scullys, Ron Santos and Bobby Knights of the world.

There's a big difference in doing a book on Mike Ditka or Harry Caray and doing one on Joe Maddon. Ditka and Caray were born long before Joe Maddon, thus they had many more years to create their stories and build on their legends. Furthermore, unlike Maddon, they both liked to enjoy liquid fortification against the unknown, which leads to even wilder tales.

I don't even pretend to be an author. This book with its unusual format is designed solely for fans. I don't really care what the publishers, editors, or critics think, but I am very concerned that Maddon fans have an enjoyable read and get their money's worth. Sometimes, the person being interviewed will drift off the subject, but if the feeling is that the reader would enjoy their digression, it stays in the book.

In an effort to include more material, the editor decided to merge some of the paragraphs and omit some of the punctuation, which allows the reader to receive an additional 10,000 words, an equivalent of 25-30 pages. More bang for the buck... more fodder for English teachers...fewer dead trees.

It's also interesting—as you'll find in this book—how some people will view the same happening in completely different terms. Most of this book covers Joe Maddon before he arrived in Chicago...as Cubs fans seem to have been bombarded with everything Maddon since he took over the Cubs.

Joe Maddon is a man in a society where orthodox behavior has stifled creativity, adventure and fun...a society where posturing and positioning one's image in order to maximize income has replaced honesty and bluntness...Joe Maddon is a principled man in a world of rapidly dwindling principles...a difference maker on an indifferent planet...a man the way men used to be in an America that's not the way it used to be...a loyal man to colleagues, teammates, and friends in an age when most people's loyalties are in their wallet...a man who is fighting the good fight and living the good life.

Finally, my Cardinals friends would be extremely upset that I'm doing my fifth Cubs book before writing another edition of a Cardinals book. I'm not going to tell them, so it's entirely up to you: Speak not to a Cardinals fan about what I've done. Not to anyone from St. Louis. Ever.

Thanks. Go now.

–**Rich Wolfe**
Lost Nation, Iowa, and Scottsdale, Ariz.

CHAT ROOMS

FOREWORD

By Geoff Gehman
Lafayette College '80

Joe Maddon '76 is playing the Pied Piper of Thanksmas, a free feast he hosts every December in a community center he helped open in his hometown of Hazleton, Pa. Wearing a red Santa hat and a blue baseball hoodie, the white-haired Chicago Cubs manager shakes hands, hugs, kisses, thumps backs, bumps fists, grins, jokes, offers sports scoops and hip blessings ("Thank you, brother/sister/man") and autographs everything from mitts to aprons for everyone from 9 to 93.

After three hours of constant good-will ambassadorship, Maddon sits down for his first interview with *The Lafayette Magazine.* He reviews a hectic five days of glad tidings in Hazleton while swallowing a fistful of vitamins and signing two armfuls of items, including a brand-spanking-new Joe Maddon bobblehead doll. Every event he emceed—a coaching clinic with a former Major League outfielder, a fireside chat with a retired pro **PITCHER***, a celebrity banquet with a Hall of Fame defensive end—promoted the Hazleton Integration Project (HIP), which he co-founded to unite Anglos and Latinos in a city where municipal officials tried to penalize employers and landlords for supporting illegal immigrants.

HIP is another mission for Maddon, baseball's most missionary, hippest skipper. The child of an Italian mother and a Polish father is renowned for getting the best out of players of many talents, temperaments and nationalities. His formula for success features daring decisions (two suicide-squeeze bunts

---

*Mets **PITCHER** Bartolo Colon is the only former Montreal Expo still in the Major Leagues.

in one inning of a playoff game), bumper-sticker mantras ("Don't ever let the pressure exceed the pleasure") and a relaxation regimen of bizarre entertainers (an animal trainer with a python). The formula has been very successful; he's earned three manager-of-the-year awards for turning underdogs into top dogs.

"We have to get past that mental block, the black/white/brown block, the language divide, the cultural divide," says Maddon, whose ancestors were named Maddonini. "We have to treat everyone with respect. There's no one better, there's no one worse."

Maddon received his first lesson in benevolent tolerance from his late father, who lived and worked a dozen blocks from HIP's community center. Joe, Sr., who co-owned a plumbing business under the family apartment, donated money to all kinds of good causes. "I can still see his desk covered in scraps of paper marked with $10 for this charity and $20 for that charity," says Maddon. "My dad didn't see colors. He had none of that superficial nonsense."

Colorblindness served Maddon well as a catcher and manager in the minor leagues, where he mixed with whites, blacks and Latin Americans. He ran his own culinary United Nations; teammates lined up to eat his crockpot pork roast and sausage simmered in his secret marinara sauce. "Baseball players get tired of fast food," he says. "After games they're so starving, they'll eat anything, even cardboard. Believe me, everybody wanted to be my roommate."

Maddon was coaching the big-league California Angels in 2004 when another loved one gave him another lesson in charity. Jaye Sousoures, then his law-student girlfriend and now his law-teaching second wife, told him he needed to do something substantial with his kinship with all races and ages. He responded by donating his sweaters to homeless people by his favorite beach bicycling paths. Two years later he launched

Thanksmas in Florida, after his first season as manager of the Tampa Bay Rays. "I needed a little bit bigger soap box," he says. "Once I got the soap box, I jumped on it."

Maddon began pointing his charity compass toward Hazleton in 2010, the year he led the Rays to a second American League East championship in three years. In restaurants and bars he heard native Caucasians blaming falling real-estate values and rising crime on a rising tide of Latino newcomers; according to the U.S. Census, the number of Hispanics in Hazleton zoomed from 5 percent to 37 percent between 2000 and 2010. The city became a national civil-rights battleground in 2006 when municipal officials passed an ordinance to fine business owners and landlords who employed and rented to unauthorized immigrants. In 2007, 2010 and 2013 federal courts ruled that the Illegal Immigration Relief Act was unconstitutional, after it had been adopted and adapted by more than 100 states and municipalities.

All this prejudice pained Maddon, who believes he grew up in the best melting pot possible. "We were built on that divide: Poles, Italians, Slovaks," he says. "It was like a subdivision of Europe. We always asked our parents to tell us stories of the old days."

Maddon took his confusion and concern to his cousin, Elaine Maddon Curry, a founder of Concerned Parents of the Hazleton Area, which helps immigrants with reading, citizenship and other services. She and her husband, fellow Hazleton native Bob Curry, took Maddon to an integrated daycare center run by a Latina. Sitting on child-size chairs, they shared wine, bilingual food and the happy din of everyone talking at once, loudly.

The story is picked up by Bob Curry, who as a Hazleton recreation director gave a college-age Maddon a job as a youth sports specialist. "At one point Joe leans toward us and says: 'What's the problem? This is exactly the way we grew up.'"

The Currys and Maddon decided that Hazleton's children deserved a more holistic, healthier childhood. In 2011 they organized HIP, which Jaye Maddon named partly to create such catchy slogans as "Get HIP!" That year the project was boosted by the first Pennsylvania Thanksmas and a sports banquet starring Yogi Berra, the Hall of Fame catcher, fabled philosopher and Maddon's pied-piper pal. In 2013 the Hazleton One Community Center opened in a former Catholic school building. Maddon attended the dedication before driving to Boston to manage a Rays doubleheader against their archrivals, the Red Sox.

Three years later, the center has become an epicenter. Elaine Curry, the program director, estimates that it serves 2,000 people per week, an impressive number in a city with a population of roughly 25,000. Subjects range from karate to yoga to Rosetta Stone language systems. Nearly 100 after-school scholars participate in weekly Skype lessons with college education majors. Summer campers study debating, fly fishing and building bridges with tooth-picked marshmallows.

HIP president Bob Curry, a former bookstore owner, calls the center "a Petri dish" for intellectual, social and emotional growth. The dish teemed with healthy cultures during the 2015 Thanksmas, which took place in the center's basement. A pretty much 50-50 Hispanic-Anglo crowd chowed down on Latin-spiced chicken, pierogies and meatballs marinated in Maddon's sauce. Pretty much every decade of age was represented. The oldest visitor was coaxed to come to help relieve his grief at the death of his 93-year-old twin.

Verina Gad, a middle schooler of Egyptian heritage, discussed the family benefits of taking a photography course. She convinced her mother of the artistic value of a picture of ferns in and out of focus. Daniela Castillo, a college volunteer, discussed the extended-family values of coaching basketball. "Something as simple as a sport can break the language barrier and bring people together," says the journalism major. "If you keep trying, kids will open up to you—more than you could ever have imagined."

The center's success can be measured by outsiders elevated to insiders. Eugenio Sosa, its first executive director, is a real-estate agent raised in the Dominican Republic and the Bronx. On his watch the center became a home for Police Athletic League games and an oral-history documentary of Hispanic immigrants in Hazleton. One of his favorite success stories involves a once-skeptical neighbor who now reminds the center's leaders to close the building's windows.

A newer non-native leader is Daniel Gutierrez, a Michigan native who last year began teaching criminal justice at Penn State Hazleton. Working with professors of sociology and social work, he's developing a center-based program to reduce the alarmingly high rate of arrests of Hispanic juveniles in Hazleton, which rose from 38 percent in 2011 to 78 percent in 2015. Finding better treatments than suspension and prison suits Gutierrez, a former migrant worker who ran a maximum-security detention center for youngsters.

The center's ambitious, adventurous spirit ruled HIP's fifth annual celebrity sports banquet, held two days earlier in a hotel ballroom. Autograph seekers circled Manny Ramirez, hired by Maddon as a Cubs hitting coach after a career as one of baseball's most feared, revered right-handed batters. Selfie snappers surrounded Ed "Too Tall" Jones, a 6-foot-9 Hall of Fame defensive end for the Dallas Cowboys. He told the 600-odd spectators that he wants to establish a HIP-like program in his native Tennessee, where childhood obesity is an epidemic.

The most moving speech was made by the most surprising star. Billy Bean, an outfielder managed in the minors by Maddon, was one of the first retired pro baseball players to announce that he was gay. His LGBT activism persuaded Major League Baseball officials to hire him as the organization's first ambassador for inclusion. He received his first lesson in inclusion at age 5, when the mother of his Latino best friend taught him Spanish.

Maddon was his usual zesty Zen self. He greeted scores of guests in a red- and blue-striped jacket over a Cubs T-shirt with his mantra "Do Simple Better." He saluted a table of old Hazleton baseball buddies and a table of Lafayette people that included Kevin Canavan '76, a Zeta Psi brother who joined Maddon at high school football games in Hazleton. HIP's "beautiful" youngsters, said Maddon, "speak better English than most everybody in this room." The key to the integration project's success, he insisted, is "the music, the magic" of constructive criticism.

Maddon vows to take HIP's mission on the road—to charity events in Chicago, postgame press conferences, even the Twitter account of his English bulldog, Winston Churchill. He expects that Hazleton natives will scold him for being an absentee missionary. "I know people criticize me because I'm not here all the time, so I have to speak up without going over the top," he says. "Criticism doesn't bother me. I'm used to it because of the job I'm in; as a manager, I get hammered from every angle. My point is: Hey, there's a lot of thin skin in this world, folks. It's not as thick as it used to be."

Albina "Beanie" Maddon was asked if her famous son ever loses his famous cool. "He takes after his father. He doesn't have a mean bone in his body," she says, sitting by the Thanksmas dessert counter in an apron with a Cubs logo. "He has a very positive, low-key attitude. He never gets riled up; the moment is never too big."

Ah, says an interviewer, but what about Joe's very disagreeable disagreements with umpires? Ah, says Beanie without missing a beat, "He's always right. He won't argue if he's wrong."

JOE MADDON FROM A TO Z

A biographical alphabet for an influential baseball manager,
quotable humorist, amateur chef and style hipster.

A   Maddon worked from 1975 to 2005 for the California **Angels**. A five-tool employee, he was a catcher, hitting
instructor, coach, manager, and cook. Teammates lined up
to be his roommate to get access to his crockpot pork roast.

B   Maddon's mother, Albina **"Beanie"** Maddon, has worked
in the family-owned Third Base Luncheonette in Hazleton
since 1948.

C   Maddon's **cutting-edge** hair styles have ranged from
Biker Guy to Surfer Dude to Zen Rock 'n' Roller. When he
managed the Tampa Bay Rays, he and his players wore
Rayhawks.

D   **"Do** Simple Better" is one of Maddon's many motivational
slogans, suitable for T-shirts, bumper stickers, sound bites,
and #hashtags.

E   Ava, a Tampa **eatery** co-owned by Maddon, offers his cock-
tail "Holy (Bleep) Batman," which is what you're supposed
to rave after one sip of the citrus-splashed cherry-bourbon
concoction.

F   Before every game, Maddon honors his late **father** by
imagining Joe, Sr. sitting in the stands.

G   Maddon credits Norm Gigon, his baseball coach at Lafayette, for helping him develop his professional skills. In
1967, **Gigon** appeared in 34 games in the infield and outfield for the Cubs.

H   In 2010, Maddon helped persuade MLB officials to rescind
an order that players and coaches wear only official pull-
overs, insisting that the **hoodie** was his cold-weather
security blanket.

I   Maddon helped organize the Hazleton **Integration** Project (HIP) in 2011 to unite Anglos and Latinos in his hometown of Hazleton.

J   HIP was named by **Jaye** Sousoures, Maddon's wife, who shares his fondness for dogs, fitness, vintage muscle cars and baseball. She played second base as a Bobby Soxer. He proposed to her at 1:30 a.m. in the parking lot of a Colorado liquor store.

K   Maddon's many acts of **kindness** include donating his sweaters to homeless beach people, shaving his head to raise money for pediatric cancer research, and launching a free holiday feast in Tampa, Chicago and Hazleton called Thanksmas.

L   "He pretty much taught me to put a sentence together," says Maddon of Sheldon **Liebman**, his freshman English professor at Lafayette. "He did a lot for my communication skills. He didn't have to put the time in, but he did." Liebman now chairs the humanities department at Wilbur Wright College in Chicago, only seven miles from Wrigley Field.

M   Maddon once hired a **magician** to loosen up Cubs players during a five-game losing streak. The trick worked: The team won the same day that illusionist Simon Winthrop turned a crushed, empty soda can into an uncrushed, sealed can full of liquid.

N   Maddon has never forgotten the 1985 pain of abandoning his favorite uniform **number**, 20, when Hall of Fame pitcher Don Sutton joined the California Angels.

O   Thinking **outside** of the box is a Maddon specialty. He's ordered two suicide-squeeze bunts in the same inning of a playoff game, canceled batting practice so players could enjoy time off, and turned the locker room into a zoo by hiring an animal trainer with a penguin and a python.

P   In 1973, Maddon told Neil **Putnam**, his Lafayette football coach, that he was giving up the gridiron to focus on baseball. It wasn't until 2014, after Lafayette's 150th football game with Lehigh, that Maddon finally explained his decision to quit quarterbacking. "I was tired of the practice, tired of the playbook, tired of the discipline. I was 19 and on my own. It was nice to spread my wings a bit and just fly. It took 40 years, but I finally got to tell Neil: 'Heck, man, that was on me, that was not on you; you did absolutely zero wrong.'"

Q   Maddon is renowned for inspiring players with **quotes** from Shakespeare to Dr. Seuss to Sugar Ray Leonard. When his team wins two games in a three-game series, he reminds players and sportswriters of the **MEAT LOAF*** song "*Two Out of Three Ain't Bad.*" He's even coined the phrase, "Meatloafing."

R   A foundation founded by Cal **Ripken**, Jr., the Hall of Fame infielder, donated $150,000 toward a new gym in HIP's Hazleton One Community Center.

S   Pete Ciccarelli, one of Maddon's minor league general managers, told *The Tampa Tribune* that Maddon's marinara **sauce** would make even an old catcher's mitt "the best meal on the block." Maddon's recipe is so secret he even refuses to share the ingredients with his mother.

T   @winstoncmaddon is the **Twitter** handle for Winston Churchill Maddon, Joe and Jaye's English bulldog, who contributes wit and wisdom about two- and four-legged creatures with a strangely Jamaican accent, mon.

---

*Phil Rizzuto is the only baseball person to earn a gold record. His radio broadcast was in the background of **MEAT LOAF**'s "*Paradise by the Dashboard Light.*" Rizzuto was the first ever Mystery Guest on *What's My Line?* in 1950.

U The **ubiquitous** coach Joe Serra recruited Maddon for the Lafayette team by taking his family to dinner, buying ice cream for his mother, and hanging out at Maddon's locker, telling the high schooler that he could be Lafayette's best quarterback, ever.

V Maddon endorsed One A Day **vitamins** for over-50 men.

W A **World** Series ring went to Maddon, 2002 bench coach of the California Angels. In 2008, he managed the Tampa Bay Rays to the Series, becoming only the fourth Fall Classic skipper who never played a Major League game.

X Maddon has won three manager of the year awards for his **X** factor of intelligence, patience, tolerance and common sense.

Y The late **YOGI BERRA***, the Hall of Fame catcher, linguist, and philosopher, was Maddon's treasured friend.

Z The late Don **Zimmer**, Berra's longtime rival/friend and Maddon's special adviser on the Rays, introduced Maddon to Berra. Maddon honored both his mentors as stars of HIP's first celebrity sports banquet.

*A young Martha Stewart was the Berra family babysitter when **YOGI** played for the Yankees.

PROLOGUE

Perhaps the best way to set the table for this book and to understand Joe Maddon is to listen to him in two diverse situations.

The first part is Maddon speaking with fans of the Montgomery Biscuits when he was still managing the Tampa Bay Rays. The Biscuits are the Double-A affiliate of the Rays in the Southern League.

The second part is Maddon talking with Rex "Wonder Dog" Hudler in Kansas City as he was getting ready to embark on spring training before the Cubs' historic 2016 season.

Here he is answering questions for baseball fans in Alabama:

"The question I get a lot is are you missing anything, is there anything you'd like to have that you don't have and, honestly, the answer is no. (General Manager) Andrew (Friedman) and all of the scouts that put this together in the winter time—that's when this all happens—Andrew and I are on the phone a lot and truly they put together a really significant team. It's really a complete ballclub. Beyond that, they are really good guys. If you were to work with us on a daily basis, we have a really good time. We laugh a lot and play hard and are very talented. Going into this season, I guess I have no excuses as a manager. I can't point to a deficiency because our guys, as a group, are doing a wonderful job.

"It's fine that we're in the same division as the Yankees and Red Sox. Their payrolls are higher than ours. That's always been the issue and it's never bothered me in the least. I've always felt that since 2006, when I got here, at that time Major League Baseball was really doing a good job of eradicating PEDs within Major League Baseball. It got to the point where there was less and less of that in the game. Without that, I don't think it matters how much money you spend. The fact that the playing field has been leveled, it's not about money, it's about who plays the game better on a specific night. If you look back at what I've said since 2006, I don't think one time have I lamented the fact that we didn't spend a lot of money. It's all about playing the game better than the other team. We have, we believe, good players and now it's up to us to be better.

"I'm with such a great group, there's a two-way street here. It starts at the top with (Owner) Stu (Stuart Sternberg) and all the ownership people and Andrew Friedman. We feel like we are family. Sometimes, it's an over-used phrase. Sometimes it's not necessarily true. The reason that it is that way is because we trust each other. If you don't have trust in the organization, you really can't thrive and survive. I don't care how much money you throw at it. It's survived and we've done so well because at the top it's so good and beyond that we trust one another and with that, there's a really open exchange of ideas. When you have a relationship built where you trust one another, you can actually be constructively critical of one another and good things happen. That pretty much sums up what is going on with us.

"Every team goes through losing streaks. I see all this crazy stuff when you lose several games in a row and that's when they need your support more than at any time. It's not about guys not caring or not trying. It's just not going well. For me, whenever it goes badly, the one thing I tell myself is, when you walk in the door today to truly be consistent. The players are doing everything they can so for me to come in and send out the wrong vibe, that just makes it worse. I've always been baffled because I played for that guy, the one that gets angry when you lose a couple of games. It has nothing to do with being angry. You've got 162 games. You're having a hard time right now. You need my support. You don't need my anger. I'm not a big guy for team meetings, I don't believe in them. Baseball is not an emotional game. We have to get your brain working.

Baseball, you have to have your wits about you when you go out there so you have to be not emotional. So, all this stuff matters. Honestly, the one thing I do, when we win, is to have the best postgame celebration on a nightly basis. And then on the other hand, I want us to lose hard for 30 minutes then leave it, don't drive home with it. If you're with me, I drive over the Gandy Bridge. I'll take that "rock" and throw it out the window into the water because I don't need to carry that "rock" home. For the coaches sitting here right now, you don't have to be angry when your team loses. They need your support more than they need your anger.

"My dad is the biggest mentor in my life. I really derived patience from my father. My father was a plumber. I'm from the northeastern part of Pennsylvania, and I promise you, I've been to Birmingham and Montgomery and when the plane lands, it's really reminiscent, topography-wise, to northeastern Pennsylvania. I feel that same vibe. My dad was actually my first mentor. Decent man, hard-working man, never missed a day of work plumber. In the baseball sense, you've never heard of this gentleman, but his name is Bob Clear. Bob Clear was a minor league coach and manager for the Angels and a bullpen coach for the Angels for many years. I thought I knew a lot, but once I met this guy I probably made my knowledge of baseball triple. Bob Clear, nobody's ever heard about except for some people who have been in the game, was probably my main mentor in the game of baseball.

"I always believed I would get a shot in the big leagues. Unfortunately, I never got there as a player and that was my first goal, obviously. I'm playing my first year of pro ball, (actually my) second year in Salinas, Calif. Wade Christopher, an old scout who's no longer with us...I'm 22-, 23-years-old and already the scouts are telling me I need to stop playing and start managing. So even back then, I knew this was something I wanted to do. I felt I needed to get to the Major Leagues as a coach. It's the same game, 60 feet, six inches. What really separates good players from not so good players is how they defend. I'm really big on trying to promote the mental component of the game. As a teacher, it's very easy to teach the physical mechanics in any sport, I believe. The more difficult thing to do is to teach the mental toughness and that requires redundancy. As a manager and coach, as you're teaching the physical fundamentals of the game, what you must do to young people is teach them the mental components. Teach them how to play the game. Guys who know how to play the game, eventually they're going to deal with failure, and it's overcoming failure that makes you great.

"This is my favorite hoodie. It has 'Rays' on it and I get to wear it, being part of the organization. We were playing up in Boston and I get this thing from the commissioner, no more hoodies, and I enlisted help from coach (Bill) Belichick with the (New England) Patriots. I don't know why, but from back in the day I've always liked hoodies. It's comfortable, it's warm. So primarily, anything that has 'Rays' on it but I do have a Lafayette College hoodie. I went to Lafayette College in eastern Pennsylvania and that's really near and dear to my heart, also.

"I was really upset when the commissioner said we couldn't wear hoodies. I thought they were taking it away for all the wrong reasons. This is very comfortable. There's so much inappropriate clothing. All these people that really have no sense of fashion whatsoever are telling me how to dress. And this goes back to my days as a player. We don't have a dress code with the Rays. I'm anti-dress code. Here's my dress code: if you believe you look fine, then wear it. If I have to force a guy to dress a certain way to get his discipline, I don't really want that guy. I can understand it in a parochial school setting or private school, where it comes down to the jealousy factor between kids where some people can afford an outfit. I'm totally into the concept of uniforms. I don't want my airplane pilot in jeans and a T-shirt. I want my pilot to look like a pilot. But in a baseball sense, we go from the clubhouse to the bus to the tarmac to the plane to the bus, nobody gets to see you. So I don't want the shortstop trying to impress the catcher with how he dresses. It means nothing to me. It has nothing to do with anything so I don't worry about that kind of stuff. I want them to be comfortable in their own skin. There's a lot of freedom here because I feel like the more freedom we give our players, the greater discipline and respect you get in return. I believe in that concept. I challenge any company that works in this area, anybody that is a boss that's listening to me right now, the more freedom you give your employees the greater respect and discipline you're going to get in return. You're not able to do that with non-accountable people like fifth graders who can't do that. But in a professional setting, I believe that works, and that's how we do things.

"Who's the funniest person on the Rays? Chico, our video coordinator. Chico Fernandez, our camp concierge. Among the staff in general, it's Chico. Chico is the entertainment during spring training. Then once we're done with it, I won't talk to him the rest of the year. I use him entirely for entertainment. When the season begins, I don't want to see him, I don't want to talk to him. He knows that. Chico is definitely the funniest guy. Beyond that, Coach George Hendrick makes me laugh. Coach Tom Foley is pretty funny, too. Among the players, David Price is outstanding. David Price, every team wants him in their clubhouse. David is pretty wide open.

"I don't get frustrated easily. On certain days, please don't take this the wrong way, I don't mind the media whatsoever, I really enjoy the exchange, but there are certain days you just would rather not have to talk to anybody. When it comes to the regular give and take of the day, there's nothing I really don't like. I do enjoy the exchange with the media. I do enjoy the pregame. I love the game. I enjoy the postgame. Honestly, I can't sit here and tell you there's anything that's frustrating. Our travel is spectacular. The hotels we stay at are great. The fans are wonderful. Listen, if you get in this position and you're upset or angry or frustrated, then God bless you. You've wanted to do this since you were 6-years-old. And for me to poke holes in it or be upset with things would really be inappropriate.

"Understand one thing if you're a young player wanting to be a professional athlete. If you think you're working hard, you need to work harder. I've never met you, I don't know you, but understand one thing, you've got to work even harder and understand sacrifice is a big word. There are some things you have to give up to be able to get to that level. What I'm talking about is the work. You've not begun, necessarily, to take care of yourself and your body. I'm here to tell you man, for the people that are over 40—which I actually am, I know I don't appear to be, but I'm actually over 40 (60 actually)—you need to take care of your mind. The less you are abusive to your body, the better your brain works. That's regarding school. And for all you kids that want to play pro ball, make sure you go to class. You want to get to a good college, junior college or college, you want to be seen and that's how you become a Major League Baseball player. So if you think you're working hard, it's got to increase. If you never make sacrifices, start understanding you need to do that now. Start eating properly, a good diet, and also be very cognizant of your mind because your mind is what is going to control your success.

"The Rays' getting great starting pitching is really about excellent scouting, No. 1, and the developmental program because they come through the minors when we get them. I'm here to tell you, we have the best training staff in all of Major League Baseball. There's no question in my mind. And these are the guys who don't get enough credit. I've never been around a bunch of veteran people that are so hands on with their players, so I think a lot of the development of our pitchers is attributable to how wonderful our team fits. The lifeblood of the organization are the scouts. I was a scout and understand that concept. We have good scouts who make good decisions. Then, of course, you get better people and once you get them you have to develop them right. Medically, I'm here to tell you, that's really important and our guys are the best.

"The most valuable asset of playing in a minor league park is I hope we remember. This serves as a reminder of where we came from. It took me a long time to get to the big leagues, a real long time. I've always talked to my kids about the struggle. It's always about the struggle and to the people who don't enjoy the struggle, you're missing out. If you gloss over that and don't understand what's going on, you're really missing the point. We normally forget the most difficult moments and enjoy the most popular, better moments. If you stop and take notice of what you're going through, eventually that's how you become successful by the life's lessons that you've learned. From our players' perspective, give back to Montgomery. Give back to your roots. Never forget. We have nothing to complain about. We're very lucky. I feel very fortunate to have the job I have, where I have it, and I hope our players feel the same way. But it never hurts to be reminded of where you come from."

THE WONDER DOG AND THE WONDER MANAGER, REX HUDLER AND JOE MADDON:

"My Mom is great. I was back in Hazleton over the Christmas holidays working on an integration project, trying to bring together the Hispanic and Anglo cultures in my hometown. My Mom gets her hands dirty by helping with all the different events. She still cooks, cleans and helps serve food. She's 83 and still works at my cousin's restaurant, Third Base Luncheonette. She flips burgers in the back. Today's what, Tuesday? She gets a day off tomorrow. She's doing great.

"I was on a 35-year program at Lafayette and eventually got my degree in 2010.

"I spent a lot of time traveling in buses and riding all over. I've always thought that I never wanted something before it was my time. I never wanted to be that prodigy who was given something before he was prepared for it. I really feel fortunate that I had the opportunities to spend that many years in the minor leagues to really refine my craft and try different things at different outposts where nobody could really see. It was pre-social media so I could make mistakes and actually survive them. I was a manager, a scout, a roving instructor, coordinator, all that stuff. I'll tell you the thing that really stands out to me for anyone who wants to coach or manage is to start out as a scout. That's probably the most invaluable experience that I've had. To be able to look at a player before he becomes prominent, I thought that was really important. Beyond that, as a rover, I went to a lot of different cities and watched different managers. I learned how they do things, both good and bad, from guys that I liked and didn't particularly like. I had this vast experience and I'm really, really appreciative of that. I don't understand how guys get to be Major League managers and not have that breadth of experience. I know I could not have done it. I don't begrudge them. I'm just so grateful that I had so many years to prepare for this, because I couldn't just jump into that seat without that kind of experience.

"My first win as a Major League manager was with the Angels in 1996 when Johnny McNamara got ill. He got phlebitis in his leg. We were in New York and I walk into the clubhouse. Billy Bavasi looked at me and said he wanted to talk. He said, 'Johnny Mac can't go. He's in the hospital. We want you to do this.' I kind of gulped. To do your first game in Yankee Stadium is something. We won, 7-1. Derek Jeter hit a home run in the first inning for the Yankees and that's all they got. Afterwards, Billy's brother, Peter, met me in the manager's office with a shot of Jack Daniel's before I talked to the press. That was an outstanding moment.

"All the managers I worked under had their strengths. Gene Mauch was the guy who I really started paying attention to when I was in the minor leagues. Gene was the Angels manager. He'd come over for the Instructional League games. I was the grunt and caught all the pitchers who wanted to throw. Gene would always come over and talk with me. I always felt that if he said something, it had to be accurate and true. Among all the people I've ever run into, Whitey Herzog has that same mystique, but the first guy was Gene. I'd talk with Gene and listen to him intently, so when it came down to understanding baseball and running a game, I thought Gene was number one. I spent very little time with Whitey, but I was so impressed with him and his mind. He was a great scout and had a great understanding of the game. Another influence was Don Zimmer, who just passed away. Working with him in Tampa Bay was spectacular. It was great to have that resource on a daily basis. We really developed a tight relationship. I was very fortunate I had a chance to work with all those guys.

"I remember my first day getting to the big leagues. I remember hitting fungos in the outfield and I remember how I was talking it up. That's just how we did things. That was a veteran team, and I played with some of those guys. I knew there was a kind of concern about the way I was. I was a little bit different. I knew all that, but I could never let that bother me, because this is who I am. If it's not going to work this way, then it's not going to work. I used to go to some of the big league games in the '80s and throw B.P. and work on some things with some players. I remember walking into the clubhouse and seeing the day's schedule written on a napkin and thumbtacked to a corkboard. I thought, you gotta be kidding me. As time went along, I got involved in word processors, and I got a Toshiba 380 computer that weighed 25 pounds that I carried around. I thought it was a better way to organize my thoughts and my notes. And I thought it was more professional. I also knew that guys said to me that a computer never won a game. I wasn't saying that, but I'll tell you this, it really helps me organize my work. What does it mean to be organized? It means you know exactly what you're thinking. If I organize my thoughts in advance, when I present it to you as a teacher, I'll have a much better idea of what I want to say. We used to put together stat sheets and charts. That was all before it was broken down like it is today. I used to put that on a sheet in the dugout, reverse splits, guys' batting averages against righties and lefties, the same with the bullpen. Prior to all the stuff you see now, we were doing it in the mid-'90s.

"When I started in the Instructional League in the mid-'80s, I had a Word of the Day for the players. I was trying to increase our players' vocabularies. I'd have a word each day in September and October, then have a test at the end of the Instructional League. Whoever won the vocabulary test won the fine money that we had collected. When I got to the big leagues, I went from a Word of the Day to a Quote of the Day. I'm really into that. Back in the '80s, I started with Stephen Covey and *The 7 Habits of Highly Effective People*. It was a time in my life when I thought I had to be more analytical. I thought I needed to read more, so I started reading a lot of self-help books, i.e. Stephen Covey, Coach John Wooden, Zig Ziglar, Napoleon Hill, Dale Carnegie. I read all that and there were a lot of good quotes, one-liners, so that motivated me to do a Quote of the Day.

"When I was coaching first base, I created Respect 90. Every baseball player should run hard to first base. That benefits their entire game. It doesn't take any talent whatsoever to hustle. If you're a 4.3 runner to first base and you hit four ground balls to the shortstop, I'm basically asking for 17 or 18 seconds out of your day at full gorilla. That's all I'm looking for. It creates a sense of competition. I would post the top three times for each game. It all began in the Instructional League at Gene Autry Park. I could make mistakes. I could do what I wanted and eventually made it to the Major Leagues. Nothing's changed. What you're seeing right now with the Cubs, and what you saw with the Rays, and what you saw with the Angels, really was born in the mid-'80s. A lot of it had to do with Angels manager Marcel Lachemann, Billy Bavasi, Bob Clear and lots of others. But Bob-a-loo, Bob Clear, was my mentor. He was the best baseball coach you've never heard of.

"I haven't thought about a Victory Parade with the Cubs. I'm so focused on my job on a daily basis and if I do that, then good things will eventually happen. When that does occur, my biggest thing is to look at the other guys. In 2015, when we won that Wild Card Game in Pittsburgh, my first thought was to look down the bench and look at my coaching staff. I realized that win helped them and benefitted their families. We went on and played the Cardinals. We beat the Cardinals, and I looked down the dugout at the players, of course, but also at our coaches and support group and how that win benefitted their families. If we do win, I'll probably look at the entire organization as a whole and at the fans, which are spectacular, and realize what it means to them. That's what winning it all will mean the most to me. Having waited so long, a lot of the fans hadn't even seen the Cubs win a playoff game, which we did last year. If we get to that point, believe me, it's not about me, it's about everybody else. And that's the way I approach it.

"It really doesn't matter if the media picks us to win or not. What matters is what we think. That's the message I brought to our players in spring training. My job right now is to help us manage expectations. The relentless execution of the process is what will help us manage the pressure of the expectations. I want to use those words as positives. The things that are out of your control, there's nothing you can do about it. Don't attempt to control the uncontrollable. Let it go. Just focus on what you want to do. I want us to be on our own little planet and rotate around our goals. I'll say thank you to the media, that's really nice and we appreciate it, but at the end of the day, it doesn't really mean anything. That's the entertainment component. I'm all for that, but at the end of the day, what the Cubs think and how we go about our day is what's important. Every day I walk into Wrigley, that's how I think, so all this other stuff doesn't bother me a whole lot.

"I'm working on my speech to the team on the first day of spring training on my new iPad Pro. I ride my bike a lot, so if I come up with a thought while I'm on my bike in the off-season, I'll jot it down. I send myself texts. I accumulate all these different thoughts and through conversations with coaches and players, it starts to conjure up and I start to know what I want to say. I'll have a couple of bullet points to expand upon. The relentless execution of the process—that's how you control the pressure and the expectations. I'll talk about that. Then I'll talk a little about our rules and regulations. You know my dress code? It's if you think you look hot, wear it. That's simply put and that's what I go with. Be on time. I don't believe in being the first one there and the last one to leave. I don't believe in that stuff. I want to make sure the guys who have not been around me understand that. The message needs to be concise. It needs to be pertinent. And not too long or the players will turn me off.

"I'm in a reading slump right now and am really upset with myself. When I sit down and think of all the different books I've read, it's incredible. The Ken Follett trilogy is the last one I've really gotten into, *Fall of the Giants, Edge of Eternity, Winter of the World*. My favorite author, Pat Conroy, was recently diagnosed with pancreatic cancer. That bums us all out. Pat Conroy is my favorite American author, maybe my favorite of all-time. Ken Follett, Tom Clancy. I love Ken Follett. I could go on and on. I've read all these dudes. It's the way to do it, man. That's a way to use your imagination and helps you become more analytical. To read is calisthenics for your brain. If you're willing to sit down and get absorbed in a good book and let your imagination take off, it's the best way you can spend any downtime. I try to get my guys to do that, too.

"I never was a Major League Baseball player. I thought I needed to spend a lot of time as a Major League coach, not necessarily to understand the game. There is so much difference between the minor leagues and big leagues. The nuances and all the little components of the game, it's totally night and day. I found that out, but the biggest thing was to find out how a Major League clubhouse works, how to deal with the media, the travel, and just talking to a Major League player. I talked with Tony Phillips as much as anybody. Tony was not easy. He could be all over the map. But as a friend, we got real close. I'm proud to say that I worked with Anthony Phillips. That guy taught me as much about being a Major League coach as anybody.

"David Ross to me is the best chemistry guy in all of baseball. We were so lucky to get him. He does make a difference, primarily by catching Jon Lester. He might grab another start now and then. Sometimes that term 'leader in the clubhouse' can be overrated, but it's not with David. You have to be cognizant that a guy like that might be what you need to get over the top. In 2008 with the Rays, we went to the World Series, and a lot of that had to do with Troy Percival, Cliff Floyd, Eric Hinske and Danny Wheeler. Those four guys were so influential. They played at a very high level, but what they did to that clubhouse with a bunch of young players was invaluable. Sabermetricians of the world don't believe in that kind of stuff because they can't evaluate what a heart means and what a brain means to the substance of the other 24 guys in the clubhouse. I'm totally into that and believe in that. And David Ross is one of the best in the business for that.

"Some of what sabermetricians do can be very helpful. In the off-season the numbers are helpful in determining acquisitions along with your organizational philosophy. That's when these numbers are really helpful. In season, the numbers for me can be very helpful. The match-ups and bullpen usage can be helpful, but if you've got the bells and whistles, don't worry about the numbers and utilize your talents. I will use the numbers in a match-up situation. If you have a lesser bullpen, you've got to do different things. If you have a match-up oriented line-up instead of having seven or eight regular players that are going to play regardless, then the numbers become more pertinent. It depends on your situation and what you've got going on. I'm big into the numbers. I keep them on a card in my back pocket. It's dripping with analytics. But at the end of the day, it's about people and players that make a difference. So when it comes down to these annual projections on wins, I always consider that kind of funny. We should have a high projection because we have a good team."

Chapter 1

HOME SWEET HOME HAZLETON:

THE BOAST OF THE TOWN

YOU CAN GO HOME AGAIN

SARAH LAUCH

Sarah Lauch is the executive producer of original content at Comcast SportsNet Chicago. She grew up an avid Phillies fan in the Philadelphia suburb of Manheim, Pa., and graduated with honors from Kutztown University. She moved to Chicago in 2004, when Comcast entered the market. She was in charge of an extremely well received documentary on Joe Maddon returning to his Pennsylvania hometown. It was one of the highest rated shows in SportsNet's history.

Comcast SportsNet didn't get to Chicago until 2004. When we came in, we inherited Fox Sports Net and SportsChannel's videotape library. Even when we weren't physically here, we still have all those games, clean video and interviews. It's nice to have their library here.

Our Web reporter for the Cubs, Patrick Mooney, has a really good relationship with Joe Maddon because he's at the park every day. He travels with the team on most occasions. Near the end of the 2015 season, Joe said, "Hey, Patrick, you should come to Hazleton this winter to my Christmas dinner and see my community center where I run my charity. We'll do a little tour of Hazleton."

We weren't sure if he was serious or not. During the off-season, Patrick kept up with Joe and was talking to his agent, and they were all onboard. Everyone loved the idea, especially after the high the Cubs were on at the end of 2015, even though the team lost. The team was way better than expected, and a lot of that was thanks to Maddon.

We were all set to send a camera person and field producer to Hazleton with Patrick. Then MLB set up a trip to Cuba for José Abreu. The team and MLB were pushing us to go to Cuba to show the goodwill tour. They thought it was really important for us to be there.

A week before we were scheduled to go to Cuba, things changed. My passport had just expired, so I couldn't go to Cuba. I was going to Hazleton with two camera people and a reporter, and Ryan was going to Cuba with José Abreu and one of our other reporters.

I got nervous. I knew the Hazleton story had the potential to show a side of the manager that most people hadn't seen. I wanted to be prepared. My job is to reveal things that people don't know about the Cubs that might be interesting. I love to do that. I search for story ideas that fans will love.

We flew in late on Sunday into the Philadelphia airport. It was an hour-and-a-half drive to Hazleton from there, so it was after midnight when we got to the hotel. We had two camera people and Patrick Mooney, our reporter. I didn't sleep much. I was nervous.

Being from Manheim, Pa., population 5,000, I was excited about going back to a small town in Pennsylvania. But I was misguided about how big Hazleton is. When we got there, it seemed huge. It's a lot bigger than Manheim. The population of Hazleton is around 25,000. It had a really nice downtown area. It was Christmas-time, so everything was decorated. It was really pretty.

Monday morning, we went to the community center. It's an old school that Joe and his foundation turned into a community center. It has classrooms, after-school care, daycare and a gym where they can do after-school activities. It's a facility where they do all kinds of good stuff.

Our first introduction to Joe Maddon's life in Hazleton was of his Mom rolling meatballs with members of his extended family. They were making food for that week's big event. Some of Joe's aunts and cousins were there. His Mom was absolutely hysterical. My nervousness went away as soon as she cracked her first joke. She was hilarious. She was so fun loving. She joked to the cameramen, "You guys need to get out of my face."

We put a microphone on her, and then Joe came in. He hadn't seen her for a while, so he gave her a big hug. She was so happy to see him and so grateful that he was going to be in town for an entire week. The first thing Joe said to us was, "Let's go to lunch at the Third Base diner." That's where Beanie, his mom, has worked forever. She just recently retired.

Joe took us to the Third Base Luncheonette. It was amazing. I walked in, and felt like I was transported back to 1930. They had round stools at the counter. Everything was original. They've updated the kitchen, but everything in the dining area was original. We talked to Beanie's cousin who is the cook. He's 70-years-old. His wife, Beanie's cousin-in-law, said, "The day that Beanie leaves this place is going to be a very sad day, and we'll all be in trouble." Beanie does a lot of the work that other people don't want to do. I'm pretty sure the day that she said she was retiring was a tough day for them.

After lunch, Joe took us on a tour of Hazleton in his car. It was a trip down his memory lane. Joe was so genuine. He was telling us stories about his childhood, little things like how he used to walk from football practice all the way up a hill back to his house. He said, "I'd walk up that hill like I was walking onto the field of Yankee Stadium, like I had always dreamt of that moment. I acted like I was in **YANKEE STADIUM*** every time I walked up that hill."

---

*The cement used to build **YANKEE STAIUM** was purchased from Thomas Edison who owned the huge Portland Cement Company.

The iconic Third Base Luncheonette where Joe Maddon's mother worked for decades until 2016. It was next to the old Hazleton High School where for years, many students ate their lunch.

The baseball dream obviously started early for him. During our tour, we learned a lot about his life in the small town where he grew up. He remembered everything. Reminiscing seemed to be cathartic for him. It was good to see that side of him. He really values his time there.

About 10 years ago he noticed that the city was changing. People weren't walking on the street anymore and kids weren't on the street playing. It really hurt him to see his town in shambles. There were businesses that were boarded up. He thought that some of it was because different types of people came into the town and got jobs there. The cost of living was so low that they infiltrated the city. Then some bad things happened. The crime rate went up and there was some violence. People were afraid to leave their houses.

He wanted to try and change that. He built the community center to try to bring the different cultures together. That's how he is as a manager, too. He takes a team of different personalities and different nationalities, and he brings them all together. He knows how to speak Spanish. He knows how to connect players. It was a melding of his baseball career with his real-life hometown.

After the tour, we did an interview with him. The Cubs had just signed Jason Heyward. He talked about that. He talked about his time in the minor leagues and how much he learned there. What he did in the minors, he still does today in the Majors. He was able to do some crazy things in the minors without so many eyes watching him. He could test the waters in the minors without getting in trouble. He thinks he's successful now because he could get away with trying things in the minors.

Joe was bitter early on in his career about not being with the big club sooner. He always knew he would be a big league manager. He had to be patient in the Angels organization. When he told the stories about all his time in the minors, I could tell that he felt he should have been in the Majors much sooner. Joe told us this story. He was on an airplane and was stuck in the middle seat. He was frustrated and angry about not getting his chance to be a big league manager. His attitude was really bad.

A woman seated next to him on the plane said, "Remember, whatever you put out there comes back to you." Joe said, "From that day forward, my whole attitude changed." He tried to emit a positive vibe, no matter what mood he was in. He was aware that if he didn't have a good attitude that it was reflecting back on him. He was working in the minors, sitting in the middle seat and so angry that he didn't want to talk to this woman, but it was a moment that changed his life.

While Joe was in Hazleton, he had a pitching and hitting clinic with some big names in the Majors. Some of his coaches with the Cubs were there along with other coaches and players that he had worked with. A lot of high school and college coaches in the area came. Joe was at the community center a lot. The kids absolutely adored him. As soon as he walked in, he had a flock of kids around him. They were so thankful for that center. A lot of the kids didn't know the background of why he helped build it, but you could tell they were thankful for a place to go after school.

Joe is a hero in Hazleton, but they treat him like one of the guys. People walked into the diner while we were there and just said, "Oh, it's Joe Maddon. Hi, Joe." They weren't crazy fans, although that might change if the Cubs win the World Series.

At Joe's first press conference with the Cubs, he said, "A shot and a beer is the Hazleton way." We wanted to start the show with that. We thought we needed to have him in a bar with a shot and a beer. But Joe drinks red wine, really good red wine. We arranged to do the shoot one night in a local bar-restaurant. We wanted to do the shoot with the shot and the beer in front of him. He was there having dinner with Rick Sutcliffe and some other baseball people. We got there and waited at the bar. I was afraid to interrupt Joe's dinner. The bartender knew that we had been waiting for awhile, so she brought all of us on the crew a shot and a beer. We drank. Maybe it was the time, maybe it was the drinks, but I finally said, "Guys, we need to get this shot. I'll go ask him."

I walked up to his table and said, "Joe, this is going to be the last time we bother you, but we really need to get this one shot." He said, "Well, I'm not drinking the shot and the beer." I said, "No problem. We just need to show you with it." We miked him up and asked a few questions at the bar. That's what we used to open the show. He said that Hazleton was a microcosm of Chicago. Family was very important and everyone was hardworking. It was exactly what we needed.

Albina "Beanie" Maddon, Joe Maddon's mother.

Joe loves Hazleton. He always goes back, and he always gives back. He talks weekly to the people that run the community center. He's very hands on. He wants to know what's going on. A lot of us left our hometowns in the rearview mirror and aren't going back any time soon. Joe deserves a lot of credit. He didn't give up on Hazleton. His involvement makes a huge difference there.

Joe bought a house in Hazleton where his family can meet up when he's in town. His sister lives in the house permanently. It's right in the center of Hazleton, and they all get together every year around Christmas. He thought it was important to have somewhere to stay when he was in town, a place that felt like home and not a hotel or rented place. He wanted a permanent residence in Hazleton. He and his wife, Jaye, stayed at the house. Jaye is amazing, too. We interviewed her for the show and she said, "I'm not from here, but I feel like I'm from here." She felt the love from Hazleton like she grew up there.

Joe's sister runs a consignment store that is co-owned with Jaye. It's in what used to be the plumbing store that Joe's dad owned. Beanie still lives in the same place that they all grew up in above the old plumbing store. Joe's house, where his sister lives, is right around the corner. You can see the Third Base Luncheonette about 500 feet down the road. And the community center is about eight blocks away.

After the trip to Hazleton, I didn't see Joe again until spring training. I thought he wouldn't remember me. But he said, "Oh, hey, Sarah, the show turned out really good. Thank you so much." He loved the show. They're going to show it this December at their annual event in Hazleton.

I cared what the Chicago viewers thought about the show, but I cared more what the family thought. We sent a bunch of copies to the diner and to his sister. They all loved it. I wanted to tell the story right and show the town in a good light. SportsNet is owned partly by the Cubs, so we have to be careful with things. But this was a great human interest story, and we wanted everyone to feel good about it. We're hoping it will be nominated for an Emmy.

At spring training, after the Cubs were done with their workouts, most days Joe got on his bike with his MP3 player and did interval training sessions behind Sloan Park. He let our reporter, Kelly Crull, go on a ride with him for a show we were doing. We miked him, put a GoPro on his bicycle and then followed them with our van. He told us how important those rides were. He believes in meditation. He schedules meditations throughout the day because he thinks they clear his mind. On the bike, he spends a lot of time meditating, even with music. It was a short bike ride, but it was nice to see Joe Maddon away from the baseball field enjoying a spin around the park.

He has a specially-built bike with really thick tires. He usually rides for a half mile or so and then does a burst of high intensity with a really high-speed pedal. Then he slows down to a normal pace, then speeds up again. It's like being in a spin class, only outside. He was fast. We had to gun the van to keep up. The camera guys in the back were having trouble shooting it. Joe saw that we were having problems, so he slowed down a little for us. Kelly was riding with him and said, "Man, you're fast. This is unbelievable."

Joe is approachable most of the time. Oftentimes, if you see an athlete or a manager or a coach, you're wary to approach. Joe just gives off a vibe like, hey, it's fine. He does listen to you. He's not just hearing you. He actually does listen. I think that's why he's so successful. He gets the players onboard from the get-go. They believe in his system. The Cubs never had a consistently good manager who listened to the team, listened to the players. Joe knows when to keep it light. He knows how to get the locker room's attention. If they win a World Series, it's because of him. There's no doubt.

When I first heard he was hired, I thought it was great. We heard about all of the wild things. He had penguins and

The house Joe Maddon bought for his family in Hazleton.

Joe speaking at Hazleton.

magicians in the locker room and all kinds of crazy stuff. For me, I love that. Some people were wondering when he was going to focus on baseball. There's a reason he does that stuff, and we've seen it now for two seasons. You have to believe in it because it's working.

Here's another thing I love about Joe. Anthony Rizzo had an event this summer. Anthony was on the way to the event when Joe texted him. "Hey, I'm giving you the day off tomorrow. Enjoy your event." Joe gets it. He understands. As much as he would love Rizzo to play every day, he gave him a break. I'm sure that Rizzo appreciated that a lot.

Everyone in Chicago loves Joe. They love when he does crazy things and double switches and has a pitcher playing centerfield. People love that, especially when they win, right? I'm glad that I'm able to see how Joe Maddon spends part of his life away from **WRIGLEY FIELD*** and share some of that with our viewers. It was very enjoyable and satisfying to go to Joe's hometown, get to understand his background and meet those great people.

*On July 1, 1943, the first night game was held at **WRIGLEY FIELD**. It was an exhibition game for the All-American Girls Professional Baseball League (AAGPBL). Portable lights were used.

THE WRITE GUY

DAVE SEAMON

Dave Seamon is the top sportswriter in Hazleton, Pa., Joe Maddon's hometown. Seamon became interested in sports journalism as a fourth grader while following the exploits of "Broad Street Joe" Maddon on the gridiron.

We didn't have a major sports team in the Hazleton area, so the closest thing we had was our high schools. High school athletes were always idolized. Joe was one of those guys. His name was always in the news. He had the nickname "Broad Street Joe," because Broadway Joe Namath was famous at the time. Broad Street was the main thoroughfare in downtown and since he was the school's quarterback, he was "Broad Street Joe." He was a great passer. He could have been a small college quarterback. Joe's one of those guys the girls wanted to date. He was always front and center in student activities, a leader in the classroom as well as the field.

People just gravitated toward Joe. They wanted to watch him because they knew something special was going to happen when he had the ball in his hands.

Our late sports editor, Ray Saul, coached Joe on his Little League team. He had stories that Joe had the "it" factor back then.

In 1971, Joe pitched in the District championship game. It was his junior year and he was a leader on that team. A lot of guys from that team went on to play at the college level in different sports. Joe was the leader on the field.

In Joe's senior year, the teams didn't have great success, but Joe had an outstanding year in all his sports. He went on to Lafayette College, where he majored in economics.

I was in third and fourth grade when Joe was in high school. I remember mostly listening to games on the radio. I followed the local athletes in the local paper and he was one of the guys I first remember reading about. Joe was *the* guy. You knew when you heard his name something good was going to happen.

I really didn't get a chance to meet him until well after that. When I was in junior high and high school, he was in college and into his minor league career.

Ray Saul always put a little snippet in the newspaper updating readers on what Joe was doing and where he was playing. Ray did that for all the local players. Joe's name was always fresh, "Oh, Joe Maddon is there now." We didn't have the internet then, so we couldn't follow the team from far away. We had to wait until *The Sporting News* came out and there was mention of something. There was always a sense of pride when he was moving up the Angels chain.

I later become a member of the newspaper staff and we did stories on Joe. He was on the field coaching when Cal Ripken, Jr. broke Lou Gehrig's consecutive games streak. You could see Joe on the field and be like, oh, he's from Hazleton.

When Joe was a coach with the Angels we did a couple of "local boy makes good" stories after the Angels won the World Series in 2002. After the Series, Joe walked into our office and started talking to us as if he had never left town. He talked about guys from way back and bustin' chops here and there. He talked about his cousins and his huge extended family.

Joe told us the Angels' whole game plan from when they played the Yankees in the playoffs. "Then we're gonna beat **MINNESOTA***. Then the Giants. We're gonna do our best to pitch

---

*Bruce Smith, the 1941 Heisman Trophy winner from **MINNESOTA**, was nominated for sainthood by a Father Cantwell, and his application is still on file at the Vatican.

around **BARRY BONDS***." He always takes time to talk with Hazleton reporters.

The thing was, Joe talked to us like we were sitting around the bar talking about the game. He made it sound so simple, which really it isn't. He went over the whole scouting report, things you wouldn't talk about with anyone else. It was the first time I got to just talk baseball with him.

The next year he was courted by the Red Sox, before Terry Francona was hired. I remember working the phones. "Is he gonna be the Red Sox manager?" Joe was going to get into a great situation there, but they went with Francona.

Joe eventually got the Tampa job. Everyone I talked to said if anyone can turn around that Tampa situation he could. He relished that challenge. He just needed a chance to show what he could do. He turned that around within a year or two.

A lot of the things he learned back here in Hazleton. We're known here for our work ethic and Joe took pride in that. His dad was a plumber and his mom just retired from the Third Base Luncheonette. They're good people and he's a good person. People see the quirky side of him with the themed road trips. When Joe got that chance he was going to be different. But he still has that Hazleton base, the work hard then we can have fun ethic.

The players loved to play for him. I got a chance to talk to Don Zimmer before he died. Don was one of his consultants, and he saw the potential of what he could do with the Rays and that Joe was on to something.

Joe comes back every off-season and has a charity golf tournament. In Tampa he has the Thanksmas celebration

---

*In 2002 **B*RRY B*NDS** received 68 intentional walks… Eight came when no one was on base.

where he helps the needy. He's brought that to the Hazleton area, too.

There has been a great influx in the Hispanic population and some of the old-timers in town weren't very receptive. There has been a lot of controversy. People weren't getting along and there were clashes or perceived clashes between the old-time residents and the newcomers. The newcomers weren't given a chance to contribute to the community. Joe saw something missing in the town he grew up in. He wanted people to have the same opportunities he had as a kid.

Last year he had a coaches clinic. He has a fundraiser every year for the community center. There is a lunch for the needy the Sunday before he leaves. There are all types of food for the different ethnicities in the community. It's just a great way to bring people together. Joe will tell you it's not just him doing all this. He doesn't want to take the credit. It's his family, friends and a lot of volunteers.

Carmine, his sister, is still in Hazleton and has a shop downtown. I think his brother, Mark, is in Florida.

Joe has a great rapport with the Hispanic population. He is very fluent in Spanish.

I try to see him once each season in Baltimore, Philly or New York. Then I catch up with him during the off-season when he's in town for that week.

We are very proud of Joe.

JOE MADDON WAS A REGULAR GUY WHO SOME DAYS WORE A CAPE

FRANCIS LIBONATI

Francis Libonati was Joe Maddon's favorite history teacher at Hazleton High School. They have kept in touch over the years.

At Hazleton High School, Joe played baseball and was our pitcher and shortstop. He also played football and was our quarterback. Some people fail to realize that. We had a quarterback that was coming back for his senior year when Joe was a sophomore. Joe actually beat him out. The other kid went to Syracuse to play tight end. That's the kind of talent he was. Joe went on to lead the team for the next three years. He led the baseball team to its first District title. It was a very competitive District 11, which had all the Allentown and Bethlehem schools. Joe always seemed to be under control. When he played quarterback in high school, I remember him calling audibles at the line of scrimmage.

Joe always stood out in the classroom. He was the captain of the class panel discussions. There were six disciplines. He would select the topics, and he would tell the five students what to do. He always asked penetrating questions. He always wanted to know the "why" of things. When we discussed the Civil War, the War of 1812 or World War II, he always wanted to know why. He separated himself.

It seemed like all the prettiest girls were paying him special attention. He was very charismatic. If you wanted to point to someone who was going to be successful in any walk of life, he was it. He chose being a baseball manager, but he could

Joe Maddon's youth revolved around St. Gabriel's Parish. The convent is on the left and the church is on the right. Digger Phelps coached basketball at St. Gabriel's in 1966 before becoming head coach at Notre Dame a few years later.

have been a governor. There always was a group of people around him.

After Joe became the Rays' manager he said, "Mr. Libonati, this organization is going to be good. There are really some great things in store." He wasn't arrogant about it. He just felt very confident. In 2008 they made the run to beat the Red Sox and lost to the Phillies in the World Series. I had undergone a stem cell transplant in October and the Rays were playing the Red Sox. He left a message for me, "Mr. Lib, I'm driving up to St. Pete. Pretty big game tonight, but more importantly, I hope that you're winning your battle against your current condition." He was on for about five minutes. It was unbelievable. It was all about my health and nothing about the game, which they went on to win.

Joe got married that year and they had a little reception in a hall here in Hazleton. He called me outside and in the trunk of his car he had a Rays jersey with my name on it. He gave me that.

The next year a group of teachers and I went down to Baltimore when the Rays were in town. In the seventh inning Harry Kalas' son, Todd, who covered the Rays for Sun Sports, interviewed me. Joe said his favorite teacher was at the game so go talk to him. After the interview a little boy came up and asked for my autograph because I had the Rays shirt on with LIBONATI on the back. Joe remembers where he came from.

Joe is the real deal. He was a catcher in the Angels organization and came home during the off-season. He said, "I don't know. I'm not hitting very well." I said, "Look Joe, there has to be a place in baseball for you. You're a people person." With his knowledge of the game and how he related so well to people, I just knew he could be successful as a coach or manager or in the front office. He still wanted a shot as a player, but I think he already was thinking about what he could do to stay in baseball.

He visited me the following Christmas and brought me an autographed Cal Ripken, Jr. bat. He was doing his annual Thanksmas event. We talked for nearly an hour about school and never about his success. It was always about you. You know how people are talking to you but not listening? He was just the opposite. He listened to everything you said, and he genuinely was interested in what you were doing.

Digger Phelps coached **BASKETBALL*** at St. Gabriel's High School in Hazleton in 1966. He used to call me "King" because we beat him twice that year. He and I got to be good friends. You talk about charisma. He was easy to talk to. We were both 26-year-old guys. He was married, and I was single.

Joe's mom called me occasionally and so did his sister. But when Joe called, on the biggest day in the Rays' history, to talk to a teacher that he had 35-40 years ago, wow! He was actually sincere. It wasn't "let me get this over with." And that's the kind of guy he's always been.

The Cubs could not have picked a better guy to break the curse. All of the adulation people have for the Cubs, Hazleton has for Joe. He started the One Community Center. He tries to bring our city together. Just as he succeeded in doing that, he will succeed in being the manager in the greatest win in the last century. He has made us proud in whatever avenue he has walked. The greatest manager of the greatest victory in baseball history should be Hazleton's own Joe Maddon.

Leo Durocher was wrong when he said, "Nice guys finish last." Not when you're Joe Maddon.

---

*Dick Groat, the 1960 National League MVP, was an All-American **BASKETBALL** player at Duke University and was the first Blue Devil to have his basketball number retired.

A COACH IS A TEACHER WITH A DEATH WISH

ED MORGAN

Ed Morgan is 83-years-old and has the best of both worlds. He summers in his home area of Hazleton, Pa., and winters in Naples, Fla. He was Joe Maddon's high school baseball coach, and in subsequent years, earned quite a reputation as an umpire and basketball referee. Later, he became a realtor. Morgan and his wife, who is a speech therapist, have three successful grown children.

I started my coaching career at a little school, Black Creek Township, which is just west of Hazleton. I coached basketball and baseball.

When Black Creek was absorbed into the Hazleton School District, I became a teacher at Hazleton High School. Two years later, I was an assistant football coach and the next year was the head coach. At that time my relationship with Joe was just as a junior high athlete, a kid that was the main show on the football team. He was a great quarterback with a good arm. I saw Joe's biggest asset was his ability to fit into any situation. Also, Joe would handle it with experience, a lot of class and a real knowledge of all sports. He was adept at playing the game, and analyzing the game.

When I became the coach, I had heard a lot of Joe and had seen a little of his play. When I got the head coaching job, Joe was coming in as a sophomore. I immediately saw that this kid had a lot of talent and knowledge of the game. He knew the game better than any person I had.

During Joe's junior year, we had a pretty good baseball team. Jeff Jones, our star outfielder and best hitter, was being looked at by some of the scouts. We breezed to the District

11 championship of the Luzerne County area. Unfortunately, there was no state championship back in 1971. We had a stellar cast of nine or maybe even 12 outstanding baseball players.

I had Joe pitch as a junior in the District championship against Northampton, and we won, 4-1. Joe even cleared the bases with a hit to give us three of our four runs. I got a call from a gentleman saying how I was an idiot for pitching a junior and not a couple of seniors. I replied, "I play the player I think can do the best. If the kid were a sophomore, or if he were black, white or green, if he lived in Hazleton city or the rural area, I always go with the athlete I think can do the job for us. That's why I had Joe pitch for us, and I was pretty well pleased with the result, weren't you?" The caller said, "Never mind, never mind."

Joe carried the team. The plays he made weren't outstanding, but his knowledge was. Here's one example: We were playing in one of the league championship games and Joe was playing shortstop. A guy hit a ball by our right fielder. The runner rounded first, rounded second and was going to third while the ball was still in the outfield. Maddon went to cut off a phantom throw and the runner fell down and hurt his ankle. We got him out at third. Joe did those things. Not that they are unorthodox, but he had the smarts to always do the right thing.

We had a good team that year. We had Jeff Jones, a great player, a speedy kid in centerfield, two big kids at first and third. We had kids that sat on the bench that I wished played for us later because they were so good. That team wasn't nine deep. There were 14 or 15 kids that were very talented. It was just one of those things where they came together at the right time.

If there was a rain out and we couldn't practice I would tell the guys to go to my classroom. They would ask why. I'd tell them we're going to learn how to play baseball. Joe would contribute a lot to those sessions.

When Joe got signed by the California Angels, he called me that night and said, "Coach I got a job." That was good news for me to hear. His ability to understand the game—and be a good all-round good kid—helped him move up the system.

He called me again when he went to the Tampa Bay Rays to be their manager. He did a real outstanding job with them and made them a bona fide contender.

I had the privilege of living in Florida when I retired, while Joe was managing the Rays. I got to see him in many, many games. I would sit right next to the dugout.

Joe had interviewed for the Boston Red Sox job that eventually went to Terry Francona. I got to meet Theo Epstein, then general manager of the Red Sox, now of the Cubs, and he wished they could have signed Joe. When I talked with Epstein, he liked Joe. Joe is a really likeable kid, real down to earth. Everyone in the Hazleton area is real proud of him.

When the Cubs job came open, Joe had a clause in his contract. He could get out if he wanted to. I thought he was going to go to Chicago. Now he's had a good run with the Cubs.

He wins with distinction, with little novel ideas like having the pitcher bat eighth. He's pointed out the reasons why.

Joe comes back to Hazleton occasionally when his team plays in New York or Philadelphia. But every off-season he returns. He started the Thanksmas program there for underprivileged kids. He bought a home for his mother and his sister back there. He's a real asset to the community. I don't know anyone who doesn't like this kid.

Now I really miss Joe. I asked him how he could desert me for the Cubs, of all the teams, a team that does spring training in Arizona. So I don't see him nearly as much as I'd like.

They do have two teams right here near Naples. The Boston Red Sox have their miniature Fenway Park and the Minnesota

Twins. They both train here so I get to see a lot of baseball. But I don't get to see Maddon as much, so that's the bad news for me.

Joe was probably the best all-round player I had. I had a pitcher named Ted Damiter who followed him. He was a dominate pitcher with the cold days here in March, and he could throw in the low 90s. He was the exact opposite of Joe. He was not an athlete. He didn't try out for other sports. If he didn't pitch, I couldn't put him anywhere. He was a wonderful kid. He came as a blessing to us. He wasn't a Hazleton boy and his father came to town for work, so we didn't have any way of following him in Little League. He was by far the best pitcher we had. He got a scholarship to Shippensburg State. I went to see his first game and he threw a no-hitter. He was eventually signed by the **METS*** and was inducted into the Shippensburg State Sports Hall of Fame.

Joe married a girl from Arizona, so he would spend his early off-seasons there.

His brother, Mark, is still in Hazleton working for a water company. His sister, Carmine, is married to a postman. I taught his sister, but not his younger brother. She was a very friendly, good student and a good human being. His family helped not only in his baseball prowess, but being a good citizen.

Joe was a marvelous citizen right through high school. In the classroom, on the field or at school itself. He was a popular guy. Everyone wanted to know Joe Maddon.

I was really impressed right away the way Joe fit in. We started using him at shortstop when he didn't pitch. He pitched for the two-and-a-half years. He showed talent. I realized Joe had tremendous potential and, as I said, that team was loaded.

---

*"The New York **METS** are my favorite squadron." —Apu, the Qwik-E-Mart store owner, to Homer Simpson in an episode of *The Simpsons*.

A hug for Mom after a hard day's work.

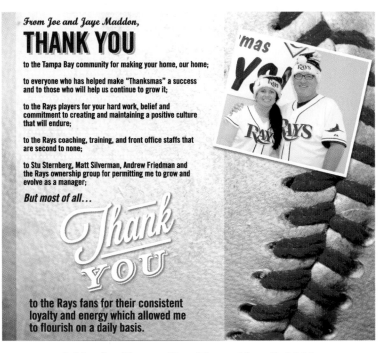

Ad in the *Tampa Bay Times*, Nov. 7, 2014.

The 1971 season was Joe's peak year when everyone realized that he was something special.

When Joe was the manager in Tampa Bay, I would go up there a lot. It was carte blanche. I could call Joe and say I was coming. When they trained, it was in a little town called Port Charlotte, which is between Tampa and Naples, so I went to many exhibition games, too.

Anytime I went to a game I'd be able to see Joe. One day they were playing the Red Sox at the miniature Fenway between Naples and Fort Myers. I didn't see Joe before the game because they had dressed in Port Charlotte and came in uniform on the bus. After the game my son, wife and I went near the bus and the police wouldn't let us through. Joe came out of the locker room and came over. We were talking when Joe said everyone was on the bus and he had to go. There was a little boy by his dad looking pretty sad and the dad said they would get a chance to talk to him, but they didn't. I felt pretty bad for him. Years and years ago, my dad would take us down to Philadelphia to old Connie Mack Stadium and we'd try and meet the manager. Now I'm being the bully and this little kid started crying when Joe had to get on the bus.

Sometimes I was fortunate to sit by the dugout and we could chat. If one of his kids would make a nice play he'd stick his head out and I'd give him a thumbs up.

I'm a baseball fan, and I'm pleased with the Phillies and the little renaissance they're on. I'm divided. I like the Phillies and the Cubs. I follow them both. I think the Phillies have a chance of being .500 in my lifetime.

If I can, I go see the Cubs when they are in Philly. I did go up to Toronto once to see Joe with the Rays. Joe introduced me to Larry Bowa, and told him I was a big Phillies fan when he played there.

Joe growing up was a Cardinals fan. His dad may have been a Cardinals fan. Joe's dad was a Culligan Man. They lived within walking distance of the high school.

Joe could have gone to other schools besides Lafayette College, but he would have only been able to play baseball or football, not both.

Like everyone in Hazleton, I'm very proud of Joe.

Jaye and Joe Maddon celebrate Thanksmas in Hazleton.

THE OTHER GUY FROM NAZARETH

BILLY STAPLES

Billy Staples is a human Red Bull living in Nazareth, Pa. Two decades ago he left a cushy job at AT&T corporate headquarters to teach in the projects of Bethlehem, Pa. He has twice been nominated as Disney's National Teacher of the Year. He has enticed world famous athletes like Tony Gwynn, Derek Jeter and **MICHAEL JORDAN*** *to come to his classroom and talk about life as they were growing up. Staples wondered: If he could motivate hundreds of kids in one school in one town, why couldn't he do it with hundreds of thousands of kids nationwide? With that, a fabulous book,* Before the Glory, *was born—a book that baseball fans love. It was published by HCI, the Chicken Soup people.*

Bob Curry and his wife, Elaine, have been with each other for 35, 40 years. Elaine is Joe's cousin. Joe came back home to Hazleton, Pa., five or six years ago to just relax and be with family and said, "I'm so proud of my hometown, but we could be doing better."

One thing led to another, and Bob and Elaine and Joe said, "Let's start a foundation and see if Tampa Bay will support it, and we'll do it here."

He started having an annual winter dinner. Exactly nine months after they got their board of directors, they bought a building. They put an elevator in. They put ungodly amounts of money in it, and it feeds children breakfast, lunch and dinner, and educates them. It's over the top. You'd have to see it yourself. Bob and Elaine are there every day.

---

*PGA tour golfer Jordan Spieth is named for **MICHAEL JORDAN**. In 1994, Jordan was called up by the Chicago White Sox from the Birmingham Barons to play in the annual Mayor's Trophy Game. Jordan had a single and double in the game at Wrigley Field.

I spoke to Joe at baseball's Winter Meetings in Nashville in December. When he heard about what I'm doing with kids and paying for college, he said, "You need to talk to Elaine and Bob."

When I came back from Nashville was when the meetings in Hazleton started to happen. Two of the nine kids that we're sponsoring through college were seniors at Hazleton Area High School this year.

The number one thing about Joe is, he has been consistent his whole life. He's no different now than he was when he was in college. All these stories are the same—that's just the way he walks and talks and thinks.

Here's a story about Joe. There was a baseball player from Puerto Rico. He was an infielder who played for the Astros and the Phillies and four or five other teams in his career. His name is Dickie Thon. Dickie didn't know jack about English, and Joe didn't know jack about Spanish, and they roomed together in the minors. Joe's great rapport with Latino players was through Dickie teaching him Spanish. I don't know how Dickie taught him Spanish.

There's another Major Leaguer who grew up, in all places, in Hazleton. He was a Cubs draft choice in 2004 and his name is Russ Canzler. Canzler went through the minor league system and wound up at Tampa Bay. Joe was in Tampa Bay. What big league manager called him up? Joe called up Russ.

I had no idea what was going on in Hazleton until the Winter Meetings in Nashville. I'd met Joe before in doing my books because I wanted to do a chapter on Joe. We were talking in the lobby, and I said to him, "Joe, we're at 36 college graduates of kids from the streets and the projects not far from Hazleton. Thirty-six! Forget about my books. What really matters is that they sell enough that the publisher donates money, and we've got a beautiful thing going here where these kids are supported. That's more important to me than asking you for an interview."

Elaine's maiden name was Maddon. They grew up right on the same block. A bunch of Maddons all lived together.

As soon as I came home from Nashville, I was doing a clinic with six or seven players and 80, 90 kids. Who's one of the players at the clinic? Russ Canzler. I'd never really met Canzler.

I said, "Hey, I was just talking about you in Nashville."

We started going back and forth.

He said, "Did you contact Bob and Elaine yet?"

I said, "No, I've been home only a couple of days."

He said, "I want to be at the meeting. I'm going to call them for you."

Canzler called Bob and Elaine. He talked to Bob for a little bit on the phone.

Bob said, "Do you have all of this information in a press kit?"

I said, "Yes, I've got it all, lock, stock, and barrel."

He said, "Come on out. I want you to see our community center."

That was it. We've been meeting ever since, probably every six to eight weeks. Maddon's fostering two kids. We're excited for them.

The community center has been around for five years. Bob and Elaine pick two seniors in high school that started coming to the community center when they were in middle school. They were two kids that they knew would a) fit our criteria on the application, and b) agree under contract to show up at the end of every semester and show my board of directors their grades. There is an agreement that the kids come back home to Hazleton for two years after graduation to live and work. That's a hard criteria. Bob and Elaine introduced us to one boy, one girl. We met their parents. We just announced these kids at our annual function in Bethlehem. We had 25 famous players for my fundraiser, and then we had the nine new scholarship kids to introduce who we're sponsoring. Bob and Elaine came down from Hazleton and were part of the crowd for that announcement.

Here's a story that Norm Gigon told me himself about Joe. Norm was Joe's baseball coach in college. I was at Norm's condo in Mahwah, N.J., seven years ago. It was in the middle of nowhere.

We were talking, and he said, "Do you want to hear a Maddon story?"

I say, "Sure, I'd like a Maddon story."

"All right, it's Lafayette College. It's where I'm coaching. And Maddon's O.K. He doesn't even come to Lafayette College to play baseball. He's got a scholarship for football, but Maddon loves baseball more than he loves football. He makes a deal with the football coach, whatever it is, the partial scholarship, and he never plays a down of varsity football.

"He's playing baseball for me. I see he's a good baseball player for Lafayette College. He might have a shot at rookie ball, low level minor leagues. On a bus ride, I tell him when it's getting near his end time at Lafayette, 'Listen, if you do get in the minor leagues, make sure that your personality is what's spread all over the place. If you want to stay in baseball, it's not going to be for your abilities. It's going to be for your love of the game and your personality.'"

Gigon said to me, "Was I wrong."

Gigon had a cup of coffee in the big leagues, and ironically, it was with the Cubs in 1967. He was a second baseman/right fielder who played 34 games that year. He died two years before Joe took over the Cubs.

You know who loves Joe? Red Sox pitcher David Price, a good, good guy. I mean, a really good guy. The way I met Joe for the first time was because of David. David was in my second book and we stayed friendly. I met David on the road, and I told him earlier that I'm from Easton, so he took me in to see Maddon for the first time. That's how I met him. I met Joe at a game in Chicago, thanks to David.

As much as Joe is the king of Chicago, and you've heard it repeatedly, it's the same Joe every day. It's just Chicago is a bigger stage.

JOE MADDON ON THE HAZLETON INTEGRATION PROJECT:

"I'll give you the CliffsNotes of why we started the Hazleton Integration Project. I went home several years ago, and I really thought my hometown was dying a rapid death. Some of it had to do with a lot of Hispanic folks who had moved into town. A lot of them were from the Dominican Republic, and the Anglo group that had been there for the last 100 years did not like these people. Neither side was getting along.

"I thought it was really vital and important to try to do something to bring the groups together, to help assimilate the Hispanic culture within our city. We thought the best way was to create a community center and then created programs and activities to attract all the kids. If the kids came in the building, the parents would hopefully follow.

"I also believed that the more we pushed these people away, the more probable it would be that our city would eventually die, and I mean that sincerely. It was really going backward. It was a dark town. There was no trust. When I grew up there as a kid, it was the most impressive, wonderful place to grow up in the entire United States, I thought, in the world. For us, as adults and the stewards in that situation, to not present the same opportunity for the kids coming up, would be totally inappropriate and wrong.

"We did something about it. We started in 2011. It began with a thought, like most good projects and situations. One of the first groups to jump onboard were the Ripkens. Actually, Billy came up. We had dinner at Martin's Restaurant in West Hazleton. He presented us with a nice check to get things rolling. The next year, during our event, Cal came up. Cal and I had a wonderful evening together, a little fireside chat talking about baseball. Again, the Ripken Foundation came through with a wonderful contribution that right now exceeds $200,000. We bought an old building. We bought the old Most Precious Blood Catholic School, 25-plus classrooms, a wonderful cafeteria, a great gymnasium. Because of generous contributions, we were able to restructure our facilities in the gym with an all-purpose floor and actually have cages coming down from the ceiling. That's all because of these guys and Mom.

"My first roommate in professional baseball was Dickie Thon—Richard Thon—who I saw in Puerto Rico a couple of weeks ago. Richard and I still remain really good friends, and because of him, I have a strong affinity for the Hispanic population. I feel honored that the Hispanics have come to Hazleton and have chosen our town to grow within. It's a great spot for their kids to go to school. There are jobs for the grownups, and they're revitalizing our city. It's coming back on its feet. There's brightness and definitely a future. Hazleton has turned the corner and is headed in the right direction."

WHY CAN'T SUGAR BE AS SWEET AS CAL RIPKEN?

STEVE SALEM

Steve Salem is the president of the Cal Ripken, Sr. Foundation in Baltimore. The **CONNECTICUT*** *native eschewed the Red Sox and Yankees growing up and became a huge Mets fan instead. His first baseball memory is that of Cleon Jones catching the final out of the 1969 World Series. Salem is a renowned baseball trivia expert.*

I got a phone call from Billy Ripken. I assume it was through blogcasting, but Bill and Joe were friends. Bill called and said, "Would you do me a favor? I need you to talk to Joe." I didn't know Joe Maddon. "I need you to talk to him about a project he has in Hazleton. Joe asked if we could help, and I'd like to help if we can." That was Billy. I said, "Of course, any time. Just have him call or email me. I'd be happy to."

We got a call from Joe's cousin, Bob Curry. Bob invited us to Hazleton to take a tour. I didn't go on the first visit. Some of my staff did. This was at the very beginning of their project. Today they have a beautiful community center.

My team went up and met with them, got the lay of the land. To support Bob and Joe, we made a $25,000 contribution. It was a nice contribution, but in the bigger picture of what they needed, a small contribution. That's how it started. They

*In 1964, the Jackie Robinson family lived with a young Carly Simon and her parents in Stamford, **CONNECTICUT**, while their new Stamford home was being built. Mr. Simon was the co-founder of the publishing company, Simon & Schuster.

had this vision of giving opportunity that had been lost to the kids of Hazleton, which is where Joe and his family grew up.

I went up there a few months later and got a tour of the city with Bob Curry and his wife, Elaine. Elaine is Joe's first cousin. It seems like everyone up there is related. They're all Joe's cousin this, Joe's second cousin, first cousin. They're all related.

In Hazleton, I felt like I had been thrown back into the 1950s. It's sort of stuck in time, and I mean that in a good way. Despite the struggles they've had like most cities similar to Hazleton, there was still very much a strong community feeling that is lost in today's society. From that point on, we started working with them any way we could. Their mission of helping at-risk kids, all kids, but focused on at-risk kids, giving them an opportunity to succeed in life. A lot of kids don't get that any more. In Hazleton, that was being lost, and that was what Joe and his family were worried about. At the same time, they were having some gang problems, crime problems. There's a large Hispanic community that's immigrated there, and there were issues that Joe was really upset about. Hazleton was no longer the town that he remembered.

One of our beliefs, and it was very clearly Joe's belief also, is that these are good kids who get caught up in something bad. If you can offer them something good before that happens, they'll stay on the right track. That's the whole idea behind the community center that they built, the whole idea behind the programs and the parks that the Ripken Foundation built. Give these kids something positive, rather than all the negative things that they're surrounded by every day. Show them that somebody really does care about them, even if you never meet them. Even if these kids never meet Joe, they know he and his family care about them, and that goes such a long way.

Joe is very involved. This past Christmas, we helped rebuild their gym. It's beautiful. It's amazing. We redid the entire gym, new everything, everything we could afford. We probably spent

$200,000 renovating the gym. We installed a new floor and got some synthetic turf that can be rolled out across the gym floor. We put in batting cages that drop from the ceiling. They can play baseball and practice baseball in the gym. There are new basketball hoops. There's a new scoreboard.

Our board chairman is Mark Butler, the CEO of Ollie's Bargain Outlet. Mark and Ollie's donated the money to refurbish that gym. They did that to honor Joe and his family, because he believed so much in what they're doing. We work in communities similar to Hazleton a lot. Joe could spend his time doing just about anything he wants. He does not need to do this. He does it because he's passionate about it. That's rare. That's why I work with Cal Ripken, because Cal is that way. I was not looking for a job, but I couldn't say no to Cal because he was so passionate about helping. Joe's the same way.

Recently, we were in Jersey City with Bob Hurley, the basketball coach at St. Anthony High School. He's the same way. There are very few. Bob could do anything he wanted. He could coach anywhere he wanted. He might be the greatest coach in the history of basketball, and he just cares about these kids, making sure they graduate from high school and go to college.

Our feeling is when you find someone like Joe, you have to help him. First of all, it's so hard to say no to someone like that. They just believe, and it's so passionate. But what's the point if you're not going to help him, if you're not going to get involved?

That's how we got involved. We've been to Hazleton five times to help them raise money. Cal's gone up there a couple of times. It's something we're going to continue to do. Our goal is to find groups like that and help them, using the bully pulpit that we have because of Cal's name, using that to help these groups like Joe Maddon's organization, help them reach the kids a little bit better. What they've done is amazing. It's really amazing.

Joe Maddon accepts the Cal Ripken, Sr. Foundation's "Aspire Award" in 2015 as Cal Ripken, Jr. looks on.

Cal Ripken.

Joe is such a genuinely nice person. The first time I spent time with him was at a fundraiser in Hazleton at the center. It was Christmastime, and he came in wearing a bright purple scarf, red sneakers, a colorful sport jacket and colored jeans. I'm thinking, oh, my God! But that's just him. It seems to me he just goes to the beat of his own drummer, and he's smarter than all of us, so who the heck are we to question anything he's doing?

Once you get to know him, you find out he's such a genuinely kind guy. When he talks about Hazleton, when he talks about the community center they built and the impact it's having on the kids, wow. When we cut the ribbon on the remodeled gym, Joe was crying, not because someone did something for him, but because of what it means to the kids in the community. He's such a genuinely kind person that you feel like you immediately have a new good friend.

He's so unique. We work with a lot of celebrities and athletes, and, unfortunately, there aren't many like him. These famous people could have such a positive impact if they chose to, like Joe has, like Cal has, like Bob Hurley has.

We honored Joe at our gala a couple of years ago. He got the Cal, Sr. Award, which is our highest award. In Baltimore every winter we have our biggest fundraiser of the year. It's called our Aspire Gala. It honors people who help carry on the legacy of Cal Ripken, Sr. It's all about helping others become successful in life, others who are less fortunate than you, learning the lessons and the skills to become successful in life.

The banquet is not a roast. It's the way the Cal Ripken, Sr. Foundation honors life's coaches. Next year we're honoring Brooks Robinson and Nancy Lieberman. In terms of fundraising, it's one of the biggest events on the East Coast. It raises more than $2 million.

Our name's getting out there more and more as we grow. This year we're on track to raise more than $30 million. Almost all of it goes back to communities. Go to our website at rip-kenfoundation.org. On our website there is a list of Youth Development Parks. Look at the parks that we built in some of the worst communities in America. It's amazing. They are synthetic turf, million-dollar parks, which we built and gave to the communities.

I have no data to back this up, but if you consider us a celebrity or an athlete foundation, we're the biggest in the country, no question. I don't think anyone's even close to us. It used to be Lance Armstrong, until he got in trouble.

If I were to text Joe right now, a guy trying to get into the World Series, "Hey, Joe, I'm going to be in Chicago. Do you have time for a cup of coffee?" He'd text right back as soon as he saw the message, "Sure, when are you coming? I'd love to." He's got way more important things than that, but he'd do it because it could help the kids. It's not because he wants to see me.

Joe is in an elite class in the baseball world. He's the best manager in the game. Anybody who wants to argue with that is a fool. More importantly, he's in the elite class of athletes and celebrities who genuinely care about making a difference. They don't just talk it. In fact, he probably doesn't like to talk about it. He just wants to do it. That's such a rare thing. That's why we love Joe.

I'm telling you, if I tried to give you 10 names like Joe and Cal and Bob Hurley, I'm not sure I could come up with 10. It's not that there aren't 10 that care, but there aren't 10 at that elite level. Another one is Bryan Cranston, the actor. He's a good friend of ours. Bryan is like that. He doesn't want it to be about him. He's passionate about his charity work.

I guess these guys know how lucky they are, and they're not fooled by their success. They know that God blessed them with special skills that He could have given someone else.

Chapter 2

LEAPIN' LEOPARDS:

A reunion of Lafayette baseballers and other friends at
famed Little Italy in New York City

CLASSMATES, TEAMMATES AND ROOMMATES

PUT ME IN COACH

NEIL PUTNAM

Neil Putnam, 80, was the head football coach at Lafayette College from 1971-80, compiling a record of 44-55-3. A native of Dennison, Ohio, Putnam played college football at Miami University in Oxford, Ohio. His coaching staff recruited Joe Maddon to Lafayette as a quarterback. Putnam now is retired in Bethel, Maine.

I've touched a lot of coaches in my travels, but Ara Parseghian was the epitome of everything. I played for Ara at **MIAMI UNIVERSITY*** of Ohio. When he looked at you, you always felt like he was looking right through you. It was always what I didn't do right, but what I did wrong, and I'd better shape up. He had that greatness about him, and he was a good coach. He handled the staff well, and we loved him as players. I felt great about John Pont, too, who took over for him.

I became a coach and left Dartmouth for Yale because, at that time, John Pont had taken over Yale. Calvin Hill was one we recruited, as was Brian Dowling, our quarterback. We called him Superman. We got him out of St. Ignatius in Cleveland. He became better known as "B.D." in the "Doonesbury" comic strip. Those were the type of kids we recruited.

Then the head coach opening occurred at Lafayette, so I went there.

We recruited Joe Maddon out of Pennsylvania, Hazleton. His mother is still working at the little luncheon place there, the Third Base. We brought him in. Of course, we didn't have scholarships in those days. We had an Ivy League approach to financial assistance. I didn't have a heck of a lot of money, but

---

*Do you confuse Miami (Ohio) with Miami Florida? **MIAMI OF OHIO** was a school before Florida was a state.

we did whatever we could do to spread it around and get the best players who could do our academic work.

Lafayette was and still is equal to any of the Ivy League schools. I have a right to say that because having coached at two of them, I can speak with a certain amount of trueness. Joe was a good high school quarterback, a great baseball player. Of course, we were looking at him as a quarterback because we needed help, and he could throw the football. The assistant coach found him up there and went up and got him.

He came to Lafayette as both a football and a baseball player. I had a rule that if a player is recruited and he looked me in the eye and said, "Coach, I want to play baseball as well as football," I never, ever said no. I just felt that that was the way we should do it. Joe came in. At that time freshmen couldn't play on the varsity team. Joe was doing a fantastic job on the freshman team. He was doing exactly what we'd anticipated. He was a leader. You know what a leader is. You can't always define it, but they have the moxie, the guts. They can see everything, and they just react. They don't talk about it. They just do, and that was Joe.

I was thinking, boy, we've got this young man. He's going to take us out of the wilderness. Joe will move up the ladder, become one of the varsity players, and in time, really be a great quarterback for Lafayette. Well, lo and behold, he knocked on my office door and came in. The open-door policy was always in effect.

He said, "Coach, I'd like to tell you that I don't think I'm going to play football next year."

Well, you can imagine me. My heart went down to my feet. I said, "Now wait a minute. First of all, you said, 'I think.' Let's get rid of that. I want to know. Do you want to play baseball?"

Of course, you can appreciate a young man saying, "I think." He was trying to bridge into it. He said, "I really want to play baseball, Coach. Baseball was always my first love. I hear that bat out there in the spring." The baseball fields were right next door to our practice fields. He said, "I just miss it."

I said, "O.K., if you've made that decision, and you want to do that, go with my blessing and be the very best baseball player you can be."

At that point, Joe indicated that he was receiving financial assistance, and it came out of the money that was allotted to the football program.

I said, "Don't worry about that. When we made a commitment to you, it was a four-year commitment, and I told you when you came that you could play baseball. The fact that you want to commit to full-time baseball, I'll miss you, but you'll never hear a word out of me about it. You just be the best darn baseball player you can be."

That's the way we left it. Time passed. I watched his career and often thought that I'd like to talk to him. I didn't know how to bridge and say, "Hey, Joe, how are you doing?" I always felt he was doing so well, he didn't need me sticking my nose in, right?

A lot of my players stay in touch. These guys kept watching Joe at Tampa, and they said, "Hey, Joe keeps asking about you. You've got to get down here to see him."

I said, "Well, I just don't get down that way. Tell him I said hello." I still didn't get on the phone, like I should have.

The next thing I know, he called. "Coach, are you going to that game in Yankee Stadium," when Lafayette played Lehigh. I said, "Yeah, the guys have me a seat. They want me to sit with the group of former players." He said, "Well, let's get together there." I said, "Joe, that's fantastic."

We made arrangements to meet at Yankee Stadium. Well, you know what that's like. Halftime, you couldn't move. It was a big game for both schools. Our side was whooping it up because we were winning. All the players had me surrounded. I kept wondering if Joe was going to show.

He didn't show. I didn't say anything. I let it go. The next day, I got a phone call. It was Joe. He said, "Coach, I apologize. I couldn't get to you. The crowd kept pigeonholing me, wanting to talk baseball. I couldn't get through." I said, "You don't owe me an apology. This is great. Thanks a lot. I appreciate it, and I can understand how you couldn't get up there. I miss seeing you."

He said, "Look, you've got to come to Chicago for a game." I said, "Oh, Joe, I'm not going to be able to."

"You big dummy, you've got your son living in Illinois, right outside of Springfield." The only thing we ever do is go to see him and the two grandkids in Chatham. We couldn't care less about the rest of the world, Mother and I. He's an only child.

I said, "I'll tell you what, we're going to be out there around the Fourth of July."

He said, "Well, you've got to come up and be my guest at a ballgame."

There we were, talking back and forth. He put me in touch with his right-hand man, and the guy made all the arrangements. I took the two grandkids and my daughter-in-law, my son and wife, of course, and we went to a ballgame in Wrigley Field. We saw the Cubs play the Cardinals. You'd have thought I was a king. My grandson, all of a sudden, thought I knew somebody who's important, right? Grandpa, he's just Grandpa. Joe gave him a cap. We got all the trimmings. Joe told the story about how he played football in front of the two grandboys. It was so generous of him. He paid me a great compliment in front of those two boys. He said, "Coach, I didn't know if I was going to have enough money to come back to Lafayette or not." It was just so gracious of him.

Years ago, I used to ask my wife, "Do you think these players will ever understand me?"

She said, "Oh, I think they understand you better than you think. You'll find out someday."

Of course, she knew more than me. Wives always do. I've seen it come back a thousand times. The players did understand.

That was Joe. I watched his career, and he's done a fantastic job. I'm afraid to call him or write him for fear I'll be a jinx.

I can tell you this. I came from a very poor family, nine in the family. I went to parochial school. I never went anywhere. The priest that taught us football and basketball and baseball

Joe Maddon (No. 22) perfecting his home run trot.

took us to see my first professional game, Cardinals against Pittsburgh. Musial was the big gun at that time, Stan the Man. I've always had a soft spot for the Cardinals, but now I'm rooting for the Cubs. Joe grew up a Cardinals fan. It was a good show at Wrigley. He's got those people humming in Chicago. He told me they were going to revamp the stadium. His offices, he's living in a closet there. It didn't matter. He hadn't changed.

I wrote him one time when he was having a little difficulty there. I wrote, "Joe, the team doesn't need you when they're winning. They need you now. Just pull out that old way of doing things, and you're going to be O.K." I had the guts to say that to a guy who's at the apex of his career, but it helped a little. He started to win again.

When I was coaching, we all wanted to win, but I tried getting across to these young men that you strive to do your very best. You're going to win some, and you're to lose some, but you always do your best, and striving to win is the important thing. When you give up on yourself, and you don't work to win, is when you're not getting out of it what you're supposed to get. This idea that you have to win, that comes because of the heart and the ability that you have, if you treat the players right.

When Joe was at Lafayette, there were no scholarships. In those days, the school was set up for financial assistance. It's just like the Ivy's still doing it. They put money aside so they can dispense it and get all facets on the campus. You've got to have music players. You've got to have poets. You've got to have scientists. Basketball players, football players. You've got to have girls. Every staff was earmarked X-amount of dollars out of the athletic department budget to run the program. That's where Joe got his money, because I said, "He's one of my guys."

We'd never take money back, once it was given to the boys. We always supported them, no matter what they did, even if they quit. A father told me his son decided he didn't want to play anymore. He was going to work in the steel mill in

Pittsburgh. The dad said, "I'm going to break both of his legs. He gave his word, and you've given him this money, and now he's going to walk away. I can't take that. It's a black mark on our family name."

I looked him in the eye and said, "Please listen to me. I don't know if I've made a mistake as a coach, but I don't think so. Your son has lost his zeal to play the game. I lose a football player if I make a mistake. You keep up this rhetoric, you're going to lose a son. I want you to think long and hard about this. There's no black mark at all. You've got a son who has the courage to walk in that door and face me and say, 'Coach, I no longer have the zeal or the enthusiasm to play football, and I'm not going to come back for the team.' He just didn't leave campus, never to be seen again. I'm not talking down to you. I'm trying to talk across the table to you. Don't do it. Admire that he had the guts. Talk about it and then support him. Or you're going to lose a son. You may find him in Greenwich Village. Don't do it."

He looked at me and said, "You know, Coach, I guess I needed that." I said, "We all need it once in a while. We all have to tell each other when we think we're out of line. You're a father. You know what to do. Just do it."

When I talked to Joe in Chicago, I said, "Joe, I remember when you left Lafayette to play baseball." I told you, "Be the very best baseball player you can possibly be. You're a hell of a lot better baseball player than you were a football player. It's just so good to see you make it. I didn't know that you were going to be that right, that you were going to be great."

I never, ever had a player that I didn't think was a top-notch person. I don't care how good they were as a player. That was an unwritten rule that was verbally given to the coaching staff. You do not recruit anyone who is not upstanding. I'd say Joe was one of the really good ones. I never had a kid I had to knock off the team. Maybe we weren't the greatest all the time, but I'll tell you what, they were all good people. I'd recruit Joe again today, even though he might leave and go to baseball. I was just pleased we got him at Lafayette. I thought Joe was a hell of a get. It turned out good for him, too.

He would have ended up starting for us as a varsity quarterback. I can't say that he would have started as a sophomore. He would have vied for the position, but I can't be disloyal to the young man who was our starter and say that Joe would have won that battle right off. You earn it on the field. We felt that he had great potential. I was trying to build the program. It wasn't on top, but I was trying to bring in the kids who would do the job. Joe was our pick to eventually be our quarterback.

I can tell you this cute story about him. We were in his office at Wrigley Field. He said, "Coach, I've been fortunate. I've made quite a bit of money. I'm going to come back to Lafayette, and I'm going to have the biggest fraternity party you've ever seen."

I said, "Yeah, that figures. Now you're going to cause the present coach heartache, worrying about you getting those kids out of line. If you come back, keep it inbounds, will you?"

He said, "Well, you're going to come, aren't you?"

I said, "I'll be the guy opening the party."

That's the fun part, going back to the school to be with the current and former players. I thought, that tells me a lot about Joe. He wants to go back and have something on the campus. He wasn't talking about being a big shot with the faculty, the administration or the athletic department. He was talking about being with the frat guys and inviting the alumni back, the guys that he went to school with. I said, "Joe, you get that party organized. I'll be there."

I always said, "Hey, it's easy to get a locker room to talk when you're winning. Show me the coach and let me in that locker room when you've got a team that's having a tough time.

That's the guy I want to be with. I want to know what he's saying because that's where the essence of coaching is. How do
you look when the chips are down? How do you handle those
situations? Anybody can brag when they just beat somebody
30-0 and you have a good season going. But what about that
coach who's struggling and trying to keep his team together
and trying to keep them motivated? That's the guy who's still
into coaching." I was never blessed with an undefeated team.
I helped coach undefeated teams. I've never had one myself.
Look at how Joe has built lousy teams into excellent teams. He
knows what it's like to struggle as a player and as a manager.

I was burnt out, to be honest with you, and I needed to
get away from everything. I was going to stay in coaching. I
looked at my wife and I thought, nope, she's put up enough
with this moving around. That was it. I've found what I wanted
to do here in Vermont. I've been happy ever since. I do miss
the intermingling with the players. I felt I needed to show some
real togetherness at home and live as a normal person. When
you're in coaching, you don't live normal.

Joe had leadership ability and could throw the football.
We call it "field vision" in coaching. When he dropped back, he

Joe Maddon (No. 12) on the freshman football team at Lafayette.

had the field vision of where to go and where to try to throw the ball, and that leadership became into the decision making, the courage to make decisions. He definitely still has that ability. I think you see that in the way he manages his baseball team. He's not afraid to make an unusual decision that someone will look at and say, "Why is he doing that?" He knows what he's doing. He knows why he's doing it. He's got the courage to do it. That's the biggest thing that I can say about him as a young player. I feel like I coached him for four years, but it really was only one.

Joe would have been great as a football player. There's no doubt in my mind about that, absolutely none. I can't prove it, because he didn't stay with us. We laughed when I told him, "You made the right decision. That's not meaning you couldn't have played quarterback. To rise where you are now, you must have really looked into a crystal ball."

Joe Maddon swinging away at Lafayette.

IT WAS A BALL

JIM CURNAL

Jim Curnal was a battery mate with Joe Maddon at Lafayette College. He now plays the Mr. Mom role as his wife is a big shot executive at Saatchi & Saatchi ad agency. He also coaches baseball at the high school level. He has studied pitching mechanics for many years, and some people consider him the most knowledgeable pitching guru in the country. Ironically, he has never shared this knowledge with Joe Maddon because he thinks Maddon would think he might be crazy. Curnal is well respected in his profession.

I have a pretty good relationship with Joe, but I respect the demands on his time. Going from Tampa to the Cubs has put him in another area code in more ways than one. We go back about 35, 40 years, but I'm very careful about not intruding into his professional life. I've shared a few of my coaching ideas from my experiences of working with high school athletes over the past 10 years. But comparing my world to his from a coaching perspective is akin to comparing Apples to Chevrolets—two totally different worlds. I've been, as well as the rest of the Lafayette group, very careful not to intrude in his world. I'll text him during the season to offer congratulations or a quick jab. He takes as well as he gives. He was kind enough to reach out to my wife and me when Virginia's mom passed away. If he asks a question, I'll offer my opinion, but that's it. As I said we all have great respect and admiration for what he does and try never to take advantage of our relationship with him

We talk about his family. We talk about my family. We talk about our mutual friends. We talk about the season in general.

I'll ask him his opinions on certain baseball issues, but more as a learning opportunity then to put him on the spot.

Three to four times a year, I get a group of friends—the Leopards from Lafayette—and we go out to dinner with him after a game. We've been to Washington, D.C., New York City, Baltimore. The dinner group has expanded to include several women who were good friends of Joe's and mine at Lafayette, who we lost touch with over the years. It's been great to reunite with them as they're good people and add a lot to the group. We had a great group of 12 Lafayette friends go to Baltimore two years ago. Joe had a special Lafayette menu created for our dinner, which was a very special gesture on his part. We presented him with a T-shirt with a picture of a Lafayette helmet that read, "From Hinkle to the Angels to the Rays to the Cubs: The Road to Success."

The Chicago move changes the logistics a bit, but we made it out this season to join the crazy Cubs fans. It was a blast. A group of seven made the sojourn to the Windy City—all good friends from Lafayette, We all played baseball at Lafayette. Joe was our catcher. Artie Fischetti played third base. Ralph Klinepeter played centerfield and pitched. Len Fruci was our right fielder. Rick Hartung was a relief pitcher. And Tom Casey played first base. They were all good players. Fischetti played for the Dodgers organization and was on his way to having a very successful career until a hand injury sidelined him.

We had a blast and got the royal treatment from Joe, as usual. We got an up close personal tour of the new Wrigley digs, including the underground clubhouse. Everyone, from the people at the front gate to the clubhouse personnel to the players we met, were extremely personable and gracious. We had a great dinner with Joe and his lovely wife, Jaye, on Saturday night that put a fitting end to a great weekend.

I believe he really enjoys these get-togethers as it provides him with an opportunity to hang with us as simply Joe Maddon, good friend. We have a very eclectic group of individuals which suits Joe very well. The bottom line is we respect his position and the demands on his time and I believe he appreciates the effort we've made to stay in contact over the years. It has meant a lot to this group of guys.

Several years ago when Joe was with Tampa, a reporter from St. Petersburg called to interview me. I said one of the things I most respected about Joe was how he handled life with great equanimity, probably because that is not one of my strengths. His view of life is colored with a great sense of balance and perspective. Off the field, I have never seen him lose his cool regardless of the situation, and have come to greatly admire that aspect of his character. We go out to dinner after the game and win, lose or draw, he is simply Joe Maddon, one of the gang.

We try to get together during the off-season. Every year a group of us from Lafayette travel to Hazleton to participate in his HIP program. They have a wonderful dinner, which is open to the public. My friends and I work the kitchen. It's our way of saying thank you by helping to support his hometown community. When we were in college, I went to Hazleton with him a few weekends to hang out with his family and friends. He often spoke of his father and the dedication his father had to his craft and his family. I always felt that Joe inherited his work ethic and perspective on life from the example his father set. As a way of saying thank you during his tenure at Tampa Bay, I sent him a framed picture of an Olympic runner crossing the finish line. The quote below the picture read, "What were you thinking of when you crossed the finish line?" The runner responded, "All of the sacrifices my father made for me." After hearing Joe speak so fondly of his father through the years, I felt he would appreciate the gesture. He sent me a very kind note.

I've gotten to know his mother Beanie over the years. She is wonderful woman who is extremely proud of all of her children and grandchildren. The fact that Joe can return to his hometown and simply be "Joey" in her eyes is a really cool thing. It speaks a lot about him as an individual, his family and the people of Hazleton.

I still have vivid memories of Lafayette baseball when Joe and I were freshmen at the Hill. The new field house hadn't been built yet, so we practiced in the old Alumni Gym at 9 p.m. It was the only facility at Lafayette. Norm Gigon, a former Chicago Cub, was the coach. Practice would end around 11, then we'd play pick-up basketball for another two hours.

Maddon came to Lafayette as a pitcher, along with Ralph Klinepeter and myself . Our spring trip our freshman year was to Tampa. We played the University of Tampa and a team from the Kansas City Royals Baseball Academy. Our transposition was a 24-hour double-decker Trailways bus ride.

We played the Kansas City Royals Academy at St. Petersburg. The Academy was a baseball school for prospects who were high school graduates, kind of a pre-minor league training camp. We played back-to-back doubleheaders and they wound up stealing something like 25 bases in four games. Gigon called a meeting the next day and said, "Hey, I'm looking for catchers."

Maddon stepped up and said, "I'll give it a shot." From what I gather, Joe had never caught before. Right then and there he donned the catching gear for the next game and learned by on-the-job training. It was interesting pitching to him for a while, but through hard work and perseverance he developed into an excellent catcher. Ralph and I always kid him that it was the best decision he ever made for two reasons: 1) It obviously started him on his career path. And 2) He was never going to get a lot of innings with Ralph and me on the mound.

Joe told a story that during the first game he caught, he missed a fastball and it hit the home plate umpire square in the mask. The ump turned to Joe and asked if he had ever caught before. Joe, being the honest guy he is, said no. The ump just shook his head and laughed.

From that point on, Joe caught every game for three years. He was a great catcher to throw to, very headsy, a very good student of the game and always in command of the situation. A reporter asked me, "Did you think he was going to be a manager in the Major Leagues?" You know, at 20-years-old, it never even crosses your mind, but I thought at the time that he was very intelligent. He had a very broad view of life and even then great balance and perspective for a 20-year-old. He never seemed to get rattled, which I thought was a strong attribute. Whether I thought he was going to be a Major League manager, a CEO or a general in the Army, I couldn't tell you, but that's what I remember about him back then.

As a pitcher you always felt that you could rely on him. He called a very good game and was a tough competitor. Rarely did I shake him off as I was afraid he would chew me out. He was all business during the game and always was willing to let

Joe enjoying a get-together with the Lafayette gang.

you know who was in charge, but he also had a great sense of humor and was not afraid to bust some chops.

I pitched an apocryphal game at Penn State that we affectionately refer to as the "Snow Storm." We were playing at Penn State in a full-blown snow storm, about 25 degrees with 25-mile-per-hour winds. I lost the feeling in my fingers by the second inning. During the bottom of the fourth with the snow coming down in sheets, Maddon came out to the mound and started getting on me for shaking him off. I asked him what he meant and he said, "Why are you only throwing fastballs?" I said, "Because my hands are frostbitten." That ended the meeting on the mound. By the way, we won in nine innings and Maddon got the game-winning hit, a double against the fence.

Our sophomore year we are playing the last game of the season on a Monday versus St. Johns. We had back-to-back doubleheaders that weekend against Gettysburg and Delaware and were out of pitchers. After the second game on Sunday, Gigon said, "Hey, I need a pitcher. Who wants to pitch?" I was 20-years-old and stupid. I said, "I'll take the ball." I had pitched on Saturday, a complete game win, so I would be pitching on one-day rest. We went to St. Johns and all things considered, I was feeling pretty good and began loosening up as the game progressed. We got to the bottom of the ninth, and we were winning. With two outs and a 1-2 count on the batter, Maddon called time out and walked to the mound. He said, "Curns, I need you to throw two more pitches." I said, "What are you talking about?" He said,"There's a pool." I said, "What are you talking about?" He said, "The bench started a pool before the game. Everybody chipped in 10 bucks and picked the number of pitches you'd throw. You're at 123. I picked 125." I looked at him and said, "I'll tell you what. I'll give you one more, and you can split the pot."

Maddon was also a very good quarterback. He was recruited to play quarterback at Lafayette. He was very controlled, very levelheaded, which suited him very well. He did not have a great arm, but he had a very accurate arm. From a mental standpoint, he displayed the characteristics and attributes that would make you a successful quarterback. He was only about 5-foot-11, but athletic. He was able to see the open receiver, and he had a good head for the game. If I were to characterize him, his style was more Joe Montana than an Aaron Rodgers, cool under pressure. I think that's an attribute that serves him well as a manager.

I get the impression that Joe has always really enjoyed what he is doing. Joe has a very persevering attitude. He's a grinder. I think he knew what it was going to take to get where he wanted to go. I can't tell you that when I knew him in his early years that he would tell you he would be the manager of the Tampa Bay Rays and the Cubs someday. But I knew he had the determination and the work ethic that, if given the opportunity, he would make the most of it. The saying, "luck is the residue of hard work and perseverance," certainly applies to Joe.

Combing these attributes with his talent, we all knew he had the ability and opportunity to go far. Even during his first few years with Tampa Bay when they were losing 100 games, he was extremely confident about the path the organization was on. He told me he was invested in "building a culture." Even after not getting hired by the Boston Red Sox in 2003, he said that despite being disappointed, he knew that his turn would come and he would get his chance to manage. He was proven right three years later when the Rays hired him and he led Tampa to the World Series.

I often saw him during spring training in Arizona during the early '80s when I was doing a lot of traveling. I can honestly say that his work ethic wasn't any different then than it is now. I would watch practice and his approach with his minor leaguers was just as thorough and professional as it is today. Probably the only thing that has changed is the Burl Ives goatee that he sports.

I played in Yankees organization and can appreciate the time and effort that a managerial career demands, not to mention the personal sacrifices one needs to make to attain his level of success. I have great respect and admiration for what he has achieved.

He is always speaking about the process, which I can absolutely relate to as a high school coach. I believe his ability to always take the long view is what contributes to his success along with the fact that he is not afraid to bring mariachi bands, magicians and snakes into the clubhouse. Not to mention the frequent pajama themed road trips.

I was in Baltimore during one of our group trips. We were sitting next to the dugout and as game time was fast approaching several of his players were still talking to fans and signing autographs. I thought that was odd and asked him about it after the game. His response was, "Hey, they have a difficult job and it's a very long season, but it's a game and they need to relax and have fun." I was impressed by his response and recognized that this uncommon approach and philosophy serves him and his players well.

After knowing him all of these years, the highest compliment that I can give Joe is that he treats everyone he meets, everyone who crosses his path, with a great deal of dignity and respect.

KNOWING JOE MADDON IS LIKE PLAYING HOOKY FROM LIFE

TOM ODJAKJIAN

Tom Odjakjian is the senior associate commissioner for broadcasting and digital content of the American Athletic Conference. He is a 1976 graduate of Lafayette and has a bachelor's degree in economics and business. He played football and baseball as an undergraduate and was Joe Maddon's teammate. He is the recipient of the George Wharton Pepper Prize, Lafayette's most prestigious honor. While at ESPN in 1994, he was named the most influential person in college sports and in 1990 The Sporting News *named him one of the four most influential people in college basketball.*

I first ran into Joe in freshman football at Lafayette College. I was a third-string safety, and he was the starting quarterback. He was always cool under pressure. We had a really good team. We were 5-1 and lost only a close game to Rutgers. Unfortunately, not enough of those players stayed with the program, and Joe gave up football after his freshman year to concentrate on baseball. His last game was as a freshman against Lehigh. He threw four touchdown passes.

We did drills against the varsity quarterback. Back then, freshmen couldn't play varsity. It was such a different time. We had only four coaches total, two on offense, two on defense. Steve Schnall was the head coach of our freshman team. We had a lot of other good players on the team. Would Joe have been the starting varsity quarterback if he had stayed with it? He probably had a good chance, if not sophomore year, probably by junior year. We had a really good back-up named Mark Jones who later became the varsity quarterback.

I was disappointed that I didn't get to spend senior year with Joe. I played one year of football and two years of baseball. I really enjoyed it. It was hard to get off the bench. It was a small school, and everybody knew everybody and stayed in touch. It was a lot of fun. We had eight guys from this little non-scholarship school that played pro baseball just from the years I was there. Joe signed right after Christmas of his senior year and went out to Iowa and then worked his way up the Angels chain. He certainly more than paid his dues.

Joe interviewed for the Red Sox job in 2003. He was the runner-up to Terry Francona. I thought, boy, that would have been so cool, considering I don't live far from Boston. When he got the Tampa job, I went to a Rays game and saw him. I said, "Oh, my gosh, nobody can win in Tampa. I'm thrilled you got the job, but how can you win here?" He was so calm. "Oh, we've got a great young team. We've got great management. You know, in three years, I think we're going to be really, really good." The next year, he was in the World Series. Tampa had been so bad for so long, I figured, O.K., he's going to lose a hundred games a few years in a row, and then they'll try somebody else. Instead, what a career he's had.

The Chicago thing has been off the charts. I read one story that they're going to rename Lake Michigan Lake Maddon if the Cubs win the whole thing. The media loves him. I knew the P.R. director for the Rays, and he said he was the luckiest guy around to have Joe as his manager. Tim McCarver said during the World Series that Joe was the best manager he'd ever talked with in preparing for a telecast. That's incredible. Joe is so unique. Because he's won, he's been able to do all the unusual things he does. He has certainly gotten a lot of recognition. He's been manager of the year three times. That may be tough to do again. A lot of times, it's easier when you're the underdog. He's going to be the favorite for a few years in a row with the team he's got now.

The 1973 Lafayette baseball team. Joe Maddon is in the front row, the second from the right (No. 22).

The 1974 Lafayette baseball team. Joe Maddon is in the front row, far right (No. 22).

I'm pretty good friends with Dick Vitale, a big Rays fan. He has seats right by the visiting dugout. A few years ago, my family went to visit Dick, and then we went to see Joe and the Rays, and we sat with Dick. Before the game, I went into the locker room with Joe and Dick. I saw a lot of people because of my ESPN background, and they'd say, "Say hi to Joe" or Joe would say hi to me in that way. I don't see him as often as I'd like. Now that he's in the National League, it's harder. The Cubs make one trip a year to play the Mets.

I went to Wrigley Field last year with my family and got to see Joe. I said, "You've set such high expectations here. The expectations are through the roof." Joe said, "Look how awesome this is. This place is packed. It's exciting."

He embraces it. When he had his first Cubs press conference, he asked, "Why not playoffs?" He's just so positive. Everybody loves him. He's incredible. I love reading stories about him. A lot of writers that I know have written about him. It would just be so awesome if he could bring a World Series title to Chicago. He paid his dues. I treasure my friendship with him and wish I could see him more often, but he's a pretty busy guy. I was surprised when Joe gave up football. He didn't have a rocket arm, but he had poise. He was accurate and cool under pressure. Joe Namath was his idol. He was cool. Joe Willie.

Joe wrote me a beautiful handwritten letter when he was in the minors many years ago. My wife found it. I don't know if I can find it again, but I wanted to send it to Joe. It was really, really nice.

I'd still look up to Joe, even if he hadn't reached this level of success. My wife teases me because she says I have a man crush on him. He's such a good person.

When Dick Vitale was at a Cubs game last month, he tweeted a picture of him with Joe. Dick texted me, "Yeah, we talked about you, O.J." That's my nickname. It's nice when Chris Berman or somebody that I know from my ESPN days runs into him.

The majority of players in the minor leagues never make it. When I think about Joe's life on the road all those years in the minors before he got to be a coach with the Angels, talk about paying your dues. He'll tell you this. He didn't get a shot as a manager earlier because he never played past Class-A ball. In sports, there's sometimes a stigma. If you haven't played at the highest level, they don't think you can manage. He obviously has a great relationship with Mike Scioscia. When Joe was a bench coach when the Angels won the World Series, that elevated his value. He was the interim manager a couple of times with the Angels. The first time he interviewed for a manager's job was with the Red Sox, and he almost got the job. I'm sure Red Sox fans said, "Who?" They hired Terry Francona, but he was exactly the type of manager they were looking for. They wanted somebody modern and with analytics. They had just let go of Grady Little, who was as old school as they come.

I went to a Rays-Yankees game in New York, and I told Joe, "I'm so happy for you." I'm sure that the fact that the Red Sox almost hired him got the attention of the Rays. He just thought it was such a great situation. He knew the stadium was going to be an issue. I remember him telling me that. It still is for the Rays, right? He just was so excited about their young players and his owner and the general manager and the support he was getting. I think he actually said, "I'm in a better situation with the Rays than I would have been in with the Red Sox." Now that's hard to imagine, isn't it?

Obviously, his record speaks for itself. And the stars got aligned so he would be with the Cubs at the perfect time. And there's Theo Epstein who almost hired him in Boston. There he is, hiring him in Chicago. He has a young team, and he's best with young players. The players love him.

I was third-string freshman safety. It was great being Joe's teammate and admiring how beautifully he played. He probably wasn't the fleetest of foot. He was so poised and knew what he wanted to do. We had a lot of good players on that team. We had a great tailback and good receivers and good defense. He was like the orchestra leader. I was on the sideline watching him with so much admiration. He just was so down to earth, so cool, so unflappable. I can't remember ever seeing Joe mad.

I went to Joe's fraternity bedroom. He told me about playing in the Colorado College League. Some of our other teammates played in the Cape Cod Baseball League, the best in the country. I wasn't good enough to play in the Cape League, but I always dreamed about it. Joe told me about playing in Colorado, and it was fascinating to hear what that experience was like. That summer in Colorado was when Joe thought he could play pro ball.

Catcher was the natural position for him because he was so smart, and he could manage the game from there. I didn't realize it at the time, that he hadn't been a catcher before getting to Lafayette. He really seemed like such a natural at it.

When Joe was traveling, it was hard to stay in touch. After he got the job with the Rays, a lot of the old Lafayette gang made a point of getting together to visit him in different cities. It's not easy on his schedule, but it's been pretty special when we've been able to do it. I haven't made all of those get-togethers, but I made a couple of dinners in New York and got to see him a couple of other times before games. He's so well liked.

There are a lot of life lessons in sports. They may not be ones that you like. I try to explain to my son why he made a team or didn't make a team. Those conversations are hard, hard for a parent, hard for a kid. Whether you got a job or didn't, got into college or didn't, life's full of disappointments. A lot of times it doesn't make sense, and a lot of times, it's not fair. Hopefully, you keep plugging away, and things will turn out good for you. Thankfully, they did for Joe.

*Danica Patrick has starred in more **SUPER BOWL** spots than any other celebrity.

A PLAY-TONIC RELATIONSHIP

BRENDA SASSO

Brenda Sasso grew up in Wayne, N.J., graduated from Lafayette College, and has returned to Wayne where she is a language arts and reading teacher. She was a close personal friend of Joe Maddon while in college and finally reunited with him a few years ago.

I first met Joe Maddon freshman year in college. Susie Tischler and I were roommates. When we first started at Lafayette, the ratio was five men for every woman. It had just gone coed three years before. Joe was a freshman like us and he would always come in and hang out with us. He was like, I don't have a chance with you, because all the upperclassmen would come to the door to meet us. It was funny.

Joe became our buddy. I had one good friend that was a girl, and Joe was like my good buddy friend all through college. We never dated. We were always just buddies.

Sophomore year, I lived on the third floor of a dorm. One Thursday night, it was always beer on tap at all the frats. He'd yell, "Can Brenda come out and play?" We'd go out drinking together. He was always the one I could talk to. We had many serious talks about life in general. He came to my house in New Jersey and visited. My dad died when I was a senior, and Joe came then, too.

On Friday and Saturday nights there were often dances. Joe and I would start out together. We'd start dancing, and he'd dance me all over. He'd see a girl that he might want to try to pick up. So we'd dance over to the girl, and he'd give me a signal. I would leave, and he'd start to try and pick up the girl. It often worked. Then I would hang out with other friends. That's the type of relationship that Joe and I had.

Senior year, I remember sitting in Jack Von Wagner's room when Joe came in. He said, "I'm leaving. I'm going to California." He had signed to play pro ball with the California Angels and was going to report to spring training in El Centro, Calif.

I said, "Are you crazy? We're almost done, and you're going to leave school?"

He did. He went to California, and we lost touch forever until Jim Curnal got us back together with Susie and others. We've been close since. He's someone I really value as a friend. He's a lot busier now that he's with the Cubs than he was with Tampa Bay. His wife threw him a surprise 60th birthday party two years ago, and Susie and I flew down to Tampa for that.

My daughter and I flew down another time to Tampa to visit him. When he was in New York last year, I went into the city to have lunch with him. It was great to just sit for hours and talk with him one-on-one because when we get together with the group, we never get to talk much. He's the type that you just feel comfortable with immediately. It was like we were never 30 years without seeing each other.

In those 30 years, I always wondered what happened to him. He was with the Angels for a long time. He filled me in on everything he did from living in his car to making it big. I met his daughter and his grandkids. I haven't met his son. He's met my kids. When he was in New York one time, my husband and I and my kids had a very enjoyable dinner with him and his wife, Jaye.

Two weeks before the **SUPER BOWL*** was in New York in 2014, Joe sent me a text, "Brenda, if I get tickets, do you want to go to the Super Bowl with Jaye?" I'm like, what? I wrote back, "Why won't you go?" His answer was, "I don't like the cold."

He was at a fundraiser. He won the tickets. Jaye came up, stayed at my house with my husband and me, and she and I went to the Super Bowl and had a ball.

Jim Curnal called me. He had been seeing Joe when he was on the road. Every time Joe came into New York, Jim would get a bunch of guys together that he played baseball with or fraternity friends or friends he knew from college, and they'd have dinner.

One night, I got a call from Jim. He said, "I was having dinner with Joe, and he said, 'When are you going to bring some women in?'" Jim asked Joe, "Who would you like to see?" Joe said, "Sue Tischler and Brenda."

Jim arranged it. The Rays were playing in Baltimore. Susie flew up. I picked her up. It was funny because we were staying at a hotel across from the ballpark. The team was flying in from Boston. We were waiting. It was about 11, 11:30. I didn't know it, but Susie and Joe were planning on surprising me by Joe coming that evening to say "hi" before everybody else got in, to hang with Susie and me.

She told me as we were having dinner, just before Joe showed up. He had jet black hair at the time because he had done a theme of Elvis Presley. He does his theme travel things, and Jaye had dyed his hair black. It was funny to see him.

He said, "I was a nervous wreck meeting you guys again." Susie and I were nervous wrecks, too, but we had a ball. My daughter was with us, too. We were all in the hotel room hanging out, drinking some wine, telling old stories. The front desk called up twice to say they were getting complaints from neighboring rooms that we were being too loud. That was our first time back together. It was like old times again.

I was shocked when Jim Curnal first called me. I was absolutely shocked because two years before, Joe was in the World Series. An ex-boyfriend of mine from college lives in Philly. He texted me, "Joe's in the World Series." I was like, holy cow! I had lost track of him and certainly wasn't keeping track of Tampa Bay. I'm not a huge baseball fan. I should be. That was the first I'd heard of Joe in baseball, that he had done well.

When Jim called, I couldn't believe it, but I was really excited to see Joe again. It was like losing a very close friend when he left before that senior year. He was so busy trying to make it without any money or anything. In the meantime, he got married, had two kids and got divorced.

He told me, "When you don't have much money, you do what you have to do." His heart was in trying to make it in baseball, and that's what he did. He did what he had to do. I can't remember if that was before he was married or after. He said

BMOC at Lafayette.

he'd slept wherever he could at one point or whatever he could afford, but he was determined to make it in baseball. That's what he wanted.

I'm a teacher and my fellow teachers said, "You're going to the Super Bowl with Joe Maddon's wife?"

I said, "Yeah, can you believe it?"

Jaye is so down to earth. It's great. She's fun to hang with. Jaye is 10 years younger than us and looks fantastic. She's very personable, although she can be very quiet. When the whole group is there, Jaye just sits back and takes it in and listens, but one-on-one, she's fantastic. When I picked her up at the airport, we went out to dinner. I had met her a couple of times before she came up for the Super Bowl. We talked like old friends. She's really personable. We just had a great time.

It's funny. She calls him "Joseph" from time to time. "Well, Joseph," and we're like, Joseph? She runs the household for him. Joe told me this story: when they went to California, he was on a road trip, and they needed a place to live. He put Jaye in charge. Jaye did the searching for the house, found the house, got it furnished, everything. They have a home on the beach in California. She furnished the whole thing, did a lot of the painting herself, everything. She manages the household, takes care of all that stuff for Joe so he doesn't have to worry about it. Now that she has two gyms she's running, she's really busy.

In college, we didn't wish that Joe would ask us out. I always considered Joe a friend. It's funny. That first night we met afterwards, he said, "Well, you went out with this one. I thought you only had this boyfriend."

I said, "No, I was dating other people."

"Well, why didn't we date?"

I said, "Because you were my buddy. You were my best friend. You don't do that."

He was, to me, too valuable a friend to ever try and date. I just always considered him my good friend. I never tried to fix him up with my other friends. He never had any problem with that. I didn't worry about it.

Joe was interested in girls and drinking. Football, for a while. Sleeping. Music. Having a good time. Joe was different from other guys. We talked a lot, just about life and what we were thinking and things like that. If I ever had a problem, I could go to Joe and talk about it.

I don't know why we didn't keep in touch after college. We both got wrapped up in our own things and went our own ways. It's been fun to reconnect. It's been a lot of fun. Like I said, since he got with the Cubs, we don't get to talk as much. We used to text a lot back and forth. Now he's very busy, but if I text him something, he at least answers back with everybody. I try not to text him too much anymore because he's got to be going crazy. He's got a lot on his plate right now.

I went to Hazleton once during my senior year in high school. I was trying to get to Bucknell University for an interview, and my father's car broke down in Hazleton. Joe keeps saying that I could have a job there if I wanted at his old school, but I don't want to move to Hazleton. I'm not going to leave my grandkids.

I love Lafayette, yeah. It was a great time. When we were there, it was all fraternities. There were no sororities. Susie and I ate down at Joe's fraternity, Zeta Psi. It wasn't that Joe would sit with us every night, but we would sit together with him a lot of times. That just kept up the friendship, too. Joe and I and a lot of the Zeta guys took geology together, and I helped them all get through the class. I was a studier. Joe wasn't.

Susie and I drive Joe crazy when we get together. We have a ball. We love wine. We'll start sipping on wine before we're supposed to meet Joe after batting practice to say hello. We haven't made it yet. He's always worrying about where we are, what we're doing. We're fun.

Joe also loves wine. The first time I was with Joe after reuniting, I brought wine, some nice bottles. Joe and I started talking wine. My husband and I collected wine for a long time. When we would meet for dinner with Joe in New York, we took in a couple of bottles of some very nice wine. That was when I took my whole family, and we met Joe and Jaye. The restaurant owner wouldn't let us open the wine. I was so upset because I wanted to taste it, too. I said, "Joe, you and Jaye take it." They took it to their room that night, and they enjoyed it.

I was watching a video on Joe on Facebook and Joe was showing the whole new area that they have at Wrigley Field, including his office. He said, "I don't have everything in it, but I have this wine rack with some nice wine." I texted him, "O.K., what's in your wine rack?" I never got an answer.

A couple of years ago he and Jaye did a tour in Napa Valley wine country and had a very nice time.

My husband likes Joe a lot. He thinks a great deal of him. He's met him a couple of times. When we get together, it's always Susie and me, and my husband just says, "You guys go have fun."

Jim Curnal is going to have a party at Zeta Psi when Lehigh plays at Lafayette this year. My husband said, "Yes, I do want to go to that." Susie's going to fly in, and the three of us will go.

Joe is one of the nicest, easygoing, caring people I've ever met.

IF THE PHONE DOESN'T RING, IT'S JOE MADDON

SUE TISCHLER

Sue Tischler enjoys the good life, living in Lauderdale-by-the-Sea, Fla. She was born in Haddon Heights, N.J., and was a classmate of Joe Maddon at Lafayette. She worked for the DEA for 22 years before retiring in 2004 in New Orleans and is currently in the real estate business..

I went to Lafayette. I was part of the third full graduating four-year class of women. The ratio of men to women at Lafayette was 5-to-1.

Brenda Sasso and I met at orientation. We decided to be roommates. Brenda was the best-looking girl of our class. She was dating a senior who was a nerd. I was dating my high school sweetheart, who was in Springfield, Mass. None of the freshmen girls would go out with freshmen guys because they had three other classes to choose from. The freshman boys would come and literally knock on our door and say, "Hey, is Brenda here?" When I said no, they would walk away. It was so humiliating.

I don't know how we first hooked up with Joe Maddon. It was probably because of Brenda. We weren't seeing anybody on campus. We were in relationships with other guys. Joe became our buddy. He would make sure that we had places to go. He would hang out with us so we wouldn't be by ourselves. We just had a blast. We were all freshmen and just hung out together. We would go to fraternity parties. Joe pledged to the fraternity Zeta Psi. They had the best cook on campus. Brenda and I ate with Joe at his frat house as dates. We ate lunch and dinner at the frat Monday through Friday. That was our meal plan.

One night we were ready to go out, but we didn't have anyone to go out with. I remember going to the fraternity. Joe was sleeping. I jumped on his bed and yelled, "Get up! We have to go out right now! C'mon!" He got up and off we went. Everything was so low key and nice. We had a great time at Lafayette. But Joe dropped out to play in the minors. We didn't stay in touch. He never finished senior year. After graduation, everybody went their own way. Later, because Joe was in baseball, he never came back to any of the reunions. I was the reunion chairman. If he was coming, I would have known.

We just never heard from him. Our reunion became a clique of the same people with the exception of one of the girls who was a year behind us. She played field hockey with us. I found out later that Joe had dated her in college.

We kept in touch with Jim Curnal, one of Joe's friends, because of the reunions. We saw each other at least once every five years. Sometimes somebody had a party or we'd see each other at the Lehigh-Lafayette football game. There was a core group that stayed in touch through reunions.

Jim would send us photos of Joe and other guys having dinner in New York. Jim would quiz us to see if we recognized who was at the dinner. In 2008, Jim called and said, "Joe doesn't understand why we don't have any of the girls from our class at any of these dinners, because we were all so friendly." Later, I was at an outlet mall in South Florida when I get a call. It was Joe Maddon. Oh, my God. We talked for an hour. It was so great to talk to him. It was when he had already become manager of the Rays. It was funny. I told him that I had been going to

*Here's a Final Jeopardy! question from April 2016. "This word dates back to the 19th century & referred to what the **SUN** did to roofless seating." The answer was: What is bleachers?

California to see a friend. He loves baseball, loves, loves baseball, and we went to a few Angels games.

I told my friend in California, "You know, a friend of mine that I used to hang out with in college was a scout for the Angels." I never realized Joe became the bench coach and was probably there at the games. I just never even thought to look him up and contact him.

We worked it out that Joe was going to come and see Brenda and me in Baltimore when the Rays were playing there. We would meet at our hotel the night before the Rays-Orioles game. He came waltzing in off the team bus, and it was like we never left Lafayette. We went right back to the 1970s. The hotel manager called twice and said they were going to throw us out if we didn't quiet down. It's just been like that ever since.

Joe hasn't changed. He's still the same Joe Willy. He's always very upbeat, always a little cockeyed, but just very open and friendly and warm. He was always ready to take care of whatever we needed to take care of so we wouldn't be by ourselves. He was the same buddy we always had.

We girls were dating other people. We didn't really fix Joe up with anyone, but we would point out other girls. Then he started dating Susie Oaks. She was the cutest girl in her class. She was a freshman when we were sophomores. Then he really got into baseball, and that was that.

When the Cubs came to Miami to play the Marlins, I met Joe's wife, Jaye. She told me that the fans in Chicago were really excited to have Joe as the Cubs manager. When Joe was in Tampa, everyone would come up to them, but then they would back off and leave them alone. When we went out to dinner in New York or Baltimore, people knew who he was, but they

---

*When Hank Aaron was director of Minor League Operaations for the Atlanta Braves in the early 90s, he had the pockets of the players' uniforms cut off so they couldn't carry tobacco.

would let him have his dinner. No one would really bother him. Recently in Chicago, Jaye said they went to a neighborhood hair place see if Joe could get an appointment, and a female customer came up and started patting Joe on the head and said, "Oh, I love your hair. Don't cut your hair." They all think they know him. He's much more of a celebrity there because it's a much bigger team and a much bigger market, and the Cubs are doing so well. Joe would never say no to anybody. But when we are with him, we're careful not to put him in a position where he has to say no. We don't ask for a whole lot. If I go to a game down here in Miami, I don't ask for tickets. We buy our own tickets. If he has time to meet us after the game, that's great. We don't go to games when they're in Philadelphia because that's his home. That's where his peeps go. We don't want to intrude on his Hazleton time.

I worked in the DEA, so I worked with a lot of men. All of them were into baseball, mostly big Yankees fans. When I told them I knew Joe Maddon they could hardly believe it. When there was talk of him leaving Tampa, I was on a cruise to Turkey. My phone bill went up to $700 because all the guys at work and my friends were texting me. "What's happening? Where is he going? We heard he's going to Chicago. Do you know anything?"

Joe always texts back. After we hooked up with him in Florida, I'd get the Rays games on **SUN*** Sports—"Where Rays Fans Live." I watched the press conferences after the games, and then I'd text him some wise-ass comments, and he would always text back. The guys at work said, "You know, he really doesn't have time for you. He gets a thousand texts a day." I said, "He always texts back." The guy said, "Yeah, prove it." I texted Joe, "Hey, I'm with my friend, John. He doesn't believe that you text back." Joe texted me right back, "Tell him, yes, I do."

*The highest paid public employee in 40 states is either a football or a basketball **COACH**.

Joe's under so much more pressure in Chicago. It's really, really big, big time. We're all so very, very proud of him. I don't text him all the time now, just when it's important. He takes time for everybody, and that's just the kind of guy he is. He's stretched thin, but he doesn't show it. All of us were at the 150th Lehigh-Lafayette football game last year at Yankee Stadium. Brenda and I felt bad for Jaye because everyone was tugging at Joe from so many different directions. He can't say no to anybody. He makes everyone feel they're special. That is his gift.

Jaye is adorable. She's absolutely adorable. It's hard to be married to Joe because he's gone so much. She makes every time with Joe special for him. He adores her. It's very difficult to make a marriage like that work. She makes him ecstatically happy.

Since we had so few girls in our class, a lot of us became very close. And, if we played together on a sports team, that really solidified the relationships. By playing hockey, I had that bond. The school was small, and we all lived on campus. It wasn't like Rutgers, where you're on a big city campus. We were all within a confined space. We went to the same places to drink. We went to the same fraternities to drink. We ate with the same people, and you stayed friends. We had a nice class.

When we played field hockey, we were **SMOKING*** cigarettes on the bus home. Half the team smoked. Lafayette was an incredible experience. I wouldn't trade it for the world.

None of this would happen today!

Go Cubs!

---

*Which player was the National League's starting shortstop in the **ALL-STAR** Game one year and two years later was the American League's starting shortstop in the All-Star Game, yet never switched teams? The answer: Jose Altuve of the Houston Astros. The Astros switched leagues in 2013.

THE DOS AND DON'TS OF PLAYING WITH JOE MADDON: DO!

BOB ARGENTI

Bob Argenti was the senior captain of the Lafayette baseball team when Joe Maddon was a sophomore. An outstanding player, he signed with the Oakland A's and played in their system for four years in Lewiston, Idaho, Birmingham and Chattanooga. His high school teammate was Jim Van Der Beek, whose son later became a well known actor.

I grew up in New Jersey and went to high school with Jim Van Der Beek. He was a couple years ahead of me. He went to Lafayette College to play baseball, so a couple of my coaches took me there on a recruiting trip and that's how I met the school's **COACH***, Norm Gigon. Van Der Beek had a nice minor league career after Lafayette. His son has the same name and is a successful actor with starring roles in Dawson's Creek and CSI: Cyber.

I was a junior at Lafayette when Joe Maddon came in as a freshman. We always had great rapport. Joe was a consummate teammate. I was team captain my senior year, which was Joe's sophomore year. That was the year he started coming on as a catcher. He really contributed as a player. He was a great teammate and a great friend. We still keep in touch.

Joe came on campus as a quarterback for the football team and was doing a great job. He was a very likeable guy, a lot of fun. There were a couple of athletes, myself, Joe, and Art Fischetti that played two sports at Lafayette. I gave up soccer to concentrate on baseball. Art gave up basketball to concentrate on baseball. Joe did the same thing, giving up football for baseball.

Coach Gigon was a great influence. He was a guy who taught you how to be a professional. We had really good and committed teams that were successful. Certainly by the number of players that went on to play pro ball, that was his gauge. We learned to play baseball not only collegiately, but also professionally.

Joe had relatives in South Florida. Joe would come to Florida in the off-season to work out when he was with the Angels and I was with the A's. We'd get together. We'd do that even when he was still in college, since I got out a few years earlier. We'd do batting practice, work on throws, and get in shape for spring training.

Coach Gigon, who had a cup of coffee with the Chicago Cubs, was very tough, very firm. He stressed fundamentals, especially defensively. He was a great hitting instructor. He was an excellent hitter in his professional career and was an **ALL-STAR*** several times in the minor leagues.

My senior year, Joe finished the season hitting two home runs in a game. He got some clutch hits against Penn State and a few other teams. We had a good group of guys. Everybody was of the same kind of blue collar player. We'd work hard and play hard. That's what Coach Gigon instilled in us.

Joe was a pitcher my junior year, when he was a freshman. We went to Tampa to play Columbia. We rode 24 hours on a bus. We got out and had a game right away. Joe got tattooed on the mound. Columbia was launching home runs left and right. He took it in stride, didn't get to down. The next game we ended up playing the Kansas City Royals Baseball Academy. He actually pitched a really good game. He gave up only three runs versus maybe 12 in the first game. That's when Coach Gigon approached Joe to be a catcher.

Our only catcher was Mike Hinkle at the time. During the trip to Tampa, Coach Gigon asked Joe if he wanted to try catching. He was a little off at first. It took him awhile. Joe worked hard and by his sophomore year turned into a pretty solid catcher. He was productive with the bat. He was a hustle type of guy and a hard working guy. To me, knowing him now and seeing him in the pro setup, he's the type of person who never stops learning. He's not afraid to learn. He's not afraid to try stuff. He has grit.

Joe was in a different fraternity than I was. It was a small campus, so you'd see everybody all the time. Joe and I would end up at Jack's Tavern, an old farmhouse-type tavern, and have a few beers once in a while. We were on a hill and at the bottom were two breweries. The joke was that we could defy gravity because we could make the kegs go uphill on their own.

When I was first married, Joe would come down to Florida. We were working out together and afterward he'd come over to have dinner with my wife and me. She made spaghetti and meatballs and Joe would bring the wine. That's his signature now, he loves fine wines. He was getting an early jump on things way back then.

Some years ago, I was in San Diego for a convention and we met up when Joe was with the Angels. Joe was a Disney employee, as the Angels were owned by Disney at the time.

The 1975 Lafayette baseball team. Joe Maddon is in the middle row, far right (No. 22).

When he was with the Rays they would come down to play the Marlins and he would get tickets for my wife and daughters.

In Tampa, Joe sometimes had a reception after the game and I went to that twice. It was very rewarding. That was when I got to see Joe as a Major League manager. He was loved by his players, coaches and the fans. I realized he had become a celebrity. He was the man. Being the teammate that Joe was, he would introduce me to everyone.

Joe's success as a manager comes from paying his dues. He rode the buses. He tells it like it is to the players. He's inspirational with his insight on things. He thinks outside of the box. He personally has changed the managerial style of the big leagues. Other teams are doing the things he started doing 10 years ago.

I am not surprised by his success.

THERE ARE TWO SPORTS IN TEXAS: FOOTBALL AND SPRING FOOTBALL

ART FISCHETTI

Art Fischetti, 63, was a second baseman, third baseman and out-fielder at Lafayette while Joe Maddon was a teammate. Coach Dr. Tom Davis convinced Fischetti to also play basketball for the Lafayette Leopards where he excelled as a point guard. He was drafted by the Los Angeles Dodgers and played three seasons in their system, hitting .319, .368, and .297 before retiring and getting into the electrical power infrastructure business. After several years of commuting three hours round trip from Long Island to the World Trade Center, he took a transfer to Houston and has lived in Texas ever since. He currently resides in McKinney, Tex., which is a half hour north of Dallas.

Joe is very, very personable. I was always very comfortable with him in several different aspects. Number one, I knew he wanted to win. I was pretty intense about winning. I'd fight to win if I had to. I knew Joe was intense to win. He and I co-captained the same team and tried to lead by example with one purpose: to win. So, right off the bat, I knew we'd get along. We were going to do whatever it took to win. He had excellent skills as a catcher. He was perfectly built for it. He wasn't afraid. He had good command and good relationships with all the players, but in particular, the pitching staff. He knew how to manage a game and approach hitters based on what their weaknesses were and planned against their strengths.

I was interviewed by *Lafayette* magazine and told them I always liked Joe. He had focus and was a dedicated sort of guy. He related well to everybody on the team and was well liked. Having a catcher who was levelheaded, solid, and stable was good. I was more emotional. I didn't like losing or not doing well. Joe was emotional and driven, but he was just not as verbose. When he signed with the Angels out of Lafayette, I signed with the Dodgers. We played against each other in Class-A ball. I played three years in the United States and one in Europe. When I stopped playing, I made the decision to go a different path. It was a bad decision, because I didn't take advantage of my baseball contacts and lost touch with guys like Joe. I wasn't willing to make the sacrifice to work my up through an organization. I knew Joe had an affinity for staying in the game. Once he wasn't able to play, he had a bead on staying in the game. I wasn't willing to forfeit lifestyle, home life, and, to some degree, money. He did that. I'm proud of him. He stuck to it. He paid his dues.

He and I got along quite well. He had a good sense of humor. I was intense on the field and foolish off it. Joe was just a fun guy to be around. We had no issues. When we got into the professional ranks, we played in the same Class-A league, the Midwest League. He signed with the Angels, and I got drafted by the Dodgers. So we met in competition in A-ball several times. We talked after the games.

We parted ways. He went on to wherever he went to his next league, and I was in the Texas League. Having waited until I was a senior to sign, my intention was to graduate a level in the minor leagues every year, so that I didn't get too old to get to the big leagues. In those days, it was different. You got to the big leagues at 25, 26. You were ancient. My focus was doing well where I was so I could continue to graduate annually, even though the Dodgers had a really good organization. Those were the Steve Garvey years.

As a result, I didn't have a lot of connection with Joe for many years. I had a baby girl. It was time for me to get out of the minor league system and go to work. I believed at the time you could be too old to go to work. I went to work and started what turned out to be a pretty fruitful supply chain career, and we just didn't hook up for almost three decades.

My wife and I went to an Astros game in 2009 when Joe was the manager of the Tampa Bay Rays. I was very happy for him. I had known that he had his eye on trying to become a manager. I always admired his commitment and focus to do something that he loved to do. I was proud of him that he had evolved to the point that he was managing a Major League team. I never wanted to bother him. At the game, my wife, unbeknownst to me, said she was going to the ladies room. But she wrote a note that she took to a security person to hand to Joe in the dugout when the game was over.

As the game was winding down, my wife told me that she sent a note to Joe. I said, "What did you do that for? Why are you bothering him?" She suggested that we go sit behind the dugout so that once Joe saw the note, he would look for me behind the dugout. The Rays won the game and Joe went onto the field to congratulate his pitcher and team. We sat down behind the dugout. As he was walking back to the dugout, he looked at me. He was not going to recognize me. The last time we spoke, I had a full head of hair. Today, I have a fully shaven head. I was staring him down. I yelled, "What's going on, Joseph?" He stared at me for a second, gave me the peace sign and got in the dugout.

I told my wife, "Thanks for trying." We drove home, and the phone rang at the house. I answered the phone. "Is this Arthur?" "Yeah." "Well, this is Joe. I've been looking all over for you. I sent security people everywhere looking for you." I said, "How was I to know you got the note?"

That spawned a whole level of contact—texts and emails—and eventually connections in New York. We go to New York once or twice a year and try to hook up at a Yankees game. I always picked a day when the Rays were there. We met him several times during his tenure with Tampa Bay. We went to the game. We'd go to the dugout before the game and say hi. He got us in the day of Derek Jeter's 3,000th hit.

We visited him and his wife in Tampa. We saw him in Houston two years ago. That was when he was starting to struggle with the Rays. I believe everything has a life cycle. At some point, change is good. I told him that despite the team's struggles, not to change his approach. If you change, then the players can see right through it. It would be disingenuous to them. It would be more harm than good, long term, if he suddenly took a different approach.

They turned around some in the second half of that season. But they pretty well fell out of the playoff picture. Then the Cubs opportunity came up. Last year for work, I went to Naperville, a suburb of Chicago. I said, "O.K., I'll call him and see if we can hook up." I'm very careful about understanding the different pressures and the different pulls on his time. I didn't want to be a nuisance. We exchanged texts, but didn't get together. I told him to keep up the great work. If he wins the World Series, he should then run for mayor.

I know what the expectations are. I'm confident that he can help lead the Cubs to a Series victory. They have the talent, and they have the right guy managing the young players. Today's players have a lot of needs, and he's savvy to that. He can tailor his approach to get the most out of each player. He's particularly adept at that.

My wife loves Joe. She's very comfortable around him. She's not a real sports fanatic. She tolerates it because of me. She's very astute about people. She just loves him to death because she thinks he's sincere. That goes a long way. All the pomp and circumstance, it is what it is, but if you peel everything back, this is a quality human being. He's someone that I would give the PIN to my bank account.

I was a pretty decent player. My statistics were very good. At the time, the Dodgers had Dusty Baker in left field, Rick Monday in centerfield, Davey Lopes at second base, Ron Cey at third base. Those were the positions that I played. In those days, when a player was drafted and signed a contract with a team, the player didn't have the flexibility that the union and the rules today afford. Once you were with a team, unless it was willing to release you or trade you, you were pretty much that team's property. I was O.K. going to Triple-A, but the Dodgers couldn't commit to me that I would play every day. They had a high draft choice—Glenn Burke—that they wanted to put in the outfield. I would have had to split time with. Burke just passed away. He was the guy who is credited with inventing the "high five" and was the first openly gay Major Leaguer. He got to the big leagues and did pretty well.

I couldn't get a commitment that I'd play every day. Once you get to Triple-A, you need to play. You need to be visible. You need to get an opportunity so they can make the decision that you need to be in the big leagues. They couldn't tell me that.

Finally, the diploma.

I asked to be traded. They wouldn't do it. I asked to be released, and they wouldn't do it. I had stolen base records in the Midwest League. I had Player of the Year awards in higher leagues, Player of the Month in a couple of leagues, All-Star Game appearances. I was O.K. I played with guys that graduated to the bigs: Bob Welch, Jeff Leonard and Pedro Guerrero.

It was very, very tough to break through in that organization at that time. Given that I had a baby girl, and I was living the minor league life, the money wasn't the same as it is today in the minor leagues. They pay you only for the six months you play. I didn't want to get to a point where I couldn't give my family the quality of life that I wanted to, and I didn't want to roll the dice and be a minor league guy for an extended period of time. That's why I admire Joe. He stuck with it. He was willing to do that and pay his dues for a lengthy period of time for the payoff of The Show. I wasn't willing to do that.

Most of today's players are lousy with fundamentals. It's either home run or strike out, and that's the end of that. Some guys are exceptions to that, like Jose Altuve, who I think is a wonderful baseball player. The money is such that it has caused different playing behaviors and obviously, in some cases, different off the field behaviors. It disappoints me to see some of the things I see. It further disappoints me to see players taking performance-enhancing drugs. That just p----- me off.

I've seen some things fielding-wise and base running-wise that I just don't get. That's the stuff that I think Joe has the patience and the focus to continually drive home. I don't. I don't have that kind of patience. At some point, you have to say, "Look, you don't get it. You have to go." Joe is able to break through because he has figured out what will resonate with that player. That's his strength. I don't like losing 40 to 50 percent of the time and then having it be O.K. I don't have the patience for it.

THE MARQUIS DE SOD

STEVE SCHNALL

Steve Schnall is a key person in Joe Maddon's life. He helped recruit Maddon to play quarterback at Lafayette College, when Schnall was the head freshman football coach. Now 73-years-old and semi-retired, he works for the New York Yankees as an adjunct scout. He lives in Myrtle Beach, S.C., next to Coastal Carolina University, where his son, Kevin, is the associate head baseball coach, head recruiter, and head coach-in-waiting. Coastal Carolina shocked the collegiate baseball world in 2016 by winning the College World Series. They also led the nation with 96 home runs.

When I went to work at Lafayette College, we recruited like hell. I was the head recruiter, working under Neil Putnam, the head coach.

Joe Maddon came in 1972. The coach that recruited Maddon directly was Joe Sarra. Joe was the guy who wound up at Penn State, a well-known assistant coach, a relentless guy. I went to the Maddon house with Joe Sarra to recruit him. He lived in a small place in Hazleton, Pa. The mom worked at the Third Base Luncheonette right next to where they lived. She was a waitress. His dad was a plumber. Joe Maddon, Jr. is his real name.

The plumber and the waitress together probably couldn't be making $5,000 a year. I went back to campus with Joe Sarra after our meeting. Maddon was being recruited by so many schools—Cornell, Penn, Miami, Minnesota—there were a million schools interested in him. This guy was a darn good quarterback, really good, but not real tall. I want to say

5-foot-11ish, a little undersized for some of the big schools. He was a super student and an overachiever in academics. He was serious. He didn't have a lot of other interests except sports. He played baseball and football. He was a great citizen in the town. He was just a mature young man for a high school kid.

I told Neil, "We need this guy. What can we do to get him?" In those days, Lafayette cost $4,500 total, and his financial aid needs came to $4,100. That was the total package. So he had to pay only $400. We were allowed to get him a summer job. Most of the kids at Lafayette were getting financial aid based on need just like the Ivy League. Summer jobs were an important deal for the kids. The players took summer jobs at an alum's restaurant or an alum's law firm or something like that and got paid whatever the going rate was.

Joe came in as a freshman. You could tell he was more mature than the other freshmen. We had great kids at Lafayette. They were all great students. No one got into Lafayette without being a great student. It was as tough as an Ivy League school in terms of admission. The admissions office wanted to make sure that everyone could graduate, and 95 percent of the kids at Lafayette graduated.

Joe asked me the first day, "Hey, Coach, do you think I could wear uniform number 12?" I said, "You can wear whatever number you want. All the numbers are open. We're a freshman team. You want 12, you've got it. Is there a reason why you want 12?"

Joe said, "Well, my favorite player is Joe Namath." Joe Namath wore 12. Charlie Johnson of the St. Louis Cardinals was his second favorite player and also wore 12. So he got uniform number 12.

I was a varsity assistant, but my major responsibility was the freshmen team coach. In those days, freshmen were separate from varsity. We had our own field. I had to work with the varsity sometimes and then bounce back to the freshmen.

Sometimes we would practice later or earlier so I could do that. We didn't have that many coaches in those days. I had three coaches working with me, and then the varsity had six coaches. I became the seventh guy, so that we could have a little more attention to detail with position players. It wasn't like today where they have 15, 20 coaches.

Joe was a quarterback. We had several other freshman quarterbacks that were really good, but after a couple of weeks of practice, there wasn't a question that Joe Maddon was the number one guy. All of the other freshman quarterbacks were good, and good enough to play at Lafayette, if Joe Maddon weren't there. Joe Maddon stood out. Doug Flutie was not yet playing, but Joe reminds me now of a younger version of Doug Flutie, that kind of ability. I want to call him a poor man's Doug Flutie. He never got flustered. He always had poise under pressure. I call it CUPA: Calm Under Pressure, Always. That meant you were striving for excellence. You were striving and not making mistakes, no mental mistakes, no physical mistakes. Yes, we made mistakes, but we would instantly correct them, and the kids bought into that. They bought into it because I sold it every day.

They also believed it because they used it as their mantra for their academics. They strived to be the best. They would strive to be 100 percent every day in everything they did. This was how I motivated them. Joe was the lead man in the clubhouse, on the field, on the campus and in the classroom. Joe was like Doug Flutie in that he could avoid pressure. He had a great ability, a great sense, great eyes in seeing the whole field, and he made the right choices.

In those days, the coaches called every play. It was Paul Brown's methodology. Joe taught me that we didn't have to make all the calls for the quarterbacks. The reason was Joe had an I.Q. of 130. That was higher than all of our coaches combined. Not combined, but most coaches, including me, were around 110. Except for a few coaches, most of them were not Renaissance men.

Joe had a 130 I.Q. It seemed higher in football. His natural instinctive intelligence was off the charts. Bobby Rue was my quarterback coach. Bob Rue and Joe Maddon had a great relationship, as we all did. We were used to calling all the plays. Bob Rue called all the plays. A few days into practice, we got to a reverse scrimmage, and Joe said, "You know, that play looks like it can't work." I said, "What would be your alternative, Joe?" "Let me go opposite with that play. They know what's coming, so they're overloading in that area. Why don't they just check with me at the line of scrimmage?" That's when he first introduced me to the "Check with me." Those were his words, Joe Maddon's words. "Check with me," and everybody in the NFL picked up on that later on. Colleges picked up on it. "Check with me."

I don't know where he got it. I had never heard it before. I was of the opinion, having learned from my predecessors, you run the play that was called. Well, all we were doing was guessing. Joe was going to make a decision at the line of scrimmage based on what he saw defensively. That was called "Check with me." He would check opposite of what was just called. Instead of going to the right, his call would be "Check with me" opposite, and then he would go to the left with that same play.

He added something we never had before. He called a run, but stepped into a pass. He called the pass, made an opening, and then stepped into a run. He was making the steps at the line of scrimmage. I'll make this analogy. In baseball, the catcher gives a visual sign of 1, 2, 3 or whatever. That is happening at every game in college and high school. It happens on every pitch. I'm going to compare that to a pitcher changing the pitch because he's not comfortable with the call. What he does is nods, no, no, no, I want another pitch. You know how pitchers do that sometimes in the Major Leagues? Well, in football, they use the same procedure. From then on, for

Joe speaks.

Joe's sister, Carmine Parlatore, mom, Albina "Beanie" Maddon, and wife, Jaye, listen.

the rest of the season, every play that we called from the sideline or by running the play in was now called a suggestion. It was never you must call this play right now, except maybe in a 3rd-and-1 when we definitely wanted a quarterback sneak or something to just get the first down. We didn't want to take a risk. We locked him in. We called it, "Lock it in."

Joe Maddon introduced us to making calls at the line of scrimmage. That's his legacy. He was one of the best quarterbacks that I've been around. He'll never go down as a great quarterback, but he should, even though it was only one year. It wasn't long because he went exclusively to baseball soon after that. He was a very good baseball player. He wanted to be a Major League Baseball player. We were disappointed when he decided in the spring of his freshman year that he was going full-time baseball. We knew that he could carry our varsity team for the next three years.

Lafayette is a unique school. It's a beautiful school. It's in eastern Pennsylvania, near the home of Larry Holmes and Mario Andretti. Tom Davis was the basketball coach. We all lived in the same neighborhood. Gary Williams lived across the street from me. He became the great basketball coach at Ohio State and won an NCAA championship at Maryland. He was an assistant basketball coach and soccer coach at Lafayette. Tom Davis became one of the all-time great basketball coaches at Boston College, Stanford and Iowa.

When we lost Joe to baseball, I was probably a little more irritated about it than anybody else. Yet, we still remained friends, and we're still friends today. I almost named my third son after Joe Maddon. I have two sons. They're named after Lafayette guys. My third guy never made it because of complications. My third son would have been named Maddon.

We follow him. Everyone in my family is a Joe Maddon fan, and everyone is a Cubs fan. We used to be Tampa Bay Rays fans. I've spoken to his team several times. That's how close I am.

Joe was a great catcher, but not a good enough hitter to make it to The Show. He was an outstanding receptor, outstanding at running his team. I'd call him a Tom Brady kind of guy at catching. The catcher, to me, is the quarterback. He was exceptional at that, but he wasn't quite good enough as a hitter. He played minor league ball for several years in the Angels organization. He bounced around towns all over the country. He had a great experience learning from different coaches—some good, some bad—how to get along with people and how to make those shifts. He learned how to speak Spanish. He spoke Spanish in high school and college, but some guys play, and they don't learn anything. He learned it. He can actually speak Spanish. He's bilingual. That's how smart he is. He's a Renaissance guy. He didn't study just for the sake of a test or to get a grade. He studied to learn stuff. That's the difference between him and the normal manager/coach in America. That's what Joe is. He's a Renaissance man. I'm always calling him that. He's not afraid to go to the ballet and actually learn something rather than just going because his wife wanted to go or his kids wanted to go. He actually goes to learn. He's a Handi Wipe. That's what I call him. He absorbs, and is one of the best in the country at it.

If you meet Joe Maddon, it's a unique personal experience. He'll meet you and greet you and smile and it's like he has known you for his entire life. He cares about people. He's passionate about people. He loves people, communicates and makes relationships with people. It doesn't matter whether you're the president or the janitor. He treats everybody the same. He has a great knack for understanding that everyone is important. He takes time to say hello to the guy that's cutting the grass. He knows that guy's name. Other head coaches don't even know the names of the secretaries. He has a passion for understanding that everyone that he meets is an important person.

I was at College of William & Mary as a defensive coach and head recruiter in the '70s. It's a beautiful school. I love the place in Williamsburg, Va. They don't like football. That's the only negative. Every day, there was a lady who came and cleaned the football coach's office. She cleaned the entire athletic department offices. Every day she came in, and I would say, "How are you, Miss Taylor? How's everything going? Thanks for helping out. Thanks for doing what you do." I said that every day. That was Lawrence Taylor's mom. Lawrence Taylor was a kid at that time. We tried to get Lawrence Taylor to go to William & Mary, but the William & Mary admissions office said, "No, you can't have him." I said, "His mom is the janitor. Can you take one risk?" He wasn't a great student. He was a little bit shaky. "Can you take one risk? The guy's going to put us on the map. The guy's going to be an All-American. He's super." "No, we can't accept him. You'll have to send him to prep school. Maybe we can take him after he goes to prep school. No guarantees." Lawrence Taylor went to North Carolina, and you know the rest of the story. The point I'm trying to make is that if I hadn't said much to that lady, I wouldn't have had a relationship with Lawrence Taylor. When I was an assistant coach with the New York Giants, Lawrence Taylor was our main guy. Anytime there was a problem, I went to Lawrence. I said, "Hey, Lawrence, take care of this, take care of that." He was like my son, and Bill Parcells never knew. It was unbelievable stuff. Relationships. That's Joe Maddon's secret.

Joe Maddon has Tommy La Stella on the Cubs. Tommy La Stella played at Coastal Carolina for my son. Tommy is out of northern New Jersey, up there in Bergen County. His dad's a doctor. Tommy was an eighth round draft pick. Joe loves Tommy La Stella. You know why? Tommy is always calm under pressure. Calm Under Pressure, Always. You can count on him to be a role model. He may be in a pinch-hitting role and then start two or three times a week. In the old days, we would have called him a utility player. Now, he's Mr. Versatility. We changed the name. He could play second, short, third, left, even right field. He's a spectacular role guy, the same kind of guys that Bill Belichick loves, the Julian Edelmans of the world, you know? No other team would have understood how to use Tommy La Stella. But Joe Maddon did. Tommy is competitive as all get out. That's why he was so upset when he was demoted to Iowa.

Joe Maddon can take guys like Tommy La Stella, a versatile player, and make him into an All-Star. After my talk in Tampa Bay to the Rays, the one guy that wanted to spend time with me was Ben Zobrist. Do you know what he wanted? He wanted to know everything about Maddon. And Joe Maddon's favorite player is Ben Zobrist, in my opinion.

Who else would ever have won with the Rays? Has anybody ever won with the Rays? Think about it. They had good managers who struggled. Joe Maddon was beating the Red Sox and the Yankees. How the hell do you beat the Red Sox and the Yankees with the Rays organization? He went to Yankee Stadium, and beat them two out of three. He went to Fenway Park, all that money they have, and beat the Red Sox two out of three.

If Joe loses, the world ain't coming to an end. Nobody has their dauber down. He's going to get them tomorrow. It's not only amazing, it's extraordinary, what he did with the Rays. Now with the Cubs, a franchise that has struggled for a hundred years, he has a chance to win the World Series.

The Cubs have injuries. Kyle Schwarber is out for the whole year. Joe adjusts. He knows how to adjust. He moves guys around and guess what? The other managers, Joe Girardi and all of those other guys who are supposed to be geniuses, they copy Joe Maddon. These other managers, who never did anything innovative, now move infielders and outfielders the way Joe does, using five infielders in certain situations, moving pitchers to the outfield. Who used to do that? I see Girardi move his line-up around every day now. I never saw him do that before Joe Maddon. He had the same line-up every day. He didn't have to think. Joe makes managers think. He's changed the whole culture of baseball by being a manager. He's not only affecting his team, he's affecting the whole game.

He's John Wooden. He's Knute Rockne. Joe loves Whitey Herzog because he was a Cardinals fan, and Whitey was an innovator, too. Those are the guys he loves.

I'm not a fun guy. I'm a sports guy. Fun to me is fundamentals. Joe Maddon would be the Pope for me. I love the Pope. We all love the Pope. Joe Maddon is bigger than the Pope.

If you want to talk about Joe, you're talking about presence on the field. On and off the field, he has great body language, great presence. He says, don't allow the pressure to exceed the pleasure. That's what it's all about. Don't allow the pressure in any scenario to exceed the pleasure of being there, of being together as teammates.

We had a thing called LIPS: Late Interval Pressure Situations. Joe calls it Late Inning Pressure Situations. Every day we started practice with LIPS. An interval is the time from the snap of the football to the end of the play. And the average time is 5.2 seconds. So we practiced everything based on 5.2 seconds. At the beginning of practice, we'd go right to a pressure situation. I made it up each day, scripted it. "Hey, we're on the two-yard line. We've got to go 98 yards. Or we're two yards away from the end zone, and we have to get a touchdown. Or we're in a two-point situation. Or we have an injured player and have to substitute. How do we handle this?"

If you look at the College World Series, Coastal Carolina didn't make many mistakes in the late innings, and that's how they won it. They got the big hits. The pitchers stayed calm under pressure. Coastal Carolina is a baseball school. They emphasize baseball. They have the sixth best winning percentage since 2000 in the whole country. It's not really that much of a surprise to me that they won. Their guys are baseball people. But guys living in your neighborhood had probably never heard of Coastal Carolina. The average Joe wants a CCU Chanticleers cap now. They had never heard of the school before because it's not a major football school.

The LIPS—Late Inning Pressure Situations—that helped Coastal Carolina win the College World Series was born back when Joe Maddon was a college quarterback. We called it Late Interval Pressure Situations. All the quarterbacks were involved. We practiced a little differently. We put the kids under pressure right away. When they were tired again in practice, we did it again. We practiced under pressure as much as we could. It didn't mean we had to yell at players. It meant we were doing things perfect. We covered every situation we could so they were never unprepared in a game. What happened if we got beat by a trick play? We'd come right back with a trick play. We put in a new trick play every week. We might not use it, but the kids loved it. They'd beg, "Hey, coach, can we use that trick play now?" They loved it because it was something innovative. It was unique. We always have punt fakes. We would practice punt fakes because the punt was often the most important play in the game. I liked for our quarterback to also be the punter. They could pass or run or punt out of the punt formation.

Of all the guys that I've coached, and I've coached some great ones, including Hall of Famers, there's never a day that I don't think about Joe Maddon. Never a day.

Chapter 3

MAJORING IN MINORS:

Joe Maddon
Catcher

THE QUAD CITIES? IT'S TWICE AS GOOD AS THE TWIN CITIES

WHEN WE WERE YOUNG AND OUR WORLD WAS NEW

HARRY PELLS

Harry Pells has been a tower-ing figure in the Quad Cities amateur and professional baseball picture for more than five decades. He also has been a very successful finan-cial advisor, when he's not wintering in Naples, Fla. Harry was in his first year as a minor league general manager when Joe Maddon reported for his first pro duty for the Quad Cities Angels in the spring of 1976.

Joe showed up with most of the rest of the team that broke spring training. A bunch of them cashed in their airline tickets and rode a Greyhound bus from California to the Quad Cities to save money.

The thing that I remember most about him as a catcher, even to this day, was he may have been average at best. He wasn't destined to play in the Major Leagues, and he didn't play in the minor leagues long. Anyone who played profes-sional ball was skilled, but he wasn't a standout catcher. What I do distinctly remember about him was his personality and his leadership skills with the rest of the players, how he mixed with the rest of the players, how he got along with the rest of the players, how he, as a catcher, controlled the game or con-trolled the attitude of the team.

When he walked into the stadium in the afternoon to head for the clubhouse and get dressed, he would almost every day stop in the office and say hi to me and to Dorothy Wulf, my assistant. He'd say, "How's your day going? How are things?" He was the only player that I can remember who did that routinely.

That was just Joe being Joe. He was very easy to get along with, very personable. If you look at him now as a Major League manager, he clearly gets along with his players. He relates well to his players. He's got a real easygoing, fun attitude about him. When you watch him manage, he's the same type of person today as he was 40 years ago.

Statistically, he was average at that level. He didn't progress. He did not go beyond Class A. The **ANGELS*** recognized that he might not have the ability to progress up the chain and perhaps make it in the Major Leagues. They, too, recognized that leadership ability he had. That's why he was a bench coach for so many years.

Carney Lansford was on Joe's team here in the Quad Cities in '76. Dickie Thon was on that team. Mark Clear was on that team, and he came back in '77. Mark made it to the bigs and pitched in the All-Star Game with Boston. Alan Wiggins played second base for us. He went up for a while and died young.

The biggest thing about Joe that I remember is how he stood out from a personality standpoint. At that age, you have kids that are 18- to 23-years-old. They're young. For most of them, it's their first year in professional baseball.

The only time I've seen Joe or talked to him since was six years ago when he was managing in Tampa. I went up from my condo in Naples, Fla., to watch the Yankees and Tampa Bay play. The Rays' pitching coach was Mike Butcher. When Joe was a bench coach with the Angels, Mike was the pitching coach. They went together to Tampa Bay for a year before Mike

---

*Here's a Final Jeopardy! question from 2015: "When translated, the full name of this Major League Baseball team gets you a double redundancy." The show's questionable answer (which all three contestants missed) was: What is the Los Angeles **ANGELS**?

left and went back to the Angels. Mike didn't like Florida. He went back to the Angels and has now moved on to the Arizona Diamondbacks. Mike is from the Quad Cities, East Moline. I saw Mike warming up the pitchers before the game, and I said, "Hey, Mike, can you please see if Joe is available for a couple of minutes? Tell him Harry Pells is out here."

Mike went in and Joe came out. Right away, we reconnected about the Quad Cities and the years back. He remembered me and definitely had fond memories of Davenport. We had a nice conversation, although it wasn't real lengthy. It was before a game, and obviously he was pretty busy before a game. That's been my only contact with him since he left here 40 years ago.

Here's a good story that typifies Joe. My assistant, Dorothy, and her husband, Frank, kept in touch periodically with Joe. When Dorothy died in 2008, Joe somehow found out. That was the year Joe shocked baseball and took the Rays to the World Series. In the middle of all that, Joe found time to call Frank with his condolences. That was 32 years after he met her that one summer.

That's all you need to know about Joe Maddon!

THE MOOSE IS LOOSE

MOOSE STUBING

Lawrence "Moose" Stubing was Joe Maddon's manager for most of Maddon's minor league career...in the Quad Cities and Salinas, Calif. Stubing was hitless in his five big league at bats, but still had a long and successful career with the Angels as a manager and coach in the minors. The Bronx born lefty lives in Palm Springs, Calif.

I coached Joe his first year out of Lafayette for the Quad Cities Angels. He was a great organizer even in those days. He put together a place for five or six players and the bus driver to live in. Nobody was making much money in those days. One of his roommates was John Flannery who reached the big leagues as an infielder with the **WHITE SOX***. I had to run John down the day he got traded, so I went to the house they shared and Joe was there cooking Italian food.

Joe was a minor league Thurman Munson of his day. Joe threw sidearm like Munson. The ball curved to second base. He was a good defensive catcher, very intelligent, and had a good rapport with the pitchers. Joe wasn't a very good hitter, below average, and didn't have much power.

Joe and Stan Cliburn split catching duties in the Quad Cities. Stan's twin brother, Stu, was a pitcher on the team. Stan is a great guy. I'd run into Stan when I was scouting for the Angels and we spent good times together. I thought Stan would be a catcher in the big leagues for years, but he was with the Angels

The 1983 **WHITE SOX were the first Chicago team to exceed two million fans for one season.*

just one season. Stan and Stu both got into coaching after their playing days and are still at it.

Stan caught more than Joe because the Angels had more money invested in him. Stan was a high round draft choice. Joe was a free agent. I had to make a decision of who would be a better catcher in the big leagues. Instructors and front office personnel came and we discussed those things.

Back in '76 I knew Joe would end up in a front office or managing somewhere.

The next year, 1977 in Salinas, I thought Joe was going to develop into a good hitter. Part of it was my fault. We didn't make him a good hitter. In the back of my mind I thought if Joe didn't make it as a backup he'd wind up in a front office. I saw him as a receiver with intelligence. The rapport he had with the whole club—not just the pitchers—was outstanding. He had a way of doing things so that everybody on the club had fun. The players had to find ways of entertaining themselves without spending much money.

To this day, I think Joe probably hates me for not catching him more, but things turned out great for him.

Here's a funny story about Joe and his meatball sandwiches. When his mother would visit from Pennsylvania, they'd make enough sandwiches to feed everyone. They were good meatball sandwiches. We thought we were actually in Italy. Joe was always thinking of everybody else.

Joe always thought before he'd say anything, and he was usually right. He didn't have to regret anything. He and John Flannery helped mature Steve Tebbetts, the biggest bonus baby on the club.

I never got mad at Joe in Quad Cities or Salinas. I didn't have to. He was smarter than me. I was a graduate of the Bronx streets, and he was a Lafayette genius. He was smart and controlled everything. He was a man ahead of his time. He should have been in the front office. Bill Bavasi, a long time high-level baseball executive, saw that in Joe.

I knew he was going to be a big league manager when he was with the organization as a minor league manager and instructor. Bavasi wanted him to manage the Angels and later Seattle. But both teams wanted a big name, so they passed on him. When I was a scout and Joe was a coach with the Angels, I knew he was going to be a manager. But you never know. I think he should have been a Major League manager earlier, and it should have been with the Angels.

I'm not surprised by his success. I was impressed early in his career by how intelligent he was. There are certain guys that can take control of the other guys on the team. He was a natural leader.

Teams today should have double the amount of scouts. There is nothing wrong with the computers, nothing wrong with the stats, but they can't communicate the way old-time scouts used to do. That scares me. The front office kids are smarter, they do their jobs better, but they don't communicate with older scouts. They don't have baseball stories.

Teams don't do a four-man rotation anymore because the agents won't let them. Think about it. You have a young pitcher. You're his agent. You have him pitch every five days. You get a few more years out of him and the agent makes more money. In reality, you're taking eight starts away from each of your four best pitchers and having your fifth best pitcher make 32 starts. It's crazy.

But you didn't have to be crazy to know that Joe Maddon was going to be successful in anything he chose to do.

A ROOMIE WITH A VIEW

DICKIE THON

Dickie Thon, 58, was born in South Bend, Ind., while his father, Fred, was a student and baseball player at Notre Dame. Thon's first two years in the minors were also his first two years with Joe Maddon as they played together in Quad Cities and Salinas. Thon had a distinguished Major League career spanning 15 seasons and was a lifetime .264 hitter. In 1983, he played in the All-Star Game and won the Silver Slugger Award. He divides his time between Houston and Puerto Rico, his native country. His daughter is a volleyball star, and his son is an up and coming player in the Toronto Blue Jays system.

Being in the minor leagues is an awakening. You find out a lot of things that help out in life. You have to persevere, gotta work hard, when you're up, stay level, and when you're down, don't get too down. It's a great way of learning how to do well in life.

Joe and I started with the Quad Cities Angels in Davenport, Iowa, in the Midwest League. He came out of college and I came out of high school. I wasn't even finished with high school yet. In those days you could sign before you finished school. Joe and I met in spring training and then we were roommates for two years, starting in the Quad Cities in **1976***.

The Quad Cities were pretty quiet. We were a very good team and the competition was very high. Joe was one of three catchers.

---

*Joe Maddon's final year in college (**1976**) was the last year that dunking the ball was illegal in college basketball. Dunks were banned from 1967-76.

He was a very good catcher. He could hit, but he couldn't run. He was very intelligent.

We became roommates after spring training. We talked about it on a bus from El Centro, Calif., to Davenport, Iowa. Our third roommate was Jerry Brust, a very tall lanky pitcher. Jerry was a very nice guy. He came from the University of **MIAMI***, so I was the young guy. We all had our duties. I was in charge of taking the garbage out, Joe was the cook and Jerry drove the car. Joe was a very good cook. I gained a lot of weight. I signed that year at 140 pounds and by the end of the season was around 180. We ate like crazy. Joe would cook Italian food every night. His spaghetti and meatballs were my favorite. Now he owns a restaurant in Tampa.

The Angels gave us money for a flight, but 10 of us took a bus for three days to pocket a little extra money. Most of the other players were from California and right out of college. I was only 17.

Joe would have liked to have played more, but we had three catchers. One of the guys made the Majors, Stan Cliburn with the Angels. He was pretty good and played most of the time. Joe was better the second season we played together, in Salinas, Calif. He was a very good receiver, I remember that. Joe was very steady and didn't complain much.

I couldn't get into the bars because I was too young. I don't remember Joe going to bars very much my two years with him, but I was so young I didn't go to the bars.

Joe was very respectful about my age. He didn't play around much. He was very steady and serious to make it to the big leagues. He was not there to make fun or have fun on anybody.

I didn't have any girlfriends in the Quad Cities. I had a girlfriend in Puerto Rico and we eventually got married. Joe dated some girls, at least two girls. He was the Italian Dandy.

*The Marlins are the only team that travels north to spring training... from Miami to Jupiter, Florida. The Marlins have never won their division, yet they have won two World Series.

Moose Stubing was our manager in the Quad Cities. He was also the manager Joe and I had in Salinas the next year. He was a good manager and we had good teams.

We had an apartment and we had to be at the ballpark at 2 in the afternoon and didn't get home until late night. We basically would eat, sleep and go to the ballpark. We didn't go out at all, but again, I was too young. The ballpark in Davenport was beautiful, right on the Mississippi River.

I remember coming back late from a ball game and I had forgotten to take the garbage out before we left. When I got back, my bed was full of garbage. Joe had dumped all the garbage on my bed and said, "That was your job. You are supposed to do it." I didn't forget the garbage ever again. He taught me a lesson.

The thing I always admired about Joe was that he treated everyone like they were special. He treats everyone like he's their friend. He didn't big league anyone. He is very humble.

We were a pretty disciplined team, always on time. We didn't mess around too much. Joe was very serious about that. He was the older guy, always making sure I was on time. The discipline thing, I never saw Joe out of place. I was lucky to have him my first year, a guy who was serious about the game. He liked to have fun, but he was serious at the ballpark.

I remember he used to read a lot and he loved wine. I didn't know anything about wine and I didn't read too much. I pretty much learned from watching how he behaved. He wasn't all over me telling me things. He pretty much left me alone.

The year we were in Salinas together, we were roommates again. I didn't spend much time in Salinas, I got called up to Triple-A after about two months. That was the last time I was a roommate with Joe. I started the season very hot so they moved me up to Triple-A when I was 18. I moved through the system really fast. I had good years with them. We would see each other in spring training, but we weren't roommates because we were on different teams. I got called up at 19 and I turned 20 in the big leagues.

I didn't see him much when I was in the big league camp. We were in different places. I was in Palm Springs, Joe was in El Centro, Calif.

Joe called me a couple times. We stayed in touch. When I was with the **ASTROS***, he called me one time and asked me to talk with Tim Salmon of the Angels. Salmon got hit really bad in the face and was having a hard time getting back. I had that same type of accident, so I called Salmon. We didn't see each other much, but Joe and I kept in touch.

I'm not surprised Joe is a good manager. He was a very good people person. He always got along with everybody. He's a nice guy, but he's a tough guy. He played football. He knows what it takes to be successful. Joe doesn't take nonsense from anybody. He's a very nice guy, but you don't want to mess with him. He's not a softy, he's a tough guy.

I saw him last year in spring training in Arizona. It had been a while, so we went out to eat. We spent some time remembering the way we were taught by our coaches. The California Angels in the minor leagues put a lot of attention on the fundamentals. He remembered that and kept those years with him. He's a very into fundamentals, play hard, run hard type of coach.

I'm still in baseball in Puerto Rico. I'm coaching winter ball. I'm involved with the Houston Astros, not the whole year, only for special assignments. If somebody needs help, I help. I'm pretty much in Puerto Rico, but I have a house in Houston.

Once the United States starts giving the importance to the World Baseball Classic like the other countries, they'll start

*Larry Dierker threw a no-hitter for the **ASTROS** in 1976 and was given a thousand-dollar bonus check by the team. He gave the money back because the team was in receivership saying "A no-hitter is a good enough reward for me."

winning. Right now the American players and fans don't understand how important it is to the other countries to beat the United States. They put in a lot of time and effort to beat the United States and it's more competition than in the big leagues.

Joe is a plus for the game, a very good guy for the game.

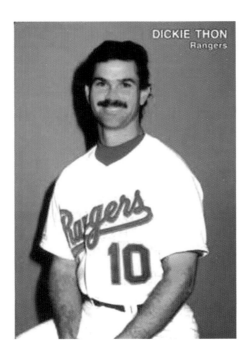

TWINS ARE PEOPLE TWO

STAN CLIBURN

When Joe Maddon reported for his first professional duties as a catcher for Quad Cities in 1976, there was a problem. The problem was named Stan Cliburn, who was a fifth round draft choice of the Angels and had signed for big money. Cliburn already had two years experience in the minors. To compound Maddon's problem, the next year Joe played in Salinas, Calif., and the starting catcher there was also Stan Cliburn. Four years later, Cliburn made the Major Leagues as a catcher with the Angels.

Cliburn ranks among the Top 10 winningest managers in minor league history with more than 1,600 wins. He hopes to reach 2,000 wins in his career. He currently manages the New Britain Bees in the Atlantic League. Stan's twin brother, Stew, pitched for the California Angels for three seasons.

Joe Maddon was an older guy coming out of Lafayette College. We all looked up to Joe. We were all a bunch of young kids. We were still all young, 17 and 18 when we got to Quad Cities in '76. Joe and I were both catchers. He'd catch a game, and I would DH, or I'd catch and he would DH. I knew I was going to get most of the playing time, being a high draft pick.

Joe was like the Wizard of Oz. He had all the answers. If anybody needed some answers, if the team started going bad, if everybody was down and out, we'd all say, "Let's go talk to Joe." One of my favorite movies of all time, especially for kids back in the day, was *The Wizard of Oz*. I said, "Joe's like the Wizard of Oz. We're off to see the Wizard because he's got all the answers."

Joe always had a way of calming the team down, particularly the younger boys, which we were at the time. Joe being a little bit of an older guy kept us all in check and kept the team loose. He always had some little antic that would keep the team loose. He took that same passion and desire that he had back in 1976 with him to Chicago and is having great success.

I ran into Joe again in '87. I was a player-coach in Midland, Tex., and he was a roving minor league instructor for the Angels. Here it was, almost 11 years since we had been teammates, and he hadn't changed a bit.

I still stay in touch with Joe. I'm managing an independent ball club in New Britain, Conn. He called me two years ago. Tony Phillips still wanted to play ball. He was 50 years old. I remember Tony Phillips well from our years in the minor leagues, playing against him, and following him to the **OAKLAND A'S***.

Joe called and said, "Man, give this guy a chance. He wants to still play ball, and he could go the independent route. He's still in great shape." He was telling me all this stuff about what Tony could do. I said, "Joe, he's 50-years-old. That's not going to look too good to sign a 50-year-old man." He said, "Well, they signed **JOSE CANSECO**** one year, and they gave Rickey Henderson a shot in the Atlantic League."

I said, "Joe, if he's that good, why don't you sign him?"

"Well, Stan, I think I'm a little smarter than that."

I said, "Well, you got me again, partner."

---

*The **OAKLAND A'S** and the Oakland Raiders are the only MLB and NFL teams to share a stadium.

** **JOSE CANSECO**'s daughter, Josie, was Miss June 2016 for *Playboy* magazine.

About a year after that, Tony Phillips passed away. But that was just Joe, being a practical young man. Obviously, Tony Phillips had come across Joe's path somewhere and Joe thought that much about him at 50-years-old to try to get him back in baseball. Who else did Joe call? He called me. That shows me a lot of respect to think of me first. That's what the baseball world is about. I talk to Joe, not a lot, but if I ever need something, I'll call and say, "Hey, Joe. We're doing this. We're doing that." Traveling through the Northeast, through Hazleton, Pa., I go through that little city and it reminds me of Joe Maddon.

I was already in Quad Cities when Joe reported. I signed in '74 with the Angels and in '75, they sent me to the Quad Cities. I knew before Joe got to the Quad Cities that he played the position I played. There are always two catchers on a baseball team, sometimes three. The starting catcher and the back-up catcher can complement each other. That's what Joe and I did. We complemented each other. I knew, as a young kid and as a high draft pick, a fifth rounder, that I was going to get more playing time because that's just the way the minor league system works.

Joe was always a guy that the pitchers loved. He was always a challenge to my position because of the in-clubhouse competition between all the players. He always kept me in check. He always kept me ready to go. He said, "Hey, you've got to perform because you've got a guy here behind you that can do just as well, given the opportunity like you're getting."

It was motivational for me. Joe made me feel like that. Even now, Joe will say, "Cliburn got to play all the time. I just carried his luggage." That really wasn't the truth. The truth was he brought mental toughness not only to me, but to the whole team, the whole clubhouse. That's why we were successful all those years in Salinas.

The impact he made has stayed with me all these years. It started in the Quad Cities in '76. In the Quad Cities, we lived

downtown at the Hotel Davenport. Joe lived there, too. I think
we all had apartments there. Joe was always cooking. He was
like a mother hen to all of us. Joe was always saying he was a
gourmet cook. He could cook anything. It seemed like every
time we'd go to his place, we had the same old thing. It was his
specialty, some Italian dish, ziti or chicken parmesan or whatever. I can remember making a smart comment, "When are we
going to have some catfish and some grits for supper, Joe?" Of
course, he didn't know what grits were back then. He probably
thought it was cement gone bad.

There was always laughter. We were good old boys, trying to
grow up in the baseball world. Joe was, no doubt about it, a big,
big part of our development, a big part of our maturity. There's
no doubt in our minds, we all look back and think about Joe
then, about which way his life was going to carry him, and that
was in leadership and leading the men because he did such a
great job of it back then. It wasn't something that developed
overnight. It was something that began 40 years ago.

We were young. We'd venture out and naturally test the
waters like all young kids do. Joe always kept it in check. He'd
say, "Guys, I think Moose might be checking curfew tonight.
You guys better be in on time." The old football coach Lou
Holtz never had a curfew. He said, "Why have a curfew? The
only players that break it are your best ones."

Joe was our player guide. He was a father figure. Moose
Stubing was my second father all the years that I played for him
in the minor leagues over there. We had become Midwest boys
in the Quad Cities, then we moved up to Salinas near Mon-
terey Beach. Someone was always saying, "Let's all go live on
the beach."

Right off the bat, the management in the front office in
Salinas saw that Joe was probably going to be a pretty good
back-up guy. He didn't have a real strong arm. He had a Thurmon Munson release. He threw the ball down to second base

just like Thurmon did. He'd catch it and release it so quick. He'd throw a lame sidearm slicing ball down to second, but he did throw people out.

Hitting-wise, he was always consistent. The Angels knew that he was going to be a good player/coach/manager one day. When he got into pro ball, he was 22, which was considered old when you were still stuck down in low Class-A ball. The years just caught up with him. I did get most of the playing time. In fact, they promoted me from Class-A to Triple-A the next year in '78. That opened up some avenues for Joe a little bit, but Dan Whitmer followed me and got the call over Joe. Dan and I played in the Major Leagues together.

I think Joe is managing in the Major Leagues, and I'm not, because he got with the right people at an early age. The Angels made him a roving instructor at a relatively young age. He got in with the right people at the right time and stayed with it. Joe got up in the big leagues with Mike Scioscia, and Scioscia gave him the opportunity to go to Tampa and start managing. Joe got into coaching in his late 20s. I stuck it out playing until I was 31, thinking I could still get back to the Major Leagues. I got in with **PITTSBURGH*** at 31-years-old as a player-coach in Buffalo in '88. I decided to forgo my playing career and got into management, which I did in the New York-Pennsylvania League.

There was controversy in the Pittsburgh front office, which was unstable. After four years, I was gone. I got picked up by the Texas Rangers to manage their Double-A team. That front office had been together 25 years, but got disrupted in Year Three, and they were all fired and gone.

In my early years of managing and having pretty good success, I never really got with an organization that was stable in the front office. Therefore, nobody moved up the ladder. The

---

*Benny Distefano of the **PITTSBURGH** Pirates was the last left-handed Major League catcher. He caught three games in 1989.

old regime got booted out, and the new guys came in. The timing never was right for me is what I'm trying to get to. The timing has always been right for Joe, because he got into it at an early age. He was with a very stable organization in the Angels. He took the most of that opportunity and ran with it.

I look back on the 17 years that Jim Leyland managed in the minor leagues before he ever got a chance. My gosh, that's a lot of time managing in the minor leagues. Here I am now, 26 years of managing in the minor leagues and still waiting for the opportunity. You just never know.

My twin brother, Stew, was going to quit after his 10th year of professional baseball. He had a job offer with New York Life. I said, "Stew, you're 29-years-old. Play one more year, even though I know you're frustrated." He played one more year, made the Angels and was fifth in the Rookie of the Year voting in '85 when Ozzie Guillen won the award. He was going to quit and go work at New York Life making $25,000 a year. Instead, he got a four-year contract for $2 million. He did O.K. by holding on one more year.

Back in the day, Elton John dressed up in funny costumes to perform on stage. I think Joe copied that fashion style. He would show up at the ballpark in a checkerboard square outfit. He'd show up with funny looking glasses, a different hairdo, and other things you didn't see very often. He was always a year or two ahead of everybody in a fashion sense. He still takes fashion seriously. The Cubs show up at the airport dressed all kinds of ways. It comes from him. It keeps them loose. He always was a guy that backed up his antics. He could always back the talk. It wasn't blue jeans and a plaid shirt with Joe. He got his fashion sense from Elton John and the great David Bowie.

Joe was always a charmer. He charmed everyone with his intellect. He's a very educated, very smart man. He was our Wizard of Oz. If anyone was having a problem, Joe would always find a way to make them feel better.

If I had to sum up Joe, it would be passion and love for people and baseball.

DOCTORIN' THE BALL

DR. STEVE EDDY

Steve Eddy grew up in the Quad Cities and was pleased to be able to play minor league ball at home. While wending his way to the Major Leagues, he attended Yale and med school in the off-season. He is now a successful doctor in suburban Phoenix.

I played with Joe in 1976 for the Quad Cities Angels, which was my second year of professional baseball. I was a hometown kid, so it was kinda special for me. I grew up in Silvis and Moline, Ill. The Quad Cities Angels were on the other side of the Mississippi River in Davenport, Iowa. My first year of baseball I played in a Rookie League in Idaho Falls and my second year was in Quad Cities. To my knowledge that was the only time I overlapped with Joe. I was 18 at the time, and Joe had just come out of college.

I'm not gonna be one of those guys now that Joe Maddon is a famous guy, to try to capitalize on it and say I was best friends with him. I remember him being an all-round good human being and a pretty good catcher. Truth is, it was 40 years ago, so I don't remember much.

He was my catcher so he tried to take charge. That year in Quad Cities was short for me. I was there for only half the season. He was an older guy who knew what he was doing. He was encouraging and called the pitches. I didn't try to call them.

Joe was a good guy, everybody knows that. We just went separate directions after the Quad Cities.

Salinas was the Angels' high Class-A ball team and I skipped that step, but Joe was in Salinas the next year. I went from low A to Double-A. I ran into him in spring training in El Centro. Minor leaguers trained there while the Major Leaguers went to Palm Springs.

The truth is I'm a fan of sports to a degree. I'll watch the **BRITISH OPEN***, the hockey playoffs and the basketball playoffs. I'm more of a guy that likes to do stuff. I fly **PLANES****, hunt, fish and play golf and tennis with my wife and kids. I have so many interests in life I don't sit down and watch sports now. I even have a hard time remembering back when I was in the Major Leagues.

I don't think getting to Yale was a lucky break. I was a small Midwestern kid. My father drove trucks and my mother was a waitress. I was just a weird bird for those parts. I wanted more for my life than working at a factory. I highly value anyone who works hard in their life. I just had something more in mind for myself. When I decided in eighth grade to be a doctor, I knew nothing about the Ivy League, but I heard one statistic that stuck in my mind: 95 percent of people that graduated from Yale that wanted to go to grad school got in. It's the only school I applied to. I did a pre-admission interview with a **JOHN DEERE***** executive who was a Yale graduate. John Deere started near where I was born in Sterling, Ill., and moved to the Quad Cities where its international headquarters is.

The John Deere guy asked, "Where else have you applied?"

"Nowhere."

"Why not?" he asked.

"I only want to go to Yale."

---

*While playing **GOLF** on 1567, Mary, Queen of Scots, was informed that her husband, Lord Darnley, had been murdered. She finished the round.

When Knute Rockne and seven others were killed in a 1931 **PLANE crash, it was the largest disaster in U.S. aviation history up until that time.

***In its early days, Deere & Company had an advertisement that stated, "**JOHN DEERE** stands behind all its farm implements except the manure spreader."

"What happens if you don't get in?" he asked.

"Well, why wouldn't they take me?"

Sounds crazy, but I had a lot of determination and blind luck. On paper I looked good. I learned later that there are thousands of kids that look good on paper. I played baseball from 1975 to '80 and went to college from 1975 to '81.

When I played with Joe in the Quad Cities, he had completed three full years of college. He also was street smart and a good guy.

ON A CLEAR DAY YOU CAN SEE KANSAS CITY

MARK CLEAR

In his lifetime, Mark Clear has had two distinct and successful careers. The Los Angeles native spent 11 years in the big leagues despite an inauspicious 0-7 start in his first minor league season. He was Joe Maddon's teammate for two years in the minors in Quad Cities and Salinas. His uncle, Bob Clear, was a very close friend of Joe Maddon, and Maddon credits Bob Clear with much of his managerial success.

Clear's second career was as a nursery owner in the greater Kansas City area. He has a 1,000-acre farm where he grows trees on half of the property and plants on the other half, which he distributes through his very successful Loma Vista Nursery in suburban Kansas City, as well as to other nurseries throughout the Midwest.

Growing up on an avocado ranch in Southern California, my dad had me up in the mountains a lot. I always wanted to own land. I started in the business in California, but you still couldn't own land. The pricing was out of the grasp of reality. When I came back to Kansas City, I was like a kid in a candy store. There was a lot of land out here, and it was cheap.

The traffic was one reason why I had to leave California. I started thinking, I've got to plan my whole day around the traffic. If I want to go anywhere or do anything, it's always about traffic. That's what's beautiful about Kansas City. It's a pretty big town. It's almost three million people, but there's no traffic compared to the West Coast.

I signed out of high school with the **PHILLIES***, but got released my first year after going 0-7. I then signed with the Angels. After another year in the Rookie League, I made the A ball club, the Quad Cities Angels. I met Joe that year in spring training. Joe was a college player out of Pennsylvania. He was a couple of years older than me, but I had already played two seasons in the minors.

Joe was always very thoughtful. He's a catcher. Catchers and pitchers usually get along really well. Good catchers know the personalities of the pitchers, and Joe was really pitcher friendly. He was a good guy. I was struggling. I had no control. I could fire it up there and have a big old curve, but I had no clue of where it was going. I was also with Joe the next year in Salinas. You think about the people who helped you in your career. I had an uncle, Bob Clear, who was a long-time coach with the Angels. He helped me get along. Joe helped me in Salinas. I was on the bubble in Salinas. Any day, I was going to get released. I said, "Hey, I need to work on the side." He said, "I'll go catch you." Joe and I would go out to the bullpen.

He'd catch me. Joe was coaching even at that time. He said, "Hey, get on top. Settle down. Slow down." He was just a teammate, a little bit older guy, a college guy. He knew a lot more about the game than I did. That's what I remember. I remember him being like a coach back then.

When I went to spring training, I'd see the guys in the minor league camp, all the guys I played with. Some guys were a little jealous. My uncle was a big league coach. They'd think that there was nepotism there. But Joe was happy for me. He'd yell, "Hey, Horse!" He was always giving me encouragement.

P. K. Wrigley and Milton Hershey were bitter business rivals. When Wrigley bought the Chicago Cubs, Hershey tried to buy the Philadelphia **PHILLIES ... and sell chocolate gum. Heshey failed in both efforts.*

Of all the coaches he came up with, he loved my uncle. He lived and breathed every word that my uncle said. Joe has that old school mindset but with the new flair of what it takes in management now. I manage a bunch of people, and I know what team building means. Back in the day when I played, there was no team building. I see what Joe does. He has dress-up days and tries other interesting stuff. He's a combination of the New Guard and the Old Guard. That's why I think he's really successful.

My uncle was a long-time minor league scout for the Angels. He came up to the big leagues in '77 as the bullpen coach. When Joe was in the minor leagues those couple of years, Bob was in instructional ball. Bob was always instructing kids. He was one of those gruff old guys. He'd tell you what he thought. If he thought you were doing something wrong, he'd tell you. There was no holds barred. My uncle had 60 years in professional ball. He had seen everything. He was a pitcher when he played. He played 19 seasons of minor league ball, but never played a game in the Major Leagues. Bob saw it all!

I know that my uncle really liked Joe. My uncle and I were close. When I was in the Instructional League in Arizona, Warren Spahn was the pitching coach. I had just completed a really good year in Double-A after I was about to get released in Salinas the year before. I made a big turnaround. I got to Double-A. I had a great year in half a season in Double-A. I was going to play in the Winter League.

Warren Spahn tried to teach me how to throw a screwball. My uncle was coaching in the big leagues by then, so I called him. I said, "Hey, this guy is trying to teach me a screwball." Bob said, "Oh, that Warren Spahn! He wouldn't know his rear from a hole in the ground!" I said, "Hey, this guy won 363 games in the big leagues." That's just how my uncle was. Whatever came across his mind, he would spit it out. By the way, Greg Maddux has more wins than any living pitcher.

Uncle Bob had 10 years in the big leagues as a coach, and then went back into the minor leagues again. I saw Joe and Bob a couple of times with the Angels. Back in '90, I was making a comeback with the Angels. I was in their spring training. Joe and Bob were there, lockering next to each other. They were together all that time. My uncle was in the minor leagues coaching, and so was Joe.

Uncle Bob died in 2010 at the age of 82. Joe said some really nice things, which I got printed out, and I've never forgotten. He nicknamed my uncle "Bob-a-loo," and said he was truly the best teacher he ever knew.

Joe said, "He was a huge influence on me. I'm not sure I'm here managing without him. He had a big impact on a ton of people. If you ever want to write a great book, Bob Clear is the best baseball coach who ever lived. He was a great evaluator of talent. He didn't tell players what they wanted to hear. He told them what they had to do to get better. He was really a legend to all those people who knew him. He was a man of honesty and integrity. He was a very special man. I was fortunate to have him as a coach in the minor league system, and he came back as a roving instructor when I started out as a minor league roving hitting instructor in 1987. He was able to teach any part of the game. He taught everything better than anyone I ever met. We would argue all the time over sometimes the smallest thing. He would challenge me. He would challenge me every day, but not as a player. I wasn't a prospect as a player. He saw me as a prospect for being a coach. He wanted me to be the best I could be. He was a mentor to all of us. He said, 'You'll be a big league coach one day, and then you'll be a big league manager.' I last saw him about three years before he died, in Anaheim. He was as salty as ever, but he just didn't move very well. I talked on the phone with him not long before he died. People like that just have to be remembered."

Those were wonderful words about my uncle and described him perfectly.

Bob and Joe were really, really close. They talked baseball all the time. They'd sit and talk. They'd go over every play and analyze what happened. I'm sure that there were other guys there that were instrumental in Joe's coaching career. Moose Stubing was one. Moose was our manager in the Quad Cities and Salinas. Moose was a good baseball man.

Moose's favorite line is, "Don't you guys be testing me now." Before we got off the bus and checked into the hotel with curfew coming up, he'd say stuff like that. He'd say, "The owl is in the air." No one ever figured out what that meant.

One night, we were in Jerry Kelly's Circle Tap in Davenport, Iowa. I was going to be the starting pitcher the next day. We were in there, way after curfew, like 1 o'clock. Out of nowhere, Moose is sitting next to me. He buys me a pitcher of beer. He said, "You may as well." I looked at him. It was me and two other players. He bought us the beer. We thought we were dead.

Quad Cities was a small town right on the river. It was a lot of fun. We'd go to the ballpark, work out, play a game then go to the bars. The Italian Village was one of the bars we went to. It was a fun place, and the owner, Jim Hancock, was super to the Angels. One of our other favorite spots was the Circle Tap.

Back in those days, we were like The Traveling Brotherhood Show. Every guy on the team was like your brother. You roomed with the guys on the road. Sometimes you lived with guys. Guys moved around all the time. Everybody was scuffling around, making 500 bucks a month. It was tough.

All of that created great camaraderie among the team. Players go through the school of hard knocks. It's not an easy road to get to the big leagues. You have to be in the right spot at the right time. You have to be talented. You have to be lucky. You have to have all kinds of stuff going for you.

When you look at Joe, he isn't very big. He wasn't buff as a player. He wasn't flashy. He was just one of those guys who knew how to play. He was a good catcher. He was a solid **.250 HITTER***. He made contact. He wasn't an out. He was a tough out. Every guy who plays in the minor leagues has talent, but Joe didn't get a big bonus to sign. The guys who sign for big money have stars by their names and sometimes get treated a bit differently.

Regarding Joe, I think that the cliché that goes with him is, "What goes around comes around." He was always there to help people, help other players. Even though he was the bottom man on the totem pole, he was still helping guys and trying to help pitchers. Seeing a guy like that being successful is wonderful payback for the way he did everything.

I met my first wife in Davenport, Iowa, at the Circle Tap. Her maiden name was Roth. She's two years younger. She's 58-years-old now. I told my daughter the other day, "I signed in '74. That's 42 years ago." I've been out of baseball 26 years. Joe and I lost touch. It's what happens in baseball. We're traveling gypsies. If I see him sometime, it will probably be like old times. I'm really happy for Joe. He deserves all the credit he's getting. He was born to be a teacher. That's what he's doing.

I'm not surprised by his success. The teaching aspect and the team building aspect, the management part of it, it took me a long time to learn that. I'm still trying to learn it. He was a natural at it. He was a natural CEO of a company or a baseball manager.

I got released from the Phillies in 1974 by **DALLAS GREEN***, a guy who played, coached, managed and was a front office

---

*The difference between **.250 HITTER** and a .300 hitter is one hit a week.

---

*Jimmy Piersall hit his 100th Major League home run off **DALLAS GREEN**. To celebrate, Piersall ran the bases backwards.

guy in the Majors forever. His young granddaughter was killed in Tucson in 2011 by the man trying to kill Gabby Giffords, the congresswoman.I got drafted in the eighth round. I got a pretty nice signing bonus along with full college tuition, but had a terrible first year. I got hurt. I had a back injury. I was 0-7 and found a note in my locker from Dallas Green. It read, "Please see me before you dress."

I went to see Dallas and he wasted no time in telling me, "We're going to release you. We're doing this as a favor to you. You can go to school and get on with your life because you don't have a good enough arm to ever pitch in the big leagues." I said, "Oh, O.K."

I went home to California and enrolled in school. I was working out on the weekends. Fast forward to 1982. I went 14-9 for the Red Sox and had been chosen to the All-Star team. I won the Boston Writers' Pitcher of the Year Award. Guess who was giving out the award? Dallas Green.

I said, "Hey, Dallas. Mark Clear. Remember me?" He said, "Yeah, I remember you." He said, "We don't get it right every time." It was pretty nice. He was classy about it.

I was at the ballpark one night in Kansas City when Joe Maddon was there with the Rays. I was up high. I went down and tried to yell at him. I didn't want to bother the guy. He was in his office. I probably should. I probably will. If the Cubbies get to Kansas City, I'm going to go try to say "hi" to him. It's just that at these ball games, all the people, it's even worse than when we played.

What I remember of Joe as a player, when I played with him, he was always everywhere. He was in the bar drinking with us. He was just one of the guys. As a catcher, he was always there to help. He was very interested in what was going on, not only with your delivery, but what was going on between the ears, too.

I feel like I'm just coming into the prime of my life. I just turned 60 and just had my 25th anniversary of being in Kansas City. I'm learning every day, trying to stay healthy. I'm an avid bicycle rider. We have a lot of trails in the area that are made from old railroad lines. My wife and I go to Lee's Summit, catch the train with our bikes, and get dropped off at St. Charles near St. Louis. We then ride back to Lee's Summit. That's a two-and-a-half day ride.

We usually stay at bed and breakfasts in one of the towns on the trail. We do 60 to 75 miles, and then we'll stay at a place. Seventy-five miles, that's not a very hard day. It's a pretty easy day.

AH, A FEMALE BASEBALL FAN, ONE OF LIFE'S MOST MISUNDERSTOOD CREATURES

CONNIE CICCARELLI

Connie Ciccarelli is a spitfire who met her soulmate, Peter, when Peter was Joe Maddon's general manager in Salinas, Calif., in 1977. Peter Ciccarelli passed away a few years ago, but Mrs. Ciccarelli has continued her friendship with Maddon.

My husband, Peter, was the general manager of the California Angels' A-ball team when Joe Maddon was playing in Salinas. That's how we met.

Joe was our back-up catcher in 1977. His dad came out to visit from Pennsylvania. Because our starting catcher was hurt, Joe started his dad's first day there. Joe went 4-for-4 with four absolute shots. Each time that Joe got a hit, his dad would go around the ballpark and introduce himself to the fans. He said, "That's my son. He just got a hit."

My husband went to Anaheim when the season was over, and he told them, "I don't know what you're planning for Joe in the future, but I want him back in Salinas next year. I don't think he's going to go anywhere in this organization as a player. He's going to manage somewhere, and he should be doing it in the Angels organization."

We were always looking for cheap ways to promote our ball club. At their age, the players usually weren't interested in helping out, but Joe was. He was real outgoing. He did our radio and TV commercials.

There are two things I can tell you. Number one, when Joe came to Salinas, and the guys got to know him, everybody was fighting to become his roommate because Joe was such a great

cook. Of course, with his Mom and his family having the restaurant back in Hazleton, Joe learned how to cook Italian food.
So everybody on the team wanted Joe as a roommate because
Joe did the cooking. My husband used to say that Joe was such
a good cook, he could take an old catcher's mitt and mix it with
his marinara sauce, and he'd have the best meal in town.

After he finished playing in Salinas, my husband and I
were living in San Diego. We were very fortunate to have Joe
and our former manager, Chuck Cottier, come down and stay
with us for a period of time. Chuck played nine years in the big
leagues and managed the **MARINERS*** for three years. Chuck is
what I would consider a neat fanatic. He'd stay in his room,
and his clothing in the closet was color coordinated and hung
properly. Nothing was out of place. He couldn't stand it if you
were finished drinking a glass of wine, and you put it down on
the table. He'd get antsy and finally say, "Are you finished with
that?" He'd get up and grab it and go in the kitchen to wash it.
My husband and I left one time for something we had to do.
When we came back, he had washed the floors.

So I had Chuck Cottier there, which was like having my
own live-in maid, and I had Joe living there, which was my
live-in cook. I was in seventh heaven having two guys live with
us that kept me satisfied as a woman. It was so nice having
two guys who were living there that could provide what every
woman's desire was: someone to clean the house and someone to do the cooking.

In the early '80s, Joe was managing in Salem, Ore. The
president of the Northwest League said, "Joe Maddon is going
to be managing in the big leagues some day." Someone asked,

---

*During the Seattle **MARINERS** first year in 1977, the distancce to the
fences was measured in fathoms. A fathom is 6 feet. For instance,
whereas one park might have a sign that denotes 360 feet, the
Kingdome sign would have the number 60...

"Why do you say that?" The president said, "Because when his players get off the bus, they always do the right things."

Joe was always very confident in what he was doing and where he was going. He had a plan, and he stuck with it. A lot of the things he's doing with the Cubs now, he started doing and preparing for years ago in Salinas. He's always believed that the game can get better if you study it hard.

A lot of the old coaches and scouts said there was no place in the game for computers. They said Joe was crazy for using a computer. Joe said, "If you criticize me for using a computer, don't turn on the air-conditioner in the car on your way home."

I'll tell you one Moose Stubing story. Moose was the Salinas manager when Joe played there in 1977. When my husband and I announced to him that we were getting married, Moose said, "Well, I hope youse guys"—everything was "youse guys"—"I hope youse guys make an investment and buy a condom to live in." That's what he said. Anyone who knows Moose Stubing, that is just so Moose.

My husband worked for the El Paso Times as a sportswriter and worked for awhile for UPI. I was born and raised in Carmel, Calif. I was working as an assistant manager at a bank, and the Salinas Angels had an agreement with our bank to do a Junior Angels program. I ran out of programs and just happened to call the office and talked to Peter, and that's how we met. We got married four months later. It was just wonderful. I was always involved in sports. We just had a wonderful life in baseball.

I don't have any dirt on Joe. He was the most likable, lovable guy that you ever wanted to meet, and he still is. Certainly when players are young, there's always something that can be of interest. Peter and I felt so blessed because we always referred to Joe as our son. He is such a wonderful person, and he is so deserving of all the success that he is having. Another deserving one is Bruce Bochy. When Bruce was playing for the

Padres, my husband was an agent, and he represented Bruce. Talk about two guys in baseball that break the mold of the traditional perception of what managers are supposed to be. They are just absolutely wonderful human beings. Their approach to the game is not through intimidation or using tactics that were so familiar in the past. They're just great, great managers and friends and tacticians. They're just great people. So we were very, very fortunate to have those two people in our lives that continue to be in my life.

You're writing a book on one of the great people of all time, not just a great manager, not just a great baseball person. Joe Maddon is a great, great person.

A HARD WAY TO MAKE
AN EASY LIVING

BILL MERRIFIELD

Bill Merrifield has the unique distinction of being penciled into the starting line-up of a Major League game, yet he never played in a Major League game. Merrifield was born in Waukegan, Ill., while his dad was a high-level executive with Abbott Laboratories. In 1983, he was taken in the second round of the draft by the Los Angeles Angels. His manager in the minor leagues his first two years at Peoria and Midland was Joe Maddon. Merrifield is now in the development office of Wake Forest University in Winston-Salem, N.C.

*Even though Bill didn't make the big leagues, his son, Whit Merrifield, made his Major League debut with the Kansas City **ROYALS*** in 2016. As an amateur, Whit Merrifield was best known for driving in the winning run in the final game of the 2010 College World Series.*

When I signed in the summer of '83, the Angels took the draft picks to Cal State Fullerton for workouts, for a week of training and tests. We all went there, and that's where I first met Joe Maddon. He was one of the coaches. I don't think at that time I knew he was going to be my manager the next year. We weren't sure where we were going to go. The top four or five draft picks that year all went to Peoria, the Angels' Class-A

*In the 1979 baseball draft, the **KANSAS CITY ROYALS** selected Dan Marino in the fouth round and John Elway in the 18th round. That same year the Royals hired Rush Limbaugh for their group sales department. Limbaugh left in 1984 for a radio opportunity in California.

team. We all played for Joe Coleman, the pitcher, who was the manager there at that time.

I went back to spring training the next year and found out Joe was going to be the manager in Peoria. I went back to Peoria, fortunately or unfortunately, however you want to look at it. I had the best time there. I had my best year and played really well. I hit 29 home runs for Joe and played really well in the Midwest League.

The reason I think I was that good was Joe came up to me in spring training and said, "Bill, you're going to be my third baseman and hit third until you tell me you're not." I looked at him and said, "O.K., but what does that mean?" He said, "If you get tired, tell me. Otherwise, don't look at the line-up. Just come in. You're going to be hitting third, playing third."

That was refreshing. Looking back, it made sense. He told me, "Bill, don't go out and get drunk. Don't go out and be stupid. Just get your rest and know that you're going to play every day." It was a vote of confidence, and it worked really, really well for me. I wasn't looking over my shoulder. I just went out and played, and Joe always had your back, just like he does now. He developed that early.

From there, I went to big league camp the next year as a non-roster player and from there, went to Double-A. Joe moved up. I played in Midland, Tex., for him the next year. That was '85. My wife came out and joined me in Midland, and she got to know Joe's first wife, Betty. It was very cool. It was just fun to play for him. I told my son, Whit, "Of all the people I'd love for you to play for, Joe would be the perfect guy because he's just the guy that everybody relates to. He wants you honestly and truly to do well." I don't think there's a hidden agenda there, at least there wasn't back in the day. I don't think there is now. You get what you get, and you get what you see. To me, he's always been a highlight of my baseball career. He was just so much fun to play for. The low minor leagues are not easy.

Joe was just very even keel. He understood the big picture. He understood it wasn't about him. It was about developing the players and getting them to perform to their ability, and that's how they were going to move. He understood it was his job to do that. The more he could get us ready and better, the better he would move. His job was predicated on getting players moving, and he did that.

As I got older, with the managers it became less about development and more about winning, more "it's about me." I had a couple of other managers who were just not fun to play for. It's hard enough to play in the minor leagues without being miserable.

For these other managers, it seemed to be about them. It wasn't about what I thought baseball should have been about. I always envisioned baseball being a team sport. It was about moving guys over and driving guys in and coming in and doing your job and being part of a team. The minor leagues turned out not to be that, especially after I got away from Joe. Joe had that calming effect on everybody. The next couple of guys I played for were almost the exact opposite. They felt like the angrier they could get you and the more upset they could get you, the better you'd play. To me, that's why I left. I left when I just turned 26. I quit because I didn't want to do it anymore. I didn't enjoy the business of baseball. I got baseball, and I was good at it, but I just didn't enjoy the business of it.

I think a lot of that had to be from the guys I played for. If I could have played for Joe, if Joe would have gone up to Triple-A and just followed me through, it would have been outstanding. I probably would have played in the big leagues. And when the Angels got Doug DeCinces to play third base, there was nowhere for me to go, really.

Joe never really got mad. He was a unique guy. He is a very, very, very smart guy, but he also didn't get real close to us. He was as close as he needed to be. It always felt like he had an open door policy. You could go in and see him at any point. He would get on you, but he would get on you in a positive way. He would remind you why you were there. He would work with you as much as you wanted to work with him.

I just enjoyed him. It was fun to go to work. It was fun to go to the ballpark. It was fun to go on road trips. It was just fun. We bused everywhere in the minors, especially in Midland and the Texas League. Trips took 5-10 hours. They took so long my shoes went out of style. Lucky Strike cigarettes had a slogan; LSMFT, Lucky Strike Means Fine Tobacco. Baseball players had a slogan: LSMFT: Lord, Save Me From the Texas League.

I didn't see Joe after I quit ball. Well, I take that back. I saw him one spring training. Wake Forest was playing in the NCAA baseball regionals in Tempe, Ariz. I went out with the team, went to spring training and saw Joe briefly. He recognized me.

Another story was this year in spring training when Whit was playing. He went in for Eric Hosmer at first base in the sixth inning of a game. Whit had his name on the back of his uniform. Joe asked his first base coach to ask that kid if his dad played professional baseball. Joe and Whit had a conversation going through the first base coach, but they never had a chance to sit down afterward. Joe would always acknowledge him and wave at him, but they never had a chance to have a conversation. But, yeah, he knew who I was, which makes me feel good.

Every time I talk about minor league baseball, I talk about two things. I talk about playing for Joe Maddon and how I dislike the business of baseball. Now it's all come full circle. I retired at Rosenblatt Stadium in Omaha, and Whit got the last hit in the final game ever at Rosenblatt Stadium. The hit won the College World Series for the University of South Carolina. My career was what it was. It wasn't what I wanted to do.

In Peoria, Rocky Vonachen, Pete's son, owned a restaurant and a bar. The Player of the Game in Peoria would always get to eat and drink free that night. So I got to do that a lot. I had a pretty good year. I was in Rocky's tavern quite a bit. Pete was unique. I remember one story, but I can't verify this. I got called out on a close play at first base, and as I was going back to the dugout, said something to the umpire and got thrown out.

The story goes that Pete Vonachen went over to the stadium's **ORGANIST*** and said, "Play 'Three Blind Mice.'" The umpire threw the organist out. That was all supposedly predicated by Pete. Joe Maddon was laughing. He loved it. Pete owned the Peoria Chiefs and was a very close friend of **HARRY CARAY****.

As a 22-, 23-year-old guy, you don't remember a lot of that stuff, and you don't know any of this is going to be significant 30 years down the road. You just show up every day, and it's Groundhog Day. You do the same thing every day.

There wasn't a lot of difference in play between Class-A Peoria and Double-A Midland. The game got a little bit faster. The guys that were good in the Midwest League went on to the Texas League. Then they weeded out guys in Double-A that went up to Triple-A, and the game became a little bit faster. The guys that you remember are usually the good guys. They're the guys that you really had to work hard to get a hit off. You watched guys like Shawon Dunston and those kinds of guys that you played against, and you remember because they were really good. You saw them as you moved up.

The play wasn't that much different. Back then, we played in all old ballparks. I didn't see a new ballpark until I got in Triple-A and played in the Las Vegas ballpark. It was brand new at the time. We were like, wow, this is really nice.

---

*The first **ORGAN** ever used in a Major League Baseball stadium was at Wrigley Field in 1941.

In the 1962 three-game playoff between the Giants and the Dodgers, **HARRY CARAY did the local color on the San Francisco broadcast with Lou Simmons and Russ Hodges.

Our shortest trip in Midland was five-and-a-half hours to El Paso. That was our shortest trip. We got on the **BUS*** at midnight and drove all night to get to Jackson, Miss., and at 3 o'clock you had to be at the field and ready to play by 5. You wonder why guys in the minor leagues can't play or don't have good stats. It's just brutal. I rode over the axle of a bus for 13 hours and had to get off and play third base in a ballpark with bad lights.

I was in my second year playing in Edmonton, Canada, which was the Angels' Triple-A team. I was on the roster, and we were on our last road trip to Vancouver. My wife was in Edmonton. The manager called me late one night in my room. He said, "Meet me in the bar."

I met him in the bar. I knew something was up. He and I didn't associate together.

He said, "Listen, you're either going to be traded, or you're going to the big leagues in the morning. I don't know which one it is, but, as soon as we find out, I'll let you know."

I said, "All right, whatever."

Early in the morning, he called me and said, "You've been traded to **PITTSBURGH**** for Johnny Ray. You're staying here."

We were playing Vancouver. That was Pittsburgh's Triple-A team. Well, in the haste, the Edmonton trainer took all my

---

*Contrary to popular belief, Michael Jordan did not buy a **BUS** for the Birmingham Barons when he played minor league baseball there in 1994.

From 1933 to 1939, the NFL's **PITTSBURGH Steelers were named the **PITTSBURGH** Pirates. The **PITTSBURGH** Pirates was also the name of the National Hockey League team in the 1920s… In September 2010, **PITTSBURGH** Penguins star Sidney Crosby took batting practice with the Pirates and hit a 370-foot "home-run" that almost cleared the park.

equipment and clothes back to Edmonton. They got on the plane and flew back to Edmonton. I didn't have anything. I didn't have a glove. I didn't have underwear. I didn't have anything. Imagine me going from the first base dugout to the third base dugout as I switched teams. I was taking some guy's job, and I was asking him if I could use his glove and wear his cleats. It was bad.

Anyway, after getting over that awkwardness, I went out and played three games. After the third game, I was told, "You've just been called up to the big leagues. The Pirates want you in Pittsburgh."

That was the September call-up. It was before cell phones and texts. My wife had to drive from Edmonton, Canada, to Pittsburgh, Pa., by herself. She had to pack up, leave the country, do the whole bit.

I got up. I went through customs. I flew. I had to go through four airports. Vancouver to Salt Lake City. Salt Lake City to Houston. Houston to Pittsburgh. I got to Pittsburgh late that afternoon. I was exhausted because I was up all night. I flew all day. I got there, and all I had was **CANADIAN*** money. I got to the gate at Three Rivers Stadium and pulled up in a cab. If you've been to Pittsburgh, you know the airport's not close to the stadium. That was probably a $40 cab ride. A lady came out. She said, "Can I help you?" I said, "I'm a new player. Can you pay the cab?" She said, "Who are you?" I said, "I'm Bill Merrifield. I just came in from Canada. I don't have any American money." She said, "Oh, O.K."

She took care of the cab. They took me into the locker room and said, "The skip wants you on the field in 20 minutes for batting practice." I was exhausted, but excited. The adrenaline had kicked in.

*The late Speaker of the U.S. House of Representatives, Thomas "Tip" O'Neill, got his nickname from an old-time **CANADIAN** baseball player (James "Tip" O'Neill) who fouled off many pitches.

I got loose. I walked out. It was just me, Tommy Sandt, who was throwing batting practice to me, three shaggers in the outfield, General Manger Syd Thrift, Manager **JIM LEYLAND*** and his coaching staff standing around the batting cage.

I started hitting. That was my first time in any big league stadium. I didn't get a chance to look around, enjoy the moment, nothing. Sandt started throwing B.P. I hit for 15 minutes, and it's not easy to hit that long by yourself. I was exhausted. Leyland was behind me saying, "O.K., hit and run, hit behind him, get him in, hit for power, hit one out." He wanted to see what I could do.

I couldn't even see where the balls were going. I hit them. I didn't know if I was hitting any out. I was just trying to get through it. He said, "O.K., we're done." I went back in the clubhouse. I changed clothes. I went out for regular batting practice and infield. I was taking ground balls at third with Bobby Bonilla, and it started drizzling. They called off B.P., and I went back inside.

Bob Kipper, who I played with in A-ball in Peoria, was on that team and was introducing me to Barry Bonds and Andy Van Slyke and all the guys. About 10 minutes into it, the clubbie came up and said, "You're starting at first base tonight. What do you need to get ready?"

Everything I had was red. I had red cleats, red batting gloves. I said, "I need some black stuff and everything you've got." My uniform was in the locker. It had my name on it. This was my night. This was my debut. Zane Smith was pitching for the Phillies, I think. He was a lefthander.

The rain delay continued. About 40 minutes later, the clubbie came back. He said, "Skip wants to see you in his office."

---

*Tigers manager **JIM LEYLAND** was once a second-string catcher for Perrysburg High School, in the Toledo area. The starting catcher was Jerry Glanville, later an NFL head coach.

I was thinking that we were going to go over signals. We were going to go over strategy. I walked in. Jim Leyland was sitting behind his desk and Syd Thrift was standing behind him. Leyland said, "Bill, we want you to go to Instructional League and prove to us you can hit for power."

I thought he meant that at the end of September, October, I would go to Florida and learn the Pirates Way. I said, "O.K., when do you want me to go?"

He said, "We want you there Monday."

That was Friday.

I said, "This Monday?"

He said yeah and just looked at me. Syd Thrift never said a word. He just stared at me.

At this time, I had 90 minor league home runs. It wasn't like I couldn't hit. I just looked at Leyland. I stood in the doorway and just looked at him, and they just looked back at me.

I turned and walked back through the locker room. By the time I got to my locker, my stuff was already packed up in my bag. I just picked up my bag, walked out and went to a hotel.

My wife is in the middle of nowhere. I didn't know how to get in touch with her. She was driving to Pittsburgh. Now we were going to Bradenton, Fla. She had to figure out how to get from wherever she was down to Bradenton. In a 45-minute window, I went from starting in the big leagues to going to Instructional League. It just got worse from there. It was just amazing how things happened.

I don't even remember where my wife was when I finally talked to her. I had to call from pay phones. I left a message with her parents, and we figured out how to connect. My dad flew out to North Dakota and jumped in the car with her and helped her drive back. It was a three-day drive.

I got to the Instructional League, and I didn't play. It was just one thing after another. I went back to spring training, and I didn't play. Leyland brought me back to spring training and said, "We want you to be the right-handed power off the bench. We'll give you a shot." In the entire spring training, I got 10 at bats. The first day they could send me down, they sent me down. Leyland said, "I don't want to b.s. you, but you never had a chance to make this team. We want you to go to Buffalo and show us you can hit for power." I was like, yeah, this sounds familiar.

It got worse. Rocky Bridges was the manager of Pittsburgh's Triple-A club in Buffalo. We were still at spring training in Florida. I said, "Rocky, what is happening?" He said, "I don't know, but I'll find out."

With about three days left in spring training, he said, "Here are your options. You can go back to Double-A and play every day or you can go on the phantom Disabled List in Triple-A."

I said, "Look, I'm not going back to Double-A, and I'm not hurt. I'll go to Triple-A with you, but tell them to trade me. This is stupid."

He said, "I'll see what I can do."

I spent two more days in spring training. I flew out with the Triple-A team to Louisville to open the season, and I was on the phantom DL. There was no telling when I was going to play again. I was in the outfield shagging balls in batting practice Opening Night in Louisville when Rocky called me in and said, "You've just been traded to Texas. You've got 45 minutes to catch a plane to Oklahoma City."

In the meantime, my wife was driving from Bradenton to Buffalo. I was flying to Oklahoma City, and she was going to Buffalo with the wives. I didn't know where she was. She was on I-95 somewhere.

I flew to **OKLAHOMA CITY***, and the team was playing an exhibition doubleheader with Oklahoma State that night. The clubbie picked me up. I got dressed. Toby Harrah was the manager. I walked in the dugout and Toby looked at me and said, "Who are you?"

I said, "I'm your new player."

He said, "Well, what position do you play?"

I said, "I'm a third baseman."

He said, "I've got a third baseman," and walked away.

I knew one person on that team. I just sat there in the dugout. We were playing a doubleheader. About the third inning of the second game, Harrah came up and said, "Can you play first?" I said, "Sure, I can play first." He said, "Go in."

I went to first base. Craig McMurtry was pitching. He walked the first batter, and I was holding the runner on. Craig came to a stretch, turned and looked to first base. He looked again. He stepped off the rubber, called time out and motioned me to come to the mound. He said, "I haven't met you, yet. Craig McMurtry." I said, "Yeah, I'm Bill Merrifield. I got here about an hour-and-a-half ago."

Then I proceeded to not play very much for the first month-and-a-half. That was the end. It was just one thing after another. I finally said, "Screw this. I've got other things to do."

It really was crazy. Wally Joyner and I were roommates and really good friends. I talked to him all the time. He said, "Why in the hell aren't you in the big leagues?" I said, "I don't know."

---

*Bricktown Ballpark in **OKLAHOMA CITY** is bounded by Mickey Mantle Drive, Johnny Bench Drive and Joe Carter Avenue. The fourth street is Flaming Lips Alley.

My wife loved baseball. She hated when I stopped playing. She was a **TENNIS*** player growing up. She traveled all the time. She loved it. She just loved the lifestyle and being with the wives. I loved the relationships. Don't get me wrong. I loved the guys I met, most of them. It just wasn't for me. She was a saint. She still is a saint, by the way.

I wasn't surprised at all by Joe Maddon's rise up the ladder. It was fun to watch, actually, and to know that I was a player for him early on when he started is neat. It's fun. It's a great memory for me. I'm so proud to be part of just a teeny-weeny, little-bitty part of his background and his history. It's fun for me to watch.

It's different for me than it would be for a lot of people to have a son playing in the big leagues. For the guy who played 10 years in the big leagues and then sees his son get to the big leagues, it's probably a matter of fact, run-of-the-mill thing. For me, it was being that close and having all of that history and having a kid who wasn't supposed to make it. I was a second round pick. I was 6-foot-4, 200 pounds, and could hit for power. I was supposed to make it, and I didn't. Now I had a kid who was a ninth round pick, was 175 pounds and without a position to play. He wasn't supposed to make it, ever. He wasn't supposed to make it out of Class-A ball. Here he is in the big leagues.

Every parent's proud, but it was more satisfying for me to say, "Look, none of you idiots know what you're doing. You prognosticators say this kid can play, this kid can't play. None of you know what's inside that uniform, what's in that player's chest and what drives them every day."

---

*In what sport was Chris Evert the leading money winner in 1974? The answer: Horse racing. The owner, Carl Rosen, named his horses after **TENNIS** players. The horse named Chris Evert won $551,063 with five wins in eight starts.

You see a kid who's 6-foot-4, 220, he's going to make it. He's a number one prospect in the organization. Well, hell, my kid won the MVP at every level he played. He was an All-Star at every level. He never made a prospect list with Kansas City. He was never in the top 40 prospects in the organization, yet he made the big leagues. Why is that? Well, because he can play, he's a good kid and the fans love him. He does things off the field. He cares about people. He does all of the stuff that you would expect somebody to do and expect a good kid to do. He has extreme confidence in his abilities and in himself. As a parent, that's all you can ask.

He was pretty good as a ninth round draft choice. He got a lot of publicity because he got the walk-off hit in the **COLLEGE WORLD SERIES***. That helped him.

It's really a shame. Baseball has become a showcase. It's a lot about entertainment. It's not about the guy. The fans aren't paying to see a Whit Merrifield come up with nobody out and a runner on second and moving him to third. They're not paying for that. They want to see him hit the ball out of the ballpark. They want to see him hit a double. They want to see him do something that they're paying their good money for, and I get that. I grew up playing the game fundamentally correct and doing it the right way. Now only the hardened baseball guy understands productive outs. The average fan that's paying these guys' salaries just wants to see you swing as hard as you can, hit it as hard as you can and throw it as hard as you can. That's what they're looking for.

Flip your bat. What kind of entertainment are you showing me because we want to go home and watch it on ESPN on *SportsCenter,* and who are the only guys that are getting on

---

*President George H. W. Bush played first base for Yale in the 1947 **COLLEGE WORLD SERIES** in Kalamazoo, Michigan. The **COLLEGE WORLD SERIES** later moved to Wichita, Kansas before settling long-term in Omaha.

SportsCenter? It's not the guy who made three productive outs that won the ballgame for you and made a great defensive play. It's the guy that hit two home runs and struck out three times. That's the guy they want to see.

When Whit was going up through the minor leagues, I said, "Look, the big leagues are about superstars and the guys that support the superstars. If you can be a guy that supports the superstars and play 10 years, you can do whatever you want to do the rest of your life. Chances are, you're not going to be a superstar, but there are going to be two or three on a team, and what are the other six guys? You know, they've got to have them, and for them to be superstars, they've got to be able to win enough to get on TV. If you can be one of those guys, you can pick your number. Go through arbitration and pick your number. But that's what it's about. The superstars are going to be the guys that everybody goes out to watch. But if you play hard and get involved in the community and you're out there early signing autographs and you're staying late and getting pictures and doing all the stuff that fans want you to do, you're creating value for yourself." Whit is like that anyway, so it's not a big deal for him to do that stuff. He enjoys the fans.

That's the way Joe Maddon was as a player and as a minor league manager. Joe always preached that it's about the game. It's not about you. It's not about me. It's about the game. Joe's an extremely bright guy. He knows the game, and he's loyal to the game and what it stands for, what it's meant, and that rubs off. Joe believes that if you do the right things, good things are going to happen. It worked out for me. The best thing in the world that could have happened for me was not making the big leagues.

People say, "What are you talking about? How did you not want to play in the big leagues?" I say, "I never said I didn't want to play in the big leagues. I just didn't want to be a professional baseball player." That's different. The profession of baseball, I wasn't interested in. But growing up, everybody wants to be a big leaguer. It's different. I watched Wally Joyner, my roomie. He had four girls. For the 13 years that he was in the big leagues, he never saw them. He was gone two weeks out of every month. He was gone a month-and-a-half in spring training. Leslie, his wife, did all the hard work while the kids grew up. His time demands were not his. When it was "Wally World" in California his rookie year, he didn't have a life.

I love Joe. I loved everything he did for me and with me. My biggest wish would be that Whit could play for him before his career is over. I think the world of Joe.

I'd love to touch base with him.

SHORT STORY FROM A LONG MEMORY

Joe and I literally closed down a bar, not in the traditional sense. We literally closed it down. I was with Joe, Bruce Hines, who was our pitching coordinator, and the manager and coaching staff of the Quad Cities Angels. We went to a restaurant-bar called The Dock in Davenport, Iowa. They turned The Dock into a Rusty Pelican. The night we went was the last night of it being The Dock. It was about 1 o'clock in the morning. We were still there. We were not horribly drunk. We weren't terrifically sober either. We were not a mess, but we were just talking. Bob Clear was there. Bob did not drink, but he laughed. We laughed and laughed and told stories and just kept going. We were nice enough, because the staff let us stay, and they tore the place down around us. They literally took pictures off the walls. They took all the tables out. By the time we were done, there was one table in the middle of this restaurant with eight or nine chairs around it, us talking, and they were still serving us drinks. It was closed the next day. It was closed for two weeks. When they reopened it, it was a Rusty Pelican.

That Davenport stadium went through a lot of iterations. We were there when it was terrible, and then we started moving around the Midwest League. We were in Peoria a little bit. When we finally got back into Quad Cities, it was really a mess. But it got sold, and they redid it, and it was beautiful. John O'Donnell Stadium was just gorgeous.

—**Bill Bavasi**, Jr., director of the Major League scouting bureau and former general manager of the California Angels and Seattle Mariners

Chapter 4

BITS AND BITES:

Former Mendel and Notre Dame star Joe Farrell was all
smiles the day the Cubs clinched.

BEGGED, BORROWED
AND STOLEN

GYM DANDIES

MICHELLE BEARDEN

Michelle Bearden was an award-winning reporter for The Tampa Tribune *for 20 years until leaving due to the* Tribune *downsizing in 2014. In April 2012, she wrote this story on the Maddons' marriage.*

The buzz was high and fast when Tampa Bay Rays manager Joe Maddon showed up at spring training in Port Charlotte in February. And it had nothing to do with the Rays' chances in 2012.

What's with the hair?

It wasn't the first time the free-spirited Maddon shocked with his locks. But this style—longish, wavy and a coffee-colored brown—looked like he was channeling a '50s biker dude, especially when he slipped on his Kaenon sunglasses.

What was his wife thinking?

Not much, it turns out. It should be no surprise that his wife of three years, Jaye, doesn't dictate style or anything else for her mate. And he doesn't for her.

The bicoastal couple who met in Southern California— where Jaye still lives most of the time—are each other's biggest fans. And that comes with an understanding. He does his thing; she does hers. That means he manages the baseball team and she manages their life.

Jaye, 49, is the CFO of the family, the analytical one who raised two sons, got her law degree at age 45 and teaches online courses in criminal justice for the University of Phoenix. She oversees their residences and rentals in Tampa, Southern California and Hazleton, Pa. She makes sure the bills get paid, the fine print in contracts is carefully read, and commitments to multiple charities, community events and family are kept.

And in December, Joe added yet another responsibility to their already hectic lives: comical English bulldog puppy Winston (follow him on Twitter @winstoncmaddon), who joins 8-year-old Great Dane rescue Athena.

"Joseph pulled out all stops on this one," Jaye says, rolling her eyes.

He told her that having a puppy would make them better people. He lavished attention on the new arrival for two months, and then...he left for Port Charlotte. Now it's Jaye in charge of housebreaking, training and arranging sitters when she travels.

"But it's all worked out," Joe insists. "She's the dog whisperer."

Jaye says their arrangement makes it possible for her husband to devote his energies to winning games, something he's been quite successful at since taking over the once-bedeviled Rays in the 2006 season. With a partner handling life's details and schedules off the field, it's easier for Joe to be himself: affable and positive with his players, the media and the public, and one of baseball's most cerebral strategists.

And yes, for the record, she did like that maverick biker look, which Joe shed in mid-March when he and 70 others in the Rays organization had their heads shaved to raise money for pediatric cancer research.

"That's the thing about Joseph," Jaye says, smiling. "It's always a fun ride. You just don't know what will happen next."

****

They were both married to other people when they met in 1995 at the Rossmoor Athletic Club in Seal Beach, Calif., where Jaye worked in accounting.

It wasn't love at first sight or anything like that, even if Joe admits he was "completely star-struck" when he laid eyes on the petite, dark-haired beauty who is eight years his junior. He liked her calm demeanor and self-confidence. She was brainy and beautiful.

Jaye and her best friend, Erin-lee Anderson, the club manager, immediately took to the longtime Anaheim (now California) Angels bench coach, who occasionally came in to work out. He was easy-going and entertaining. Best of all, he left game tickets for the baseball-crazed women. They all became fast friends, even if they only saw Joe a few times a year.

Friendship blossomed into romance years later after their marriages broke up. The two had a lot in common: They were geeks about fast cars, sports and high-tech toys. It was kismet. Here was a woman whose first car was a dark gold 1968 Camaro, no less. Joe loved that she was as comfortable with her femininity as she was hunkered down in a man cave with a cold one and a game on the big screen. It was easy hanging out together.

"I never guessed they would eventually end up together," says Anderson, now an independent casting producer. "But knowing the both of them, it makes sense. They're both down-to-earth people with a beautiful zest for life. All the success they've had hasn't changed them at all.

"I would say they are perfectly matched."

Each is deeply rooted in family. Besides their extended clans, Jaye has two boys and Joe has a son and daughter. They have the same priorities. Though Jaye is more subdued, she was charmed by Joe's quirkiness.

"She's got a great laugh. And I can make her laugh, which is very important," Joe says. "We always have a blast."

Like a lot of professional couples who get together midlife, they had some balancing issues. Joe's Angels team was World

Series-bound, winning it all in October 2002. Jaye, meanwhile, was buried in textbooks. After years of juggling motherhood, working several jobs and attending night school to earn her bachelor's degree, the goal-oriented woman wasn't through yet. She started law school at 41.

She was in her second year at Western State University when she and Joe began dating. Jaye knew things were getting serious when he took her home to Hazleton to meet his family and see the old neighborhoods he roamed with his sister and brother. He shared stories of his grandfather, an Italian immigrant who worked in the local coal mines, and his late father, a plumber. She met his Polish mother, Beanie, 79, who has been working at the Third Base Luncheonette since 1948.

If there was one thing that could capture Jaye's heart, it was a man who embraced his roots. That meant something to her.

She grew up a tomboy in a boisterous home in Fullerton, Calif., the fifth of Ted and Eileen Sousoures' six children. She played second base for the town's Bobby Sox league and tinkered with cars. Like the Maddons, the clan didn't have much money—they had to scrimp to send the kids to Catholic schools—but they had plenty of love. Her parents instilled values of hard work, independence, good humor and loyalty.

"Maybe that's what attracted me to Joseph," she says. "He had all those qualities. He felt like home."

All the baseball travel, school studies and family obligations could easily torpedo a relationship, so they had a two-week rule. No matter what, they would carve out time for each other at least twice a month in their Southern California base.

What they hadn't counted on was Joe's being wooed for the Rays job in November 2005. Even before an offer was on the table, he told them he needed to schedule some time off to attend his girlfriend's graduation from law school the next May. No problem, they told him.

But there went the rule.

"I said, 'Dude, could you move any farther away than that?' But this was Joe's dream, and it had such potential," she says.

So they made another pact. We're going to be a bicoastal couple, they declared, and we're going to do it better than any other couple in the history of baseball.

She thinks they're doing a good job so far. During the season, they squeeze in at least a week together every month, either at their Mediterranean two-story home in South Tampa or on the road. They talk every morning and every night, with maybe a text or two during the day. She gets that being married to a baseball guy means sacrifice. A sign in the kitchen says it all: We interrupt this family to bring you this baseball season.

When Jaye's in California, she has DirecTV and MLB.com. Technology allows her to watch her husband make his moves from thousands of miles away. That includes when he uncharacteristically loses his cool and argues with the umps.

"I'm always thinking, 'Whoa, babe, be careful. This is gonna cost you some money!' But how about the time he actually threw out the umpires?" she says. "I was laughing hysterically!"

And, she says, dropping her voice, "To be honest, it made me kind of hot. You go, Joseph!"

****

Unconventional is the best word to describe Joe Maddon's management style.

There are the themed road trips—Jaye's favorite was the overnight flight out West when everybody wore pajamas on the plane—and motivating his players with quotes from Dr. Seuss to French philosopher Albert Camus. While Boston Red

Sox manager Bobby Valentine famously put the kibosh on any alcohol consumption in the clubhouse, Joe enjoys a glass of a fine Spanish red in postgame interviews with the media. Ever since Jaye introduced him to wine, that's his beverage of choice.

He doesn't lock himself in an office to work on equations and devise some of those rather unusual on-field chess moves he makes from the dugout. Instead, his best ideas come when he straps on his helmet and hits the road on his racing bike. He cycles as much as 100 miles a week. (Jaye's bike has a basket on it, signaling it's mainly used for pleasure cruising.)

As solid and dependable a person as he is, she says, "You learn to expect the unexpected with Joseph."

In June 2007, she met him in Denver, where the team had an interleague series with the Colorado Rockies. Though it was late, Joe said he wanted to take her on a road trip to Boulder, where he played semipro ball for Bauldie Moschetti's Boulder Collegians in the mid-1970s. Show her his favorite haunts, take in some of those great memories.

In the dark, he couldn't find Scotty Carpenter Field, the old ballpark where the team played. So after a meal of burgers, fries and beer at his old hangout, the Dark Horse, he headed over to Moschetti's store, Baseline Liquors, where cash-strapped players such as Joe would work to help pay the bills.

On bended knee in the parking lot, Joe proposed to his future bride. It was 1:30 a.m.

Moschetti died in 1994. Bill Singh, who now owns the store, says the legendary coach and general manager would have loved that Joe declared his everlasting love to Jaye in such a sentimental location.

The next year would be the roller-coaster ride of a lifetime for the couple, with the death of Jaye's mom and the improbable road to the World Series. Two weeks after the Rays lost in five games to the Philadelphia Phillies, they married in a small ceremony at Jaye's family church, St. Julianna Catholic Church in Fullerton, followed by a big shindig on the Queen Mary in Long Beach.

Though the wedding photos and the two-week European honeymoon—her first trip there—suggest a fairy tale, Jaye knows that's not the case. Commuter marriages and blended families require a lot of give and take. Her eldest son, Ryan, 25, works and lives near the Maddons' 1928 Spanish bungalow in the charming Belmont Shores neighborhood in Long Beach; Dylan, 18, graduates from high school next month. Joe's grown kids, Sarah and Joey, and his two grandchildren are in the Phoenix area.

Some people don't understand why she doesn't live full time in Tampa. Besides wanting to be near her sons, she has a brother with brain damage who lives in a convalescent home about a half-hour away. Since their father's death a year ago, the Sousoures siblings are responsible for overseeing his care.

"Jaye and Joe's (California) place is the home base for us now," says older sister Terry Sousoures, a flight attendant for United Airlines. "With both our parents gone, we needed a gathering place. And Jaye stepped right into that role."

Sousoures has a lot of respect for her sister, who overcame the odds to finish her schooling and raise her sons. She admits she was a little surprised when Jaye started bringing Joe around. Who's this old guy? Sousoures thought. Turns out, the white hair was deceiving.

"Jaye has always looked way younger than her years. So they're a lot closer in age than people might think," she says. "I don't think this would have worked when Jaye was in her 20s. Having experience and wisdom makes her a much better partner for him now. They really complement each other."

Joe is known as the impetuous one who makes decisions without thinking them through (remember Winston?). Jaye is on the opposite end of the spectrum, considering all options first. An avid chef, the kitchen is Joe's territory; she only cooks if there's a blender involved.

The one area where they are in complete harmony is their shared zeal for cars. Their collection keeps growing. There's Aunt Hen, a '67 Ford Galaxy 500 convertible named for Maddon's late Aunt Henrietta; Bob-a-loo, the '72 Chevelle named for Bob Clear, one of his mentors; Gwelda, Jaye's 911 4S Porsche (it's her mom's middle name); and Bella, the family's newest addition, a '56 Chevy Bel Air, complete with fuzzy dice and a bobbing hula girl.

"Bella just means beautiful," Jaye says. "I said enough already. We had to quit naming all our cars after dead people."

****

Joe is the spotlight guy. It comes with the job. He's comfortable with the television cameras. With his funky eyewear and talked-about hairstyles, he's recognized most everywhere he goes in the Tampa Bay area.

Jaye, on the other hand, prefers anonymity.

She can do without social events, unless they contribute to a good cause. For the past two years, she's worked with the PACE Center, a nonresidential counseling and education program for girls ages 12 to 18 who are at risk of dropping out of school or getting into trouble. Executive director Sally Zeh says Jaye led a drive to collect school supplies, donates clothing to "Beth's Closet," a dress-for-success initiative, and brought some of the girls to a ballgame, where they went on a shopping spree in the team shop.

What impresses Zeh is Jaye's sweet nature and how humble she is. Once she called the center and said, "Hi. I'm Jaye Maddon, Joe's wife from the Rays. I'm not sure if you remember me."

"Of course we remember her. She has gone above and beyond to help us here. And the lesson the kids are getting is that strangers are willing to love them and help them better their lives. The girls are hungry for that kind of encouragement," Zeh says.

Angelica Craig is one of them. Now 19 and living in a residential facility, she keeps a picture taken of her and Jaye at a Rays game. The two keep in touch by phone, with Jaye encouraging her to finish school and stay focused on her goals. Craig wants to be a chef one day, and she was invited to help cook at the Maddons' Thanksmas charity dinner, which feeds hundreds of needy people in the Tampa Bay area every year.

"She's been an inspiration to me," Craig says. "She makes me feel special, which is something I haven't always felt."

When the Maddons go out to dinner in the Tampa area, well-meaning fans stop by their table for autographs or to chat. She knows that comes with the territory in being married to a local celebrity. At Cook's Kitchen, one of their favorite neighborhood spots for homemade soup and salad, Sally Cook instructs her staff: Don't stare and don't bother them. Treat them like all the other customers.

"They're just the nicest people," says the British chef. "Perfectly charming, really. And both of them are quite arresting-looking."

In Belmont Shores, with her partner on the road, Jaye walks the streets with Winston and eats at her favorite raw-foods restaurants without interruptions. For several months, hairstylist Shelby Buckley listened to Jaye talk about her husband, Joseph, who lived in Florida.

Finally she had to ask: Why are you married to some guy who lives across the country?

"So she says his name is Joe Maddon, and he's the manager of the Rays," Buckley says. "I tell my brother, a huge Angels fan, and he goes nuts. She was just so matter-of-fact about it."

Now that she's met Joe—and fixed one of his bad do-it-yourself dye jobs—Buckley understands their arrangement and why it works.

"They're living in this world, and they're real. They make the most of every day," she says. "I love their spirit and the energy they give out. And all the work they do in the community shows what remarkable human beings they are."

Joe says no one has to tell him he's a lucky guy. Meeting Jaye, and convincing her that marrying him was a fine idea, is the best thing that ever happened to him. Even better than that 2002 World Series win with the Angels.

Says Joe: "I'm way over my skis with her. Sometimes, you just hit gold."

FANECDOTES

Joe Maddon is not your man if you want a manager who can stand up in a clubhouse and draw on his own experiences as a big league player when he makes demands of his team.

Of the 30 Major League teams, 26 have managers who had at least a cup of coffee in the big leagues.

Maddon does not qualify for that. He never played past Single-A ball.

Maddon suspects that may be the primary reason he never has interviewed for a big league managing job outside of the Angels, the only organization for which he has worked. And he may have a point, because otherwise Maddon brings the kind of credentials that would attract attention: bright, organized, honest, innovative, personable, communicative, with a broad background as a minor league manager, hitting instructor, player development executive, and big-league coach.

Maddon loves Bruce Springsteen, is hoping to catch Simon and Garfunkel soon, and is well-read, counting Pat Conroy *(Prince of Tides, Beach House)* as one of his favorite authors. Angels people praise his sense of humor and uniformly positive outlook on life. And he said he always has counted Boston as one of his favorite stops.

What makes him best qualified to manage the Sox?

"Myself," he said. "I think I'm an organizer. I know I am. My good training in different positions in the past has given me specific ideas about what I like to do offensively, defensively, and with a pitching staff.

"I don't want to sound pretentious, but the stuff I bring is a baseball thing. I've been doing this for a long time, and I've had some really wonderful mentors."

Mentors like former Angels coach Bob Clear, pitching guru Marcel Lachemann, former Red Sox hitting coach Rick Down, Dodger hitting coach Ben Himes, and former infielders Bobby Knoop and Larry Bowa as major i uences in developing his philosophies.

Maddon knows his way around a computer.

"I've been using one since 1990," he said. "I use it as an organizational tool. I like looking at numbers, but I like making them simple. For me, the most important thing is to take a lot of numbers and simplify them. Players can't hold onto a lot of stuff during a game. There's a fine balance between giving them information and still allowing them to play unobstructed."

But for all his affinity for stats, and his enthusiasm for the intricacies of the game, Maddon has clarity about what separates the successful managers from the also-rans.

"Understanding the pulse of the players," he said. "That makes all the difference."

That's something you understand, whether or not you played in the big leagues.

—**Gordon Edes,** *The Boston Globe* writer on Maddon interviewing for the managerial position with the Red Sox in 2003

He's an outside-the-box thinker. He used to ride his bike in Mesa, Ariz., and lie on a yoga mat on the grass in our front yard and do yoga in his Spandex. Everybody could see him, but he didn't care what anybody thought.

When we were young, we didn't spend a lot of time on the road with him. It was tough. We only got to see him a couple of months out of the year. When he was with us, he was a great dad.

—**Joey Maddon**, Joe's son

I can respect him for what he's done and what he's achieved, but it came at a high price.

After the season one year, he had a box of stationery. I asked him what he was going to do with it. He said he was going to send each player a handwritten note and tell them how much he appreciated them.

—**Betty Maddon**, Joe's ex-wife

Joe is a brilliant marketer, very creative. He branded Tropicana Field as "The Pit." When Joe was here, it took on a life of its own. It sparked a booster club called Maddon's Maniacs, 500 of our loudest and proudest fans. He met with them throughout the season. He led their section in cheers. It was a big plus.

No one is beneath him. He knows all the security guards by names.

—**Darcy Raymond**, Tampa Bay Rays Vice President, Marketing & Entertainment

I never heard a sidewards word about Joe. True, he's sometimes driving in his own lane on the freeway of life, but count me in as one who thinks that's a great thing.

—**Bob Hards**, radio announcer for the Midland (Tex.) RockHounds

I'm really excited to be a Cub. You have not won a World Series since 1908, and that makes it even more attractive. I'm really jacked up about this entire moment. I'm really looking forward to get going. We start in Mesa in a couple of days. So I'm going to go back home tomorrow for Valentine's Day. I already sent Jaye, my wife, a nice bundle of flowers. Sunday, I fly to Arizona where my grandkids and my kids are, and we start spring training out there. I'm really excited about that. As a manager, you're just about winning. It's about winning and that's it. You win. You take wins really well. You take losses harder than anybody else. It's not about individual awards ever for me. It never has been.

—**Joe Maddon**, before his first spring training with the Cubs

I sent Joe a rather strange email. It was in 2009, Opening Day of the (Port) Charlotte Stone Crabs. Who in the world would buy a Class-A team of the Tampa Bay Rays and move them into Port Charlotte after the Rays finished in last place every single year? But, as it turns out, when we got involved with the Stone Crabs, our ticket sales in the Florida State League were great.

I went to Port Charlotte for Opening Day. The home clubhouse set-up was really, really nice. I took it upon myself to go into the manager's office and use his bathroom. I dropped trou. I sat on the seat. I took a picture and sent it to Joe. The email read, "We're enjoying Opening Day in Port Charlotte. I got the best seat in the house!"

—**Billy Ripken**, former Oriole and co-owner of minor league baseball teams

I started broadcasting for the Angels in 1999 and stayed until 2009. I was in the locker room one day when Joe coached with Mike Scioscia. I was waiting outside the manager's office to talk to Mike. I heard a heated exchange. When it was over, out came Joe. He winked at me and smiled. I loved it. That's what you do in business. Sometimes you're going to disagree and argue. But he knew I heard everything. He wasn't angry. He was just doing his job as the bench coach.

Joe knows how to talk to guys. He knows how to share. Joe Torre was the same way. They both understand the art of communication. Torre, with all his experience, was like a father figure. Joe Maddon, with how smart he is with all those books he's read and his vocabulary, is really something.

—Rex "Wonder Dog" Hudler, former Maddon player, 10-year Major League veteran

Of course I knew that I'd start a fashion trend with my black glasses. I'll tell you how that happened. I was with the Angels and I'm a bench coach and I'm buying those little readers out of Walgreens and all the other places. I kept scratching them up and my eyes kept getting worse. So I was living in Brea, Calif., and there's this cool little eyeglass joint and I walk in there one day with my wife Jaye—that's when we were still going out— and I chose them. I knew I was going to get hammered by the old school, Jarrod Washburn, Darin Erstad. They're all going to give me a hard time, but I said it's about time we brought the look into the clubhouse. Eventually, like all the time, corny becomes cool and cool becomes really cool and then it takes off. Starting about 2003, maybe something like that, but it truly was because I was tired of it and furthermore, I wanted to give Jarrod Washburn a hard time.

—Joe Maddon on his choice of spectacles

Joe enrolled as a freshman in 1972, my second year at Lafayette. There were 2,000 students at Lafayette. Five hundred had to be engineers, and they had to have a certain number of women. They had just started admitting women. Recruiting was a little tough, but it's a great school, a great small liberal arts college. Joe Maddon was in the Zeta Psi fraternity and was friends with some of my basketball players. Jay Mottola and Tracy Tripucka were my co-captains and best players. Today, Jay Mottola is the head of the Metropolitan Golf Association of the New York City area. Tracy is an executive with a New Jersey bank.

Joe was a highly recruited quarterback out of high school. He got letters from Duke, Minnesota, Pitt, Miami, Notre Dame, Penn, Cornell, Brown and others, but he went to Lafayette. A lot of people thought that if he had kept playing football, he might have been able to play in the NFL. He probably would have been the starting quarterback at Lafayette as a sophomore. He went to spring practice as a freshman and then quit, got in his Volvo and drove home to Hazleton. His dad didn't speak to him. One reason he quit was because when he was playing football, the baseball team was having practice in the same facility. He could hear the crack of the bat every day. It was too enticing. I think that's why he chose baseball over football.

Growing up in a small town in Western Wisconsin, I was a huge Milwaukee Braves fan. I still love baseball.

—**Dr. Tom Davis**, former basketball coach at Lafayette, Boston College, Stanford, Iowa and Drake

I talked to Larry David. It's official. Joe Maddon will be on *Curb Your Enthusiasm* this coming season. Season Nine starts shooting in January or February, so it'll be before spring training. I'm assuming he'll play himself, maybe a character? Maybe a young nurse?

—**Jeff Garlin**, regular on HBO's *Curb Your Enthusiasm* and a lifelong Cubs fan

Joe Maddon had become such a well liked and well regarded fellow that when the opportunity arose for him to go to the Chicago Cubs, the people of Tampa sort of wanted what was best for him. This isn't enough of a baseball-loving town, yet, where people get offended when somebody leaves. It was, thanks a lot, Joe. You made lemonade out of lemons. You took this team with not a lot of money and a weird funky stadium and made them more of a community-based ball team. They weren't the bottom dwellers that they had been for years and years and years.

I use some of Joe's philosophy for a journalism class that I teach. Joe said, "Teach one new thing a day. Just because these guys are pros and make millions of dollars doesn't mean that they won't be distracted when an airplane flies over the field. At practice, teach one thing a day and limit it to that."

Joe was and remains an interesting guy because he's a departure from the typical baseball skipper, what with this reliance on statistics and his use of computers in the clubhouse and his interesting off the field antics and lifestyle. I think he had a fine wine collection in the clubhouse. He was constantly encouraging the players to loosen up. When he ran the show, they were always doing funny stuff. They traveled to certain places, and they all wore plaid suits. He also had the mohawk, which he dyed blue at one point. Tons of folks in Tampa followed suit. Pretty soon, you saw little kids all over the area sporting blue mohawks.

Joe got people involved in Rays baseball because of the winning, but also because of his quirky personality and his style. People who never paid attention to baseball here before him started to tune into Rays games because they were finally fun to watch.

—**Ben Montgomery**, writer, *Tamp Bay Tribune*

Joe Maddon is still looking pretty good. I just saw him walking around the Winter Meetings, and I'm worrying that we're approaching peak Maddon. He had some Vans on, a cool pair of jeans, and a nice, fashionable, military-esque jacket and was pretty much put together like an aged millennial. Not that

that's a bad thing. If you feel young, you are young, to some degree. But seriously, the dude turned 62 before spring training, and I worry that he's going to keep this Cool Dad thing up past the point where he can really pull it off. It's still working for him, but there's a fine line between trying and trying too hard. It's going to take quite an effort for him to maintain.

—**Craig Calcaterra**, NBC Sports on ranking the best-looking MLB managers. He ranked Joe Maddon ninth out of 30.

On a Tampa Bay website they had a bio on Joe Maddon. One of the questions was: "Who was your biggest baseball influence?" Joe answered, "Norm Gigon." That was one of the nicest surprises I got and it made me feel really good. I went to a banquet in Hazleton and Joe's mother gave me a big hug. When Joe saw me, he seemed very excited. That night, the mayor gave Joe the key to the city. During his speech that night, Joe said, "I want to recognize my old college baseball coach, Norm Gigon." He had me stand up. Then he said, "O.K., how old do you think this guy is?" Joe had white hair at the time, and I probably looked younger than him, but it made me feel good.

—**Norm Gigon**, baseball coach at Lafayette when Joe Maddon played

We played together in 1977. Joe was a Renaissance man. He was a college guy. He brought a real flair into minor league ball. Most of us would be in the locker room reading *The Sporting News,* and Joe would be reading *Rolling Stone*. We got about $7 a day in meal money. So we had to get pretty creative. Joe would send us to go buy the groceries. Then he'd do all the cooking. So all we had to do was shop and clean up.

We used to give clinics in small towns for kids. I was with Joe one time, and when it was over, I said, "Jeepers, Joe, you sounded like a real coach." He said, "Don, I'm going to manage someday. I really like this." Later, when I got out of baseball, I got a job coaching varsity baseball, and I asked Joe for a piece of advice. He said, "Teach one process really well each day. Don't try two. Even guys who make millions of dollars are amazed when a jet flies overhead. Don't lose them."

This guy has a plan for everything. We roomed together on the road in Salinas. We checked into a small hotel, and we were getting ready to leave, and I heard something clink into the ashtray. Joe and put a dime and a nickel into the ashtray. I asked, "What are you doing that for?" He said, "If I come back and either my dime or my nickel is gone, I know I can't trust this place." Toward the end of the year, he was still doing it. One day we come back to the hotel, and in the ashtray there was a dime and five pennies. Joe said, "I think they're messing with my head. I've got to take a walk."

I have a friend who's a huge baseball fan. He's a guidance counselor at my school. I asked him if he would like to go see the Rays. Joe said, 'When the game is over, come to my room. We did. My friend was so happy. He got to talk about baseball with a Major League manager, and then Joe started asking him questions about his life, 'How do you get kids to focus?' that sort of thing. Wow.

When David Price came in in Game 7 of the ALCS, my friends said, "Don't they have anything better?" I said, "This is not a hunch. Something happened along the way for Joe to say this guy can be in the position right now, and he was."

—**Don Lyons**, a minor league teammate of Joe Maddon

Joe comes from a great family, with good parents. We used to call Joe's dad Yogi because he was built just like Yogi Berra and had the same voice. He passed away when Joe was still a bench coach for the Angels, so he never had a chance to see him as a big league manager. Joe's mom, Beanie, still works at the hoagie shop around the age of 80. Joe's four uncles were in the plumbing business with his dad.

I was in the Army when Joe started playing in high school. I thought he was a better football player then baseball player in high school. He chose baseball over football, and I thought he was wrong. But he was right, and it all worked out for him.

Joe was a Cardinals fan growing up. I remember his father being a Yankees fan. I was a big baseball fan, but I don't even watch the All-Star Game anymore. I think of the greatest hitter of all-time, **TED WILLIAMS***, in the 1941 All-Star Game. It was the 10th inning and Joe DiMaggio hits what should be a double play, but the first baseman pulls his foot off the bag. Next batter is Ted Williams who hits a three-run homer to win the game. The main thing is they are still in the game in the 10th inning because it meant something. Now they just play three innings or they just don't show up. Williams was drafted into the military twice, so he missed the five best years of his baseball career, right in his prime. He was a pilot, went on missions and was shot down. How many home runs could he have hit?

Joe is an honest guy, a smart manager. He has the ability to communicate with his players, fire them up and motivate them. Joe is willing to take chances on different strategies. I like his style. I only wish he would have managed the Yankees.

—**Ron Marchetti**, family friend in Hazleton, Pa.

Joe Maddon was my manger for three of the four years I played professional baseball.I was lucky. I have total respect for Joe.

Mike Piazza once got a free half-hour hitting lesson in his backyard from **TED WILLIAMS, who was a friend of his father's.*

My junior year at Arizona State I was playing second base against Stanford. I had two line shots for doubles and made three really good diving stops in the field. Maddon was scouting but I had never heard of him before. Through the grapevine, I heard that he told someone, " Steen made $30,000 extra today."

Probably thanks to Joe, the Angels drafted me. He called me " Steen Dog". After almost every conversation, he would say " You've got to have fun, Steen Dog. You've got to have fun. You've got to enjoy what you're doing.This is a game." Well, yeah,you can be serious and have fun.If you're having fun and you're more loose, you're probably going to produce better. That's what the Cubbies are doing. Same old Joe.

When the Angels would come to Tempe for spring training, I had just started working for Starbucks. Joe was the Angels bench coach for Mike Scioscia. I would go in the locker room at Diablo Stadium. Joe and Scioscia would complain about the crappy coffee. So I provided Joe and Mike with all the Starbucks they wanted as we sat and talked baseball.Did that every spring till Joe went to Tampa.

One night in the Rookie League when Joe was our manager, his wife and their first child were on the bus with us as we were making a long road trip. We had just played a night game ,it's after midnight and we still have hours to go. He's taking his family which is cool.

We're trying to sleep but the baby's screaming, crying, carrying on, "waah, waah". Some player yelled " Hey Joe, put a (boob) in that kid's mouth so we can sleep!" Because his wife was there, Joe had to at least pretend he didn't like it but we knew him well enough to know that he was probably laughing inside in agreement.

In '94 during the players lockout I tried out for and made the Mariners. We were playing the Angels one day and I made two spectacular defensive plays. Joe yelled out from the Angels dugout " Why didn't you do that _ _ _ _ when you were with us?"

Joe is a nice guy but he has high expectations. You don't see it externally but ,trust me, it's there. I could not have played for a better manager. I would love to see him again.

—**Greg Steen**, Carlsbad, Ca., regional manager for Starbucks, key member of Arizona State's last NCAA title team.

Greg Steen.

Deb Kucharyski and Marlene Nosbusch have solved the curse.

Chapter 5

EXTRA INNINGS:

EXPERIENCE IS WHAT YOU GET WHEN YOU DON'T GET WHAT YOU WANT

THE SON ALSO RISES

BILL BAVASI, JR.

Bill Bavasi, Jr. is a graduate of the University of San Diego. He was a general manager for six seasons for the Anaheim/California Angels and four-and-a-half seasons for the Seattle Mariners. He also was an assistant to General Manager Walt Jocketty in Cincinnati prior to becoming the director of the Major League Baseball scouting bureau. He is the son of longtime MLB executive Buzzie Bavasi, and the brother of Peter Bavasi, also a former MLB executive.

That's nice of people to say that I helped Joe, but basically, Joe has done everything on his own. I ran into him in 1981. I had just started working for the Angels. He had just been hired to scout the Four Corners and manage at Idaho Falls, his first managerial job.

I knew who he was. I came across his file. There was a player questionnaire that all the players filled out when they joined the organization, and one of the questions was, "Who was your hero growing up?" You would read a lot of things in those files, and for a lot of kids their hero growing up was a player. Joe put his dad. Joe said his dad was the best professional he had ever seen. It was just a real nice thing. It wasn't a typical player questionnaire answer. I chuckled at it. Then I met him soon thereafter at Idaho Falls.

When I met Joe, I was really young myself. I didn't have any kind of position where I was judging anybody. I just liked him. He was a good guy. I hadn't been around him that much. You go see a guy manage a club. You're there for four or five days, and then you take off. I wasn't attempting to evaluate anyone professionally. I was really young and still feeling my way and just took a liking to the guy. If he wasn't as successful as he is, you wouldn't know who he is, but there's a whole bunch of other people who would, from Hazleton to the lower minor leagues when he played. He was obviously a decent college athlete. He's obviously a sharp guy. He holds a spot in a lot of people's hearts because he's a good guy. He's a fun guy. He's a smart guy. He's generous to a fault. He's a good soul.

Soon after that, we dealt with each other a lot. I was an administrator in the minor leagues. Back in those days, there was one person that ran the scouting and the minor leagues. In our case, there was one assistant—that was me. We wore a lot of hats, compared to today. It was a smaller shop. So you got to know everybody. Any relationship you have in baseball isn't built instantaneously. It's usually built over a number of years. There's a trust factor and performance factors. It's a tough business. Everybody binds together as they go through it, but that takes time. I didn't just go to Idaho Falls and met a guy, think he's a good guy and then he became Joe Maddon, the manager of the Cubs. It takes a lot of time.

I'll give you an example of the kind of guy he is. The Angels general manager for most of our career when we were together was Mike Port. Mike recognized solid people real well. I didn't have to sell Mike on Joe. When we were there, Joe rose through the ranks. For three years, we had a roving hitting coordinator and a roving pitching coordinator. That's all we had. Mike and I wanted to add a roving defensive coordinator.

We convinced Joe to take that job. He preferred to manage. I had really pushed to get this defensive coordinator position. If we didn't have somebody good doing it, and there was any sort of failure, I would never have been able to add another position again. I felt that I had one shot at this. We had given him bad teams in Double-A. They weren't good. We were all aware that it had nothing to do with Joe. He took the defensive coordinator job and a month later the Major League club took our hitting coordinator. We gave Joe the hitting coordinator job. It's a longwinded story to get to the significant part. I went to my boss, Mike Port, and told him, "Look, we really ought to make Joe the field coordinator." We didn't have a field coordinator. We had the hitting coordinator, pitching coordinator and defensive coordinator, and they all got along. The farm director at that time—me—ran the three of them.

It dawned on me one day that I wasn't running anybody. Joe was running it. I told my boss, "Look, we really need to make this guy the field coordinator, and the biggest reason is because he is the field coordinator. We just don't know it."

Joe personified an old saying that I completely understand and believe, and that is: true leadership is 20 percent given and 80 percent taken. The field coordinator job, he just took the job. I didn't give it to him. He just took it. He took it by doing it because the pitching coordinator and the defensive coordinator trusted him. They trusted him, so he directed everything, and he did it in such a way that they felt every bit a part of it.

That experience made him a real good baseball psychologist. He knows how to get through to people. He took that job because he was good at it, and people trusted him, including me. We rose through the organization together.

I felt early on that Joe should be a Major League manager. I grew up in a time when guys didn't need to play in the big leagues to manage in the big leagues. Walter Alston was a pretty good manager. He had one at bat in the big leagues. There were a bunch of those guys back then who didn't have a day in the big leagues.

It never really dawned on me that Joe was going to have to work against that. He never really did. Anybody that knew him, you knew right away that he was a big leaguer. He just came off as a big leaguer.

I never had to sell anybody on him. It was just a question of when his time was going to come. He probably wasn't going to get the same immediate opportunity to manage that a Pete Rose would get, but he was going to get a chance to manage. It was just a question of when. I was the farm director. Then I was the assistant GM for about six months, and Whitey Herzog, the general manager, wanted to retire. They were going to sell the club. I didn't know it. They weren't going to go out and invest a lot of money in a new GM or start any new programs. Whitey had done a good job, setting us up with a good farm system. We had done a good job with the farm system. Our scouting director was wildly successful in signing real good players who ended up winning the World Series there.

Everything was on track. When Whitey retired and they knew they were going to sell the club, they just didn't tell me or anybody else. I was pretty young when I got the GM job. We went through a manager and then when we replaced Marcel Lachemann, Disney owned the club.

Marcel had been a first-time manager. I had agreed with my new owners that the next manager had to be someone with experience. That's how Terry Collins got the job. Then Terry Collins resigned in '99. And I resigned right after him. Joe took the manager's job on an interim basis. He was managing the club. I thought the new GM, Bill Stoneman, might give Joe the job.

Bill wanted to get his own guy, someone he knew so he could take a fresh approach with the organization. Bill hired Mike Scioscia, and they were smart enough to make certain that Joe stayed. The proof is in the pudding. Joe became an integral part of what Mike Scioscia was doing with that club. They did a really good job with the club in winning a World Series in 2002.

Well before I left, I thought it was going to happen for Joe. When we named Marcel Lachemann the manager, I just didn't think it was time yet for Joe, especially with the club we had. It wasn't a very good club when I first got it. Then, with the new owner, we needed to hire someone who had managed before. That's how Terry got the job.

When Marcel left, for me the answer was yes, Joe was in the hunt for the Angels job. But the owner did not want to hire someone who had not managed before. They wanted somebody with experience managing a Major League team. Most all the guys that we interviewed had managed. We had a few that we considered, like Joe and Ken Macha, who had not managed at the Major League level. But when the decision was made, it was as much a boardroom decision as a baseball decision.

I'm not complaining about that. I completely understood how that went. Our previous manager was a guy that had not managed in the big leagues ever, and he didn't have the success we wanted. I saw why the new owners were a little gun shy. They wanted to rely on someone who had managed before.

It was obvious to me that Joe would be a good manager. Joe is real smart. He puts together a good plan, but a lot of people are smart and put together a good plan. Joe has every intangible—mental, psychological and spiritual—someone needs to have to be a successful Major League manager.

What makes Joe Maddon a difference maker? There aren't that many, the guys who are difference makers. Walt Jocketty used that term. No matter what you think of Joe or anyone else, they are difference makers.

Joe has the stamina to stick to a plan day in and day out, and that is very underrated in baseball. It is a real challenge to find someone who can stick to their plan. Part of that is having the good sense to adjust your plan from year to year or even day to day, and not be stubborn. There's a difference between stamina and stubbornness. Stamina is when you have a good plan and can stick with it and evaluate it every day and reevaluate it every day. He can do that. Stubbornness is when you come up with a plan, and you just stick with it, come hell or high water. That's not Joe. Joe's always going to try to find a better way of doing things.

In Anaheim, I worked for the Autrys for two years, and then Disney inherited me. I was with them for four years. They were real good to me. I felt that they didn't have a lot of confidence in me at the end. I thought they needed their own person. I had a year left on my contract. I negotiated my way out of there.

When I was with Seattle, regarding Joe being the manager there, it's a bad story that I'm not ready to tell. All I'm going to say is that he should be managing the **MARINERS*** today. That was a bad move, a decision I did not agree with. Ownership made the decision to exclude him from the list of finalists.

Seattle was not the place for me. I got there in '04 and got fired in June of '08. For the '05 season, we were looking for a manager. I had to present a list of finalists to our majority owner. All I can tell you is I submitted a list and the list I got back of approved names did not have Joe on it. That ownership group did not discuss those things. It just got handed down, and that was that. There is more to that story. I'm just not telling it. I'm not ready to share all the details. Joe has an idea. I told him a little bit about it.

Joe and I stay in touch. The beautiful thing about texting is that you can stay in touch with people and continue to get advice from them. Just before I left the Reds, I was working on a project. I contacted Joe and got some great advice. Later, when he was considering what to do with his future, we chatted.

Through texts and phone calls, we've kept in touch, but not as much as I'd like. When we didn't take him in Seattle, it

---

*Mike Piazza is the lowest draft choice (the 1,390th player, chosen by the Dodgers) to make the Hall of Fame, and Ken Griffey, Jr. is the first No. 1 overall pick (chosen by the **MARINERS**) to the make the Hall of Fame. Both were inducted in 2016.

probably damaged our relationship to a certain extent. I know it damaged me. It was really a big blow. I had to wear it. I had to eat it. I was hired by the guy who took Joe off the list, so I was conflicted. I was also really embarrassed.

I talked to one club official who interviewed Joe the same year. We were chatting, and the official said, "You know, when we interviewed Joe, we didn't take it seriously. We assumed he was going with you. We weren't sure if he was taking us seriously, either. We thought for sure that he was going to the Mariners because of your relationship."

That's one of the toughest things in my career, to know that I didn't get him to Seattle. But I went to the Mariners knowing who I was working for. I knew what the story was. I knew everything. I didn't have any room to complain. I didn't have any ground to stand on. I knew who I was working for. I knew what they were like, and I knew what was going on.

I wasn't surprised when the Rays hired Joe. He had interviewed with Boston, too. I liked the Boston situation better because there were more resources there.

Everyone should be really impressed with the job he did in Tampa Bay. They don't have the resources that a Boston does or the Cubs do or the **YANKEES*** do. You can name a lot of teams. They're probably in the bottom 10 percent as far as that goes.

I was excited that he got the opportunity, and how successful he was there. He was swimming upstream all the time. I never ever heard him say or show any frustration, though. He was always positive, saying, "Yeah, of course we're going to win here. We're going to be fine."

---

*What "performance-enhancing substance" composed of various aromatic hydrocarbons produced during destructive distillation had perhaps its most infamous use at **YANKEE** Stadium on July 24, 1983? That is pine tar, and that was the date of the famous Kansas City Royals/George Brett "Pine Tar Game."

I went to Tampa with the Mariners one time. We played O.K., but we should have beaten them senseless, and we didn't. We split the series. Joe and I went to dinner a couple of nights. I went down and picked him up at his clubhouse. I walked into the Rays' clubhouse and the team was very young. But the atmosphere in the clubhouse was like it was a bunch of veteran guys that knew they were going to win. They weren't good, yet. But he had instilled confidence. It wasn't just confidence. It was a calmness and enjoyment of what they were doing.

I thought it was a great move to go to Chicago and a great move by the Cubs. He replaced a guy that a lot of people liked, Rick Renteria. Rick has a great reputation in the game, and he always will. It's no fun when you replace a guy. But, at the end of the day, it was the right thing for everybody. Rick was not going to get treated that well, and it would have been a rough year for him. Walking in there, it was probably not the easiest thing in the world for Joe. But the Cubs made the absolute right move. Obviously, they're good and they're winning. Nature takes its course. If you're trying to get better—and you owe it to your fans to get better and you owe it to your owner to get better—then you do what it takes to get better.

The Cubs did that. They didn't enjoy doing what they did, because they liked Renteria. They really liked Rich. I think Joe being the sweetheart that he is probably felt a bit awkward taking that job, but it was the absolute right thing to do. It was the right thing for him to do, and it was very much the right thing for the Cubs to do.

If Joe had gotten the Mariners job, I'd probably still be in Seattle. I think Joe might still be there. Look at that club. In 2007, we had a club that won a bunch of games in a row, then lost a bunch of games in a row. We had good streaks and bad streaks. I'm confident that Joe would have done in Seattle what he's doing with the Cubs. The Cubs probably have a better club than I put together. I will gladly accept my lion's share of that blame. I guarantee you that, as a general manager, I would have made a move or two different if he were with me. Whatever I put in the clubhouse, I think he would have gotten more out of it.

When there's a managerial opening, you get calls from people speaking up for themselves who want the job. There are people who will call on behalf of somebody. It might be an agent. It might be a friend. It might be a former player. It could be anyone. But at the end of the day, you put together your own list. In Seattle, I said, "I'm going to give you two lists. One list has managers who have experience, and one list has managers who have not managed in the big leagues before." List 1 had four names on it. And List 2, the one with no experience, had one name. It was Joe, and that's it.

You can't judge baseball managers on their record. Some guys have better clubs than others. I see a special ability in Joe to combine intellect with a ton of common sense. He self-evaluates very well. He will put together a plan, and he will stick to that plan, but he'll evaluate that plan constantly. If he thinks he can do something better, he's not afraid to say, "Hey, I'm going to change my own plan." He will stay on that hour after hour and day after day.

Joe enjoys his downtime. He's not neurotic. He's not crazy. He enjoys his family. He's a normal guy, but he's got a lot going for him. He has the great personality. He's funny and his mental stamina is really something that is special.

Probably what drew us together in the beginning is that we have very similar senses of humor. What I think is funny, he thinks is funny. What he thinks is funny, I think is hilarious. Don't underestimate that. That is the basis of a lot of friendships in this world.

There's a team aspect to baseball. There's so much time spent with each other, so much time spent on the road with each other. You're fighting for the same thing. Even with free agency and the way rosters are transient, players end up pulling together. That's another thing Joe is good at. He's grown up with the free agent era. He's grown up with transient rosters, and he's been able to galvanize guys and make them one, make them believe they're one.

I don't really know how he does that. He creates a calm environment. They are confident. They are calm. They fight hard. They play hard, but they enjoy themselves.

I talked to Joe after he opted out of his contract in Tampa. When I hung up, I thought, he's going to get more money than he ever dreamed of. I wanted Joe to make as much money as he could, because he would do good things with that money. He'll live his life right and do projects like HIP. He'll put every spare dollar into doing things for other people.

Rafting on the Deshutes River heading towards Benham Falls near Bend, Oregon (circa 1980). Front of raft on left is Don Long, now the hitting coach for the Cincinnati Reds, behind Long is Maddon and front right is Bill Bavasi, currently the Director of MLB's Scouting Bureau.

Well, the baseball boys found Benham Falls!

Cal Ripken,Jr., Dave Winfield and Joe Maddon share a wine
toast. Before Maddon, the Cubs spent more time in the cellar
than Ernest and Julio Gallo.

JOE MADDON: AN ARMY OF ONE

STEVE VICK

Steve Vick has dedicated his life to helping other people through the Salvation Army. Vick worked closely with Joe Maddon on Maddon's fantastic Thankmas program in Tampa.

We got a phone call from Joe's foundation looking for a place to do a Thanksgiving meal. It was between Thanksgiving and Christmas, so they wound up calling it Thanksmas. Joe came and cooked an Italian meal for the homeless living in our shelter and those that were around. The people from the Rays—players, coaches, front office personnel and Joe himself—showed up every time and helped cook.

Not only did they provide the food, they brought items of clothing. One year they brought jackets. We gave one to every person that came through the door. We served about 250 people. They also brought shoes for the kids.

The best was how easily Joe and the players mingled with the guys, ladies and kids in the program. They became part of the group immediately. Joe talked baseball with the gentlemen. Everyone signed autographs. They just really took care of the people every time they came in.

They brought everything, used our kitchen and prepared everything on site. They also did the serving. The men and women sat down, and Joe and company served them like it was a real restaurant. Then they sat and talked with everybody.

The smiles on the people's faces and the gratitude they showed. They knew it was somebody special doing things for them. They knew that the Rays didn't have to do it, but they did. They were really gracious and happy.

It doesn't get real cold in Tampa, but enough to where one needs a jacket every once in awhile. Those things are extremely helpful to people. And the shoes for the kids, it's hard to explain how much that means for a family.

Joe's wife came and was a part of everything we did. Joe even did a lot of the cooking. It was as if he were a part of the crowd. I was there for 11 years and Joe was the only celebrity-type who would do something like this.

Joe also helped with the Salvation Army Night at the ballpark. Someone from our group got to throw out the first pitch. The Rays gave a donation and one of our brass bands played the National Anthem. Joe was a big part of making all that happen.

Joe was very humble. We brought in the TV stations and newspaper reporters. Joe just wanted to help people the best he could without looking for any media coverage.

Thanksmas was done in 2015, and Joe came back even though he was managing the Cubs.

I don't think the Salvation Army could ask for a better friend than Joe Maddon.

JOE MADDON ON HIS ANNUAL THANKSMAS DINNERS:

"Thanksmas is something I began when I was working for the California Angels, the Anaheim Angels. I used to ride my bicycle between Sunset Beach and Newport Beach, up and down, and I ran into a lot of homeless folks. It really bothered me because a lot of us see the homeless as being invisible, and a lot of us see them as being people who don't want to work. People think the homeless are bad people. All of these stereotypes have been drawn, but they're not true. There are a lot of single moms involved. There are a lot of kids involved. There are a lot of families involved.

"In talking to the Salvation Army people in the Tampa Bay area, a lot of the people who used to donate are now in need, based on the economic situation of the last several years. After talking with some of the homeless, some of them through their own reasons or beliefs are there because they want to be there. But that's a small minority. A lot of them are veterans and a lot are people who have met with hard times.

"Anyway, the Thanksmas situation is our way of giving back. Since I'm a Polish-Italian from Hazleton, we provide spaghetti and meatballs, sausages, and some pierogies. We've done that with the Salvation Army in Tampa. It's something I also started at the Chicago Help Initiative last year. It's a program I'm really interested in growing nationally. I have a bigger soapbox in Chicago, so hopefully it will grow bigger over the next few years and bring some help to those who need it."

LIVIN' THE DREAM WHILE TRYIN' NOT TO SUCK

JACOB CHANDLER

Jacob Chandler truly is living a dream. The Mendota, Ill., native stumbled across a unique idea less than a year ago and is having the time of his life. He formed a company called KORKED and has raised more than a quarter of a million dollars for Joe Maddon's charitable foundation.

The idea for KORKED started in June 2015. I was working at a digital marketing agency, and my investor reached out to me. He had two companies being sold, and he was looking to do something in the baseball industry. He knew that in college I started my own apparel company. He called me, and we started brainstorming.

We're both baseball guys. We really liked the idea of doing a baseball apparel brand because we're baseball nuts. We liked everything about it, but there really wasn't too much out there to serve the niche of baseball. There wasn't anything for baseball specifically. We felt that it's a sport of unique subcultures and attitudes, so it would be something really cool to get into. We wanted to work with the sport and tap the personalities. That's how the idea of working with Joe Maddon came about. He's the modern day Yogi Berra of memorable quotes. He's baseball's rock star.

We realized that we both knew a guy named Joe Ferro who knew the Cubs' hitting coach, John Mallee. Joe Ferro and John were talking one day. They thought it was funny that Joe Maddon told the rookies last year when they came up, "O.K., just try not to suck." Javier Baez, in a postgame interview last year, let it out that Joe just told him to try not to suck after he struck out, and that helped him to loosen up.

We thought it was funny. About a month before spring training started, we made a quick mock-up of what is now our infamous "Try Not To Suck" shirt, and sent it to John Mallee to give to Joe Maddon. Joe saw it and laughed. He just loved it. We started talking to Steve Alexander, his business agent, and found a way to work with Joe and his Respect 90 charity. That's how we got together with Joe.

Growing up a Cubs fan, I saw all of these big league managers and players that were superstars. They almost seemed unreachable. It was pretty surreal to go to Arizona during spring training and meet Joe. We went out to spring training the week before the shirts launched. I remember stepping back for a second and thinking, holy cow, if I would have thought that I would be able to do this a year ago, I would have thought I was crazy. But it was surreal, to say the least, to be able to get in contact and to be able to work with Joe. It was cool to be able to help his foundation, too.

The shirts sell for $29.99, and it's basically all online. We're in some retail locations in the Chicago area, too. Joe's charity gets 35 percent of the overall revenue, which is over 50 percent of the profits from the shirts.

The first day the shirts went on sale, it worked out perfectly. I'd like to say we planned this for months, but we came up with the concept a month before we launched our website. We launched the website in early March 2016 without any of the Maddonism shirts. We knew that we were going to put one up shortly because we were talking with Maddon.

I woke up the morning of the launch knowing that the team was going to wear the shirts that day. We didn't know really what would happen. I got a text from one of my friends in Michigan who is a Cubs fan. He wrote, "Dude, Carrie Muskat just tweeted out a picture of your 'Try Not To Suck' shirt." I'm like, what? Carrie Muskat is a Chicago reporter who has covered the Cubs for nearly 30 years.

I got on Twitter and saw that she tagged us in the photos, and that the whole team was wearing the shirts. That's when it hit me, this is really happening right now. In my head, I was like, there's no way we're actually going to be able to get the Cubs to wear our shirts. They're the most talked about team in baseball. It didn't seem like it would happen.

The first day that the team wore the shirts, ESPN covered it, Comcast covered it, the *Chicago Tribune*, everybody. I remember seeing the sales numbers that first day go up and up. At the beginning of the day, I'm like, if we make it to $10,000 in sales today, that would be terrific. That would be crazy. By the end of the day, it was over $30,000. It was pretty eye opening to see that and how that happened. It was just rather unexpected. It was pretty cool, a pretty wild first three days of the company there. We got pretty lucky.

That's how the shirt launched, and then it carried momentum. Once the whole team was wearing it, we didn't really have to reach out to get our wholesale and retail accounts. They came to us and came to our website asking if they could get the shirts in their stores.

We're in all Clark Street Sports locations in the Chicago area. We're in the Merchandise Mart. We're in Wrigleyville Sports. We just got approached by Scheels. They have a lot of stores in Iowa. They're looking to pick us up. We're also in Rally House, which is opening four stores in Chicago. In total, we're in around 20 stores. They mostly carry the Maddonism products. Our "Try Not To Suck" shirt is our biggest seller, but "Do Simple Better" and a few of the other ones are really selling well.

We didn't need a license from MLB. You can work with two players before you need a license. We're working with Joe, and we're also working with Jose Altuve of the Houston Astros.

We're in the process now of getting approved by the Players Association. We're just waiting on them to get back to us.

Jose is a cool guy. He's really down to earth with really good stories. He knows what he wants. He went to a tryout camp in Venezuela one Saturday, and everybody passed on him. All the scouts did. He was too short. He wasn't good enough. But there was one new scout there at the next session, one different guy. That was the guy who actually gave Jose a chance. Today, Jose is an All-Star and the American League batting champ at 5-foot-6.

But back to the licensing situation. We don't know how much the license will cost. That's a big question. I know they take a royalty on all the licensed products you sell.

We have more than the "Try Not To Suck" shirts. For Joe, we also have multiple variants of the "Try Not To Suck" shirt. We're even trying to expand that into different markets. We're going to do one where it's "Try Not To Suck" on the front and then on the back it's "Respect 90." We're going to get Bryce Harper to wear it and promote it. We're going to work with Joe to see if we can use the **MONEY*** that that shirt brings in to help fund charities in the Washington, D.C., area. We have "Do Simple Better," which is another one of Joe's quotes.

Another shirt that's done really well is "If You Look Hot, Wear It." At spring training this year, he told the team what they could wear and what their dress code would be. He said, "You can wear anything you want, basically, as long as you look hot." So we had to make a shirt out of that.

We have a few new ones that are available. We did "Anxiety Lives in the Future" with a *Back to the Future* vibe to the shirt. We also have "Embrace the Target" and "The Process is Fearless."

---

*In 2014, only 24 of the 300-plus Division I colleges made **MONEY** with their athletic departments.

We didn't meet with Joe at spring training. I was communicating with him for a while through John Mallee, who is now one of my friends. I talked to John, John would talk to Joe, and then John would get back to me. We had our first impromptu meeting with Joe this year at Wrigley Field. I was able to get batting practice passes. My brothers went with me to the second Cubs game of the year. We were on the field watching Kris Bryant hitting in the cage. I'm just in awe of how hard he's hitting the ball. We're standing there talking, and Joe just comes up and talks to us for a little bit. For me, it was surreal. This is Joe Maddon. I know I was already working with him, but it was the first time I'd met him in person. It was cool. He's just a really laid-back guy, the kind of guy that you'd want to hang out with and talk to. We talked about a few different shirt concepts, and he thanked us for the work we'd been doing and how it's helping his foundation a lot. It was cool.

I don't know the exact amount that we've raised for the foundation. We cut them a check for around $300,000 for the first three months of sales. We deposited the check in an escrow account for the Respect 90 foundation. I don't know what the total has grown to, but it's a healthy amount. I'm excited to see what he does with the money, and how it helps the Hazleton community. It's doing a lot of good.

It's been a good ride. That's why it really caught us so off guard. I don't like saying it that way. We knew something would happen when you get the whole Cubs team wearing your shirts, but it's just gone above and beyond our expectations. Joe does a really good job promoting it. He talks about it in his press conferences. The media really gives us a lot of attention when it comes up. They do realize that it is helping the community and raising a lot of money for charity. It's been a wild ride so far.

The shirt is not available at Wrigley Field, but our main vendor is Clark Street Sports. They have a few stands around Wrigley Field that sell the shirt. We've had so many people rip

off and knock off the shirt. I went to the second Cubs game of
the year, and walking around the stadium there were at least
five people standing on the corners selling shirts that didn't
have a license. There were at least five people that we saw selling "Try Not To Suck" shirts that wasn't helping the charity.
Clark Street Sports has really helped out a lot with that. We got
some cops out there and were able to stop those people from
doing it.

We're close to stopping it all. My partner and I were at a
game a month ago. We were sitting there before the game and
watched B.P. I said, "Hey, do you want to go outside?" We had
to pick up our tickets from outside the field anyway. We went
and got our tickets and decided to walk around the stadium
once to see if anyone was still selling the bootleg ones.

We didn't see anybody selling bootleg T-shirts. I was like,
wow, this is awesome. They've actually stopped. After the
game, we were waiting for John Mallee to come out. We were
going to hang out with him. We saw a guy who was wearing
a knock-off "Try Not To Suck" shirt with a duffel bag. He had
quite a few shirts in the bag. We walked over to him and said,
"Hey, man, you were told by the cops to stop selling this." His
excuse was that he was going to stop selling them, but he had
400 of them printed. He didn't want to waste his money and
just throw them all away, so he was going to try to sell what he
had left. We said, "You can't do that. It's a trademarked design."

We stopped most of them, but it's still out there. There are
people on Amazon and eBay selling bootleg ones. We're trying
our best to get them all down, but it seems like once we stop
one or two, five more pop up.

Our goal is to work with all the pros that we can. There are
so many unique personalities in baseball. Joe is the first one to
help out a charity. We want to do that same thing with Altuve.
His collection, when it comes out, is the Big Dreams collection. Everything's going to be somewhat motivational. He's a

small guy who nobody gave a chance, and he's arguably the best player in baseball right now. We want to do that with him and then also work with other pros. Maybe Bryce Harper and his Harper's Heroes foundation. It all comes down to if we get approved by the MLBPA.

I don't know if we can work through another company and go through their license. That could be an option. I'm not sure if we'd be able to. I think that we have a really good chance to be approved by the MLBPA. It's just taking a little bit longer. If not, we would still design cool shirts just around the sport of baseball. We're also a lifestyle brand that does stuff outside of what Joe Maddon has. We have some shirts that go along with lifestyle, with baseball. If we don't get approved, it would be a bummer, but I think we would still be O.K.

Bryce Harper left us VIP passes when he was in Milwaukee a few weeks ago. We had Kris Bryant text him. They played youth baseball together growing up. Kris texted him, "Hey, I have these guys that want to meet you." Bryce has already talked to Joe about the structure. That's how Respect 90 "Try Not To Suck" shirts came about. So we talked to Bryce before the Brewers game, told him how much we had raised for Joe's foundation. That got him to perk up. His foundation helps kids with cancer. He wants to raise money for that. It was one of those things where it was good to have the political context because he knows Joe. He seemed really interested to do stuff.

I'm living a dream for real. I have to pinch myself sometimes. The first few days that it happened, I was like, is this real? Is this a dream? I like apparel. I'm a huge Cubs fan. There's not really too much more I can ask for. I'm a baseball guy, and I'm getting to meet all of these pros that, a year ago, I thought were unreachable.

I went to spring training this year. We had the family pass on the players' side, and I was just standing there talking to one of my parents, and this guy from MaxBat, the bat company that has a slightly different handle. This guy comes walking up to my right. I can see him out of my peripheral vision. This guy is huge. Who is this guy? It's Kris Bryant. He came up and started talking to all three of us. He's just a cool and nice guy. If somebody would have told me that a year before that I'd have a backstage pass to spring training, and I'd be able to meet Kris Bryant, I would have said, "You're a liar. That's not going to happen." It's beyond my wildest dreams.

Kris Bryant is a really nice guy, really down to earth. Bryce Harper is down to earth, too, in really the same way. From what the media puts out, you'd think he'd be a cocky, arrogant person, but he was the opposite from what I found out, talking to him. Kris Bryant is really, really nice.

The Maddon stuff will last for a long while. It's doing well. Next year, we want to do the same thing, just with new sayings. As long as the Cubs are winning, people are going to love them.

I named our company KORKED because I'm a Cubs fan, and Sammy Sosa corked his bat. We wanted to be not so traditional and spell it with a C. We spell KORKED with a K, partly because I was a pitcher. We also reverse the second K, like you do when you're keeping score and a player is called out on strikes.

When I meet these baseball guys, I want a picture with them, but I don't want to look like a jock sniffer asking, "Can you take a picture with me?" Unfortunately, I don't even have a picture of me with Joe Maddon.

I try to be nonchalant about a lot of stuff. My friends back home know about the Joe Maddon stuff. I'm from Mendota, Ill. It's really a small town. I was covered by the Mendota paper and in the LaSalle-Peru paper. I went to college in Kenosha, so the Kenosha paper covered it. One of my other partners is from Kenosha, too. It was a good story for them.

We didn't do any shirts before "Try Not To Suck." Literally, I couldn't have asked anything better to happen. We launched our website for the first time on March 4, 2016, and then the Maddon shirt launched on March 6. My background is in consumer marketing. We do a lot of Facebook and Twitter ads and built a pretty big audience on Twitter, where we have over 70,000 followers. At Facebook, we're at 40,000.

The first two days, we were sure we'd sell a decent amount, but it was a whole new level when Joe came on board. There's a whole lot of media covering it.

My website is www.korkedbaseball.com.

IT WAS MAGIC I TELLS YA!

SIMON WINTHROP

Simon Winthrop has performed more than 8,000 magical corporate and trade show performances worldwide, and is an author and a world renowned expert at deception and mentalism. He once performed 16 straight hours for the Saudi Royal Family's palace after arriving from three nights of performing in London. The Chicago native resides in the Las Vegas area and has been called upon twice by Joe Maddon to loosen up the Cubs' clubhouse.

I got a phone call at breakfast from my agent. He said, "A baseball team has seen you perform, and they were wondering if you'd fly to New York tomorrow because the team has been in a slump and needs some magic."

I looked over at my pancakes, I looked at my schedule, and I put my fork down. My schedule was free the following day. He didn't tell me the name of the team, but said, "Are you a fan of baseball?"

I said, "Yeah, sure, I guess."

He said, "Be in New York tomorrow at 3 o'clock."

I said, "Actually, I am available. O.K."

I got off the phone and booked the next flight out of Las Vegas to New York. I didn't realize until after I landed which team it was. I get crazy requests all the time to fly to the palace of the royal family in Bahrain or to get on a plane and fly to Indianapolis for a Formula One race. I get requests regularly.

But this one was really special. I took Uber to Citi Field where the Mets play. Vijay Tekchandani, the Cubs' traveling secretary, was waiting for me at the stadium, and he took me to a room next to the team's locker room. I'm not comfortable telling you how much it cost the Cubs to hire me. My rates vary. Once I realized that it was the Cubs that I was going to work for, I Googled them on my cell phone in that room and found out Joe Maddon was the manager. It was literally just a couple of minutes before meeting him. I'm embarrassed to say it because I get so many emails and phone calls from Chicago Cubs fans on Facebook that are buddies of mine who would say, "Are you kidding me? You met Joe Maddon?" as if he were a god.

I was whisked to Mr. Maddon's office. He met me, shook my hand and said, "I've done some crazy things in the past. We've brought in wild animals and stuff like that. We think you're great. Can you dazzle the team?" I said, "Sure."

Joe said, "We'll come get you when we're ready." I told Vijay that I'd like a five- or 10-minute warning before they were ready so that I could get prepped. I didn't get to see the locker room in advance. Normally, I spend several hours in a showroom or a ballroom to feel the space, feel the vibe, get the energy, really "own" it, pre-think my game and put my game face on.

But, sure enough, when they wanted to roll, they rolled. Vijay came to get me, but I figured I still had five, 10 minutes before I was going into the locker room. Instead, it was like a scene in a boxing movie, where the boxer goes down that long hallway, the music's playing, and the crowd is going crazy. That's exactly how it felt. I didn't have time to think or to get into the zone. As Vijay was walking me toward the locker room, Joe was already introducing me. I could hear him say, "We've got some magic for you...We want to bring back the magic for you...He's from Las Vegas...and his name is Simon...and...here...he...is."

He literally paused his words. He looked down the hallway and saw me, and he was timing my entrance perfectly.

I had zero time to get prepped. I dropped my small bag of tricks—my props like a pen, a pencil, a marker, a deck of cards, my laptop—right outside the room. I didn't even bring it into the locker room with me. It was as if I was thrown into a pit of lava. That room was hot, not hot temperature-wise, but hot in the energy. It was like a firecracker. There was really no time for me to even think. Here I was, I was hot, just go for it! That's exactly what the vibe in the room was. I was on fire, and the team was connecting with me in an amazing way. Afterward, people were high-fiving me and holding their bats up to me and saying, "Please touch the bat. Please touch my bat." I touched all their bats. It truly was magical.

Now I understand the magic about Joe Maddon and why people love him so much. He looks at you. He shakes your hand. He's got this infectious personality, this smile, this energy. It's on. I got a little extra thrill because most of the magic was done specifically for the team. I did one illusion just for him that he really loved. One of the players had a soda can that was crushed and empty on a paper plate. I just looked over and said, "Joe, here, touch this." Joe touched it, and all of a sudden, the can refilled and resealed. I shouted, "Open it! Open it!" I yelled at Joe a little bit. Sometimes you've got to give these big powerful people some energy. I was yelling at him, and the team's looking at me like, is this guy crazy, yelling at Joe? What's going on?

Joe touched the can. "Open it! Open it!" I'm screaming. The team is mesmerized. He said, "No way." He just kept saying, "There's no way. There's no way."

He opened it, and everyone heard that whooshing sound a can makes when it's opened, a real can. The room erupted. I wish I had a video camera in the locker room because the whole room went viral crazy. It's hard for me to describe. It was like a wave. The whole room was bouncing, jumping and screaming. The energy was unbelievable. There were people watching from the hallway. The reporters weren't allowed in the locker room, but I could see people's heads. All of a sudden, that room went from 30 people to 50 or 60. I don't remember. It was all a whirlwind at that point.

When I finished my work, Joe didn't say anything directly to me. He just kept muttering uncontrollably, "That's awesome. No way." The reason the room erupted was everyone was looking to see what Joe's reaction was. People were blown away, but it reached a different level—let's call it an otherworldly level—because Maddon was freaked out as much as he was.

They had me come back a second time last year. The second time I came back, believe it or not, I happened to be—I don't know where I was in the world—oh, yes, I do. I was in San Diego, and I was with a client at a casino in San Diego. The client asked, "Can we have a glass of wine? Your show is unbelievable. Let's relax before you call it a night."

I said, "O.K." A game was on TV in the casino bar. This was the Sycuan Casino in San Diego and the Cubs were on. I sent a text message to the guy who booked me the first time, the traveling secretary. I wrote, "What a game!" He responded, "We need some of your magic tomorrow more than ever. Can

you be at Wrigley Field tomorrow before 3:00?" I answered, "Sure, let me work on it. I might need to get a private jet." He answered, "Whatever it takes, we need you."

I figured they didn't really want to pay for a chartered plane. Luckily, I found a flight that landed at O'Hare at 1 o'clock. The Cubs provided a driver who got me to the dugout by 2, and the game started at 3. That was a really tight schedule.

I have to admit, the first performance, the team crushed it. The second one was the final game that they had to win, and the magic wasn't so great. I heard from some of the players afterward that it didn't go as well because the star pitcher, **JAKE ARRIETA***, wasn't in the room.

Now that I've spent a little bit of time watching the Cubs—they let me stay and watch the games after my performances—they're my favorite team.

*From June 21, 1915 through April 25, 2016, **JAKE ARRIETA** had a 20-1 record with a 0.86 ERA in 24 starts. He had more no-hitters (two) than losses. His only loss was at the hands of a Cole Hamels no-hitter for the Phillies.

TAKE THIS JOB AND LOVE IT

REX HUDLER

Rex Hudler is a TV color commentator for the Kansas City Royals and was a Major League player for 14 seasons. He was a first round draft pick of the New York Yankees in 1978. During his career, he was known by the nickname "Wonderdog" after the character from the old Super Friends *TV series. He has broadcast Royals games the last five years and prior to that did the same for the California Angels. He is also the president of Team Up for Down Syndrome, which raises money for Down Syndrome research. Hudler and his wife, Jennifer, have a 19-year-old son who was born with a chromosomal abnormality.*

I've been the color analyst for the **KANSAS CITY*** Royals for five seasons. The family has been here for four. My daughter went to Kansas State. My three boys could end up going there, too. They all play ball. One of my sons has Up Syndrome, so he isn't in the veteran league. The world calls it Down Syndrome. They all have positive energy and unconditional love. That's why we call it Up Syndrome.

Albert Pujols' daughter is 19, the same age as my son. She also has Down Syndrome. Albert and I both raise funds and awareness for the Down Syndrome community. We try to do what we can.

I signed with the Anaheim Angels in 1994 out of nowhere. I had come back from Japan and signed with the San Francisco

---

*The **KANSAS CITY** Chiefs have nothing to do with Native Americans. They were named after Kansas City Mayor H. Roe Bartle, nicknamed "The Chief." Bartle helped lure the AFL's Dallas Texans to Kansas City in 1962...so owner Lamar Hunt renamed the team in Bartle's honor.

GIANTS* in 1993 and they let me go. The Angels let me platoon, share playing time, with Harold Reynolds at second base. The '94 season went along pretty good. Buck Rodgers was fired after 40 games and was replaced by Marcel Lachemann. We needed a first base coach. Lachemann had been in the Angels organization a long time, so he brought into the Major Leagues, for the first time, a coach by the name of Joe Maddon. Joe had been in the Angels system for 19 years.

When Joe came to the Majors he had this wonderful enthusiasm. He had energy that normally a young player would bring, but for a young coach like him...he was special.

A few of the veteran guys on the team—Mark Langston, Spike Owen and Chuck Finley—were skeptical of Joe, calling him a "rah-rah, pom-pom carrying" coach that was just happy to be in the big leagues. It's very typical of veterans to think of young players or coaches that way. It's all part of the ego trip.

I said, "Hey, this guy has what we need." We needed his positive energy. We needed that enthusiasm.

Joe was meticulous and sharp as a first base coach. He carried a stopwatch, like most coaches do now. He timed everyone running to first base. When you made contact and ran the 90 feet, Joe was timing it. He was in charge of making the lineup card every day. Joe Maddon brought the Computer Era to the Major Leagues. While I was there from '94 to '96 Joe had computer printouts of the lineup cards. Joe posted the top three times from home to first base each game. We liked that. We would check out the board, and it would take us a long time to decipher all the stuff that he put on it.

Before Joe, all we had was a chalkboard that had messages like: "4:00 Dressed," "4:15 Stretch," "5:00 Hitting" and "11:00 Buses." For years, that's how management relayed messages to

---

While in high school in North Carolina, GIANTS pitcher Madison Bumgarner dated a girl named Madison Bumgarner, no relation.

the players. Joe was an innovator. He brought in all this stuff. We started competing with each other, in-game, going 90 feet. That added an extra charge. Joe also was putting up a quote of the day from the many books he read.

On a day-to-day basis, Joe was starting to weave his way into the fabric of baseball management. It was wonderful to be at the beginning stages of Joe's coaching career. He wasn't afraid to be himself. I was one of the few guys to stand up for him at the beginning. I let him know we needed his energy. He thanks me to this day for sticking up for him. I'm thankful that I got to be a part of the early days of Joe Maddon.

We had painful moments. In 1995 we won our final five games of the regular season to set-up a one-game playoff with the Seattle Mariners to decide the West Division title. Randy Johnson pitched for the Mariners and Mark Langston pitched for the Angels. We lost, 9-1. That was the closest I got to post-season play.

When Marcel Lachemann resigned during the 1996 season, John McNamara took over. John got sick, and Joe Maddon became the interim manager for the final 22 games. That put Joe on my roster of managers I played for: Yogi Berra, **BILLY MARTIN***, Earl Weaver, Buck Rodgers, Whitey Herzog, Red Schoendienst, Joe Torre and Terry Francona. I'm proud to say I played for Joe Maddon. All these years later, I think he has become a future Hall of Fame manager. I really appreciate the way he went about his work.

I was not surprised when Joe got the Tampa Bay Rays job. Mike Scioscia deserves a lot of credit. He mentored Buddy Black, who got a managerial job with the Padres. Joe left when he got the Rays job. Ron Roenicke got a job with the Milwaukee Brewers. Mike Scioscia is a manager who gets his coaches prepared to manage in the big leagues.

*Peter Billingsley, the young man in *A Christmas Story*, later did ads with Reggie Jackson and **BILLY MARTIN**.

Joe has done everything you possibly can to be a field manager. He has done scouting, the background work of an organization, roving instructor. He has worn every hat. If there was ever a manager to be totally prepared to be doing what he's doing now, it's Joe Maddon. The main thing a manager needs is good communication skills. Joe Maddon has that.

Baseball is like life. You have to show up every day and produce. You have to learn how to deal with failure. If you can endure a career in baseball like I was able to do, I consider myself a successful failure. I believed I was going to be a big leaguer when I signed at 17-years-old with the New York Yankees. But it took a long time to grow up physically, and to find myself. Even after 10 years of minor league baseball, I knew I could make it. It took a lot of help from coaches like Joe Maddon, and I finally made it.

Being a 10-year guy is something I'm proud of. My stats wouldn't even get me on the streets of Cooperstown. I have the ugliest numbers for a guy who played as long as I did. I was about enduring. I was a 10-year minor leaguer, a 10-year Major Leaguer and spent a year in Japan. I'm proud that I hung in. I tell that to guys in the minors now: just hang in there.

Joe Maddon hung in there better than anyone.

HEAR ME NOW, LISTEN TO ME LATER

BILL RIPKEN

Bill Ripken began his career with the Baltimore Orioles in 1987 under the direction of his father, Cal Ripken, Sr., alongside his brother, Cal Ripken, Jr. This was the first and remains the only time in Major League history that a father simultaneously managed two of his sons. Bill Ripken played 12 years in the big leagues and, in 2002, was inducted into the Maryland Sports Hall of Fame. He and his brother, Cal, own two minor league baseball teams including the (Port) Charlotte (Fla.) Stone Crabs, the Class-A affiliate of the Tampa Bay Rays. In 2001, the Ripken brothers founded the Cal Ripken, Sr. Foundation, which works throughout the country helping Boys and Girls Clubs and other youth organizations. They have reached more than 500,000 youth in all 50 states. Today, Ripken is an analyst appearing across MLB Network's programming, which he joined in 2009.

I'm going to take you back to a couple of conversations that I had with Joe, and some of the things that I learned early on about Joe. When Joe first got the gig in Tampa as the manager of the Rays, they had been a perennial last place team. When I was covering the baseball, it was one of my duties to interview Joe Maddon. I saw Joe at the Winter Meetings in Nashville, when he was getting ready to take over the Rays. Joe was coming out of the Angels organization under Mike Scioscia, getting his gig in 2006. Everybody's got to start somewhere, right?

I looked at him with that thought process in mind. I said, "Hey, Joe, American League East, dude? Tampa Bay Rays? Last place. The year before that, last place. The year before that, last place. The year before that, last place. Really? American League East. It's the Yankees. It's the Red Sox. The Orioles have been there before. Toronto's done it before. You've got the Rays, Joe. Joe, it's the Rays. Is there any 'Woe is me' going on right now, and what have I gotten myself into?"

He said no. He talked to me for a little bit, and the more he talked, the more I started to buy into Joe Maddon and the Tampa Bay Rays. In his third season, Joe Maddon took the Tampa Bay Rays from the perennial last-place team that they were, to the World Series. They are in the World Series.

Going back to that first conversation with Joe, I'm thinking, man, this dude's confident. He's got conviction. He's got a plan. He's full of s---. But I thought it was really cool, though. Never the "Woe is me." He said, "If you're going to get your start, you might as well do it in the American League East with the big boys, and let's see what we've got." I learned right then and there that no challenge was too big for Joe Maddon. I don't say he was full of s--- anymore because he did what he set out to do.

Fast forward to the 2008 World Series. I had a little one-on-one time with Joe down in the TV truck during the World Series. If you know Joe at all, if you've followed his career, you know that he does things a little differently. He had team dress-ups on road trips. The year that they went to the World Series, mohawk haircuts were involved, including Joe Maddon himself with a mohawk. Earlier in that year, one of his players didn't run hard to first base, and that player was benched.

I brought it up to Joe in his office at the World Series. I said, "Dude, which one is it? You're sitting here with half a mohawk." It was starting to grow in and looked disheveled, not an attractive look. I said, "Is it this? Because how can you have this and bench a player for not hustling? What is it?" He said, "No matter how a man wears his hair, it doesn't have any bearing on how he runs to first base."

My takeaway from that day was, "He's unique. He's different. There's no doubt about it." But when we sign up for something, we must pull from the same rope. He was letting me know that we don't use our differences as excuses. We use our abilities to be unique, our differences as a strength, and, when we all form as one and we pull from the same end of the rope, we can get the job done.

Those two conversations went a long way with me. I think about those two days when I covered the Rays at the time and now when we cover the Cubs, moving forward. If you're a betting person, bet on the Cubs to get rid of that jinx, that long, long-time jinx of them never winning, because this is the right man for the job.

IF YOU'RE LUCKY ENOUGH TO HAVE JOE MADDON AS YOUR DADDY, YOU'RE LUCKY ENOUGH

TIM SALMON

Tim Salmon was a Major League outfield for 14 years, hitting just one shy of 300 home runs and compiling a .282 lifetime batting average. The right fielder hailed from Phoenix, Ariz., and attended Grand Canyon University. He signed with the Angels after being chosen in the third round of the 1989 amateur draft. He and Joe Maddon were so close that teammates referred to Joe as Tim Salmon's "Daddy." Salmon wrote a wonderful autobiography, Always an Angel, *which was an essay on faith and competition.*

When I got drafted by the Angels in 1989, the scout who drafted me got ill. He didn't come to my house to sign me. The Angels sent their minor league director, who was Joe Maddon. Joe was the first representative I met with the Angels. He came to the house to try to sign me to my first contract. Our relationship really goes back to the very first day of me being an Angel.

At the time, the Angels were looking at drafting a bunch of pitchers, and they did. My stock had fallen in the draft, and the Angels felt fortunate to get me in the third round. I was one of the top prospects for the Angels that year. They called Joe my Daddy. He was in charge of overseeing every aspect of my development. From my very first day of signing, all the way through the minor leagues, Joe was an integral part. We developed a great relationship over the years.

I made it to the Major Leagues in '92 and within a couple of years, Joe moved up, too. He got called up to be a coach. It was a nice reunion. Joe's been with me my whole career. To this day, when I see him, we pick up like long lost friends.

When he first came to my house, I had never heard of him. At the time, I was expected to be a first round pick. When I fell to the third round, I was disappointed. The Angels' goal was to pick all pitchers, but they couldn't believe that I had fallen to the third round, so they took me. The Angels didn't contact me right away. They waited. It wasn't like today. They waited. It was three or four days before anyone contacted me. They were trying to figure out whom to send to negotiate, because the scout was sick. When Joe came, we were really disappointed. I thought, what kind of organization is this? They draft you, and then don't contact you for three or four days? I wondered if it was a negotiating ploy.

The only difference between Joe today and Joe back then is the color of his hair. He's always been the same person. He was very disarming and personable and charming, real down to earth. I always felt he was shooting straight with me. He's the same Joe Maddon who sat across the kitchen table with my dad and me back in '89. He was just very genuine, and put us all at ease after our initial frustrations. He kick-started things. Not just anyone could have done that.

He helped me in the minors. He was involved in a lot of different aspects of my development. He was very hands on, and he was very out of the box. I had come from a college program—Grand Canyon—where we spent three times the time working on our swing and hitting than other programs. Having a guy like Joe was perfect for me because he was always creating a new technique. He was always skinning the cat a little differently than what was normal. In that day and age, he was still old school. It was probably frowned upon. It was maybe looked upon as being "Little League-ish" or, "That's great for the minor leagues, but that's not really what we do in the big leagues."

He was always looking for different ways to teach something. He was open to all the different possibilities and suggestions. He had an open mind to everything. When I look at who he is today, he's exactly the way he was back then. We're in a culture. We're in an environment that embraces that now. Baseball was very old school when I came up in the late '80s. He's a gadget guy. He's college, whatever. However they might have termed it, that's maybe what the knock on him was.

Billy Bavasi, Jr. and Joe were real close. Billy was our minor league general manager. When he got the big league job, he embraced Joe. He's the one that gave Joe his opportunities in the big leagues. Joe still had to prove himself at the Major League level.

The Angels were at a crossroads in the organization. They had committed to the youth movement. Joe was the guy that was very hands on. He was very familiar with me and Jimmy Edmonds and Garret Anderson and Chad Curtis and Damion Easley and Gary Disarcina. They were all his minor league guys. They felt like having him on the Major League staff would be beneficial, which, of course, it was.

What I don't want to gloss over is the fact that he had relationships which maybe made things work out or made things easier for a Major League manager to deal with. He had to prove himself. Mike Scioscia and Joe thought a lot alike. Scioscia was very analytic, and so was Joe. Joe was very intuitive. He could see a lot of things in the opposing coaches. Joe was very good at picking signs, for instance. He would really pay attention to what the coaches in the other dugout were doing. Those early years with Mike, we had a lot of the signs coming from the other dugout. We knew when to pitch out. We knew when there was a hit and run on. We knew different things, and as much credit as Mike gets for that, he really relied on Joe and Ron Roenicke. Those were just phenomenal at stealing signs.

At the same time, Joe was an out of the box thinker. He did conventionally things right in line with Mike. Mike liked to call the game from the bench and do hit and runs and other things to catch the opponents off guard. The game was very traditional. Situations dictated bunts. Situations dictated hit and runs. Mike said, "Why do we have to wait for that situation? Why can't we create those situations?"

Mike relied on his coaching staff quite a bit. And Joe and the other coaches learned from Mike, too. That was evident when Joe went to Tampa. A lot of that same style continued, and a lot of that success continued. One of Joe's strengths is that he's not a conventional guy. He's just a very out of the box thinker. Whether it was in the minor leagues working on some aspect of hitting using Wiffle Balls or Ping-Pong balls or colored balls or tennis balls, there was always this goofy gadget trick that our organization was doing because Joe was in charge. That's who he is. He is willing to try anything and everything to make a teaching point. Who he is today is exactly who he was then.

Joe is very good at communicating, and he's very good at embracing people's personalities. When we were at the Angels, we had a guy, Jimmy Edmonds, who was very much like a player today. Everybody called him a hot dog. He had a personality that was against the grain for the old school mentality. The organization eventually parted ways with him because of that. They didn't think he could be a team player.

Joe embraced Jimmy's style. He let him be different. What motivated Jimmy was different than what motivated other players. Joe recognized that at the end of the day, if everyone was motivated, we were going to win.

When you looked at his teams in Tampa they were full of all of those types of young players. I don't want to call them brash, but there was a definite style to those teams. From the outside, it looked like the inmates were running the asylum. I heard stories that the young guys ran the clubhouse. There weren't veterans around to keep them corralled. That was fine with Joe. He found a way to keep them corralled on his own. He allowed them to express themselves, and he allowed them to have fun on the field and off it, and guess what? They won. They had talent, but he was able to keep all that talent and all those personalities in line with the common goal of winning. And they won big.

Mike Scioscia was on the front of that wave. In the early 2000s, the game changed even more, with the young players and the ideologies of some of the new generation. Joe's on the front end of those changes now and has embraced it with all the things he does on and off the field. He keeps things light and loose. He gets it.

Joe was always trying to figure out how to keep things loose. It's a grind, 162 games in 181 days. Who wouldn't go crazy? Who wouldn't lose excitement and joy for the game? He would ask, "How do we keep it loose? What do we have to do to liven up things or give guys a break?"

Today, they talk about how Joe Maddon doesn't allow his coaches to come in before noon. Well, back in the old days, there was a mindset that if you're not getting into the clubhouse before noon, you must not care. Joe said, "That's ridiculous." A guy could come in at 3:30 or 4 and probably be in better shape to perform because, guess what? He spent two more hours at home with his family. When he got to the park, he was fresh.

Joe saw value in that, something an old school mind couldn't embrace. I remember Opening Day one year when I was working for Fox Sports West. The Angels were playing the Rays, and I went to the Rays clubhouse at about 4 o'clock. Joe wasn't in his office. Opening Day. I asked one of the trainers, "Hey, where's Joe?" He said, "Oh, he takes the late bus." "He takes the late bus?" That didn't surprise me. It was Opening Day, but that's the way he is.

He had guys like George Hendrick. When George played, George was totally like Joe. George said, "Hey, you know what? Batting practice is overrated." George would show up at 6 for a game. He said, "Hey, as long as my mind is sharp, and my body's loose, I can play the game. I don't need to be there at noon."

The George Hendrick that I knew as a coach and the George that the media knew as a player, it's the same guy. But the media burned him early in his career, and he shut them down after that. His teammates always loved him. He would tell me stories as a coach. He was so funny. He talked all the time. I remember the stereotype. I pictured George Hendrick in the '70s, a militant, the big afro. He's one of the greatest guys around. He said, "Hey, the guys that I'm going out to battle with every day, those are my boys. The media's not." He wasn't going to give the media what they wanted. He's one of the greatest guys I've ever been around in the game.

He and Joe are likeminded. George told me Vietnam stories and things that he did when he played. He said, "Hey, we're playing a game of baseball. Vietnam, I got shot." You want to talk pressure and stress? Well, George was an anomaly in his day. Everybody else had that grinding mentality, that old-school mentality. He said, "No, sorry, this is fun. This is meant to be a game. I've been shot at by the Viet Cong. I'm not going to get caught up in your life."

George ran to the beat of his own drum. The players today are more like George was back then, and that's the way Joe Maddon is, too. Joe gets the absolute best out of a player like George when other manages would bench him. Joe majored in economics in college, but it's like he majored in psychology.

Joe has a great perspective on life. He has a great feel for the heartbeat or pulse of his team, what they're feeling. He's willing to try anything he can to keep the team's vibe going in the right direction.

Joe wrote the foreword to my book, *Always an Angel: Playing the Game with Fire and Faith*. We just reached out to him. It was a natural. When the book came out, he was having success in Tampa. You're always looking for an influential person to write the foreword. In my book, I had some good stories about Joe and wrote about our relationship. The ghostwriter who worked with me suggested it. I said yeah. We called Joe. It was a no-brainer. Joe was more than happy to do it. All of the proceeds from my book went to my foundation which supports local Orange County charities assisting children in need.

Joe and I had a really great relationship. He took a great interest in me, in my life, in my family, in my kids. Even to this day, he remembers my kids' names and my wife's name. It's just like old friends. We can relive stories from years past. He went to Tampa and established his name. And now he's building on that in Chicago. You look at him from afar, and you think, holy cow, this guy's like a rock star! What's he going to be like? I walked into his office while he was managing the Rays. He had media guys in his room, and he just stopped everything. "Tim!" He sat down and we talked for the next 20 minutes while all these other people waited. He values relationships. He values people. That's a unique trait for people in that position. He always has time for people. I think that's one of his greatest qualities.

When he got remarried, I went to his wedding in Long Beach. I was happy to be invited. They called him my Daddy when I was a player. It was meant as a derogatory term, but I've grown to understand that he really was like a Daddy. He looked after me.

The only negative thing anyone can say about Joe Maddon is that he's too nice.

JOE MADDON ON TIM SALMON:

"When the phone in my hotel room rang that night and the voice on the other end said, 'Something really bad happened here today,' I knew it was about Fish. I just *knew*. Like a parent knows. Fish, of course, is Tim Salmon.

"The bond between us began when Timothy was a freshman at Grand Canyon College in Phoenix. I was the minor league hitting coordinator for the California Angels and was scouting for them during the months of January and February. That was how I first discovered Grand Canyon's big, hard-hitting right fielder. He had terrific seasons there as a freshman and sophomore and was on just about every Major League scouting director's wish list for the June 1989 draft. But his production fell off some in his junior season, and many teams pulled off from him. I was very glad they did, and when he was still available in the third round that spring, we took him. I knew we had a steal and I was very proud to be present soon after when we signed him.

"It was the next year, when I was the Angels' minor league field coordinator, that I got that phone call from Timothy's manager, Nate Oliver, at Palm Springs in the Class A California League. Nate told me that during their game that day, Timothy had been hit in the face with a pitch and it was ugly—really ugly. It was the type of injury that can keep a player from wanting to go back into the batter's box altogether.

"It was the second time in two years of pro ball that he had been hit in the face by a pitch. A lot of guys would have walked away. Instead, it became what I believe was a defining moment in his career, an early challenge that he would meet head-on with courage and strength that came from an enduring faith and a very close, loving relationship with his wife, Marci.

"I soon got him in touch with Dickie Thon, a former Angel who had been hit by a pitch that had broken the orbital bone around his left eye in 1984. Dickie's counsel helped, but mostly it was Fish's incredible perseverance that got him back during his Major League career from injuries to his foot, wrist, hand, shoulder and knees.

"When the time came for him to return to playing, I was insistent that he not return to Palm Springs even though he had very little time above rookie ball. I didn't want him going back to that park. So he instead went to Double A Midland and before long demonstrated that he was going to be a Major Leaguer for years to come.

"He was like Clark Kent. He could step into that phone booth and come out Tim Salmon. He went into that phone booth many, many times during his career, whether it was overcoming an injury or helping take the Angels organization to its first World Series championship and elevating it to the elite status it now enjoys.

"Fish truly epitomizes what is so good about the Angels. He is selfless. He revels in victory regardless of his own performance. I always told him, 'You have five physical tools. Find a way to use one of them to help us win every night.' No one understood that better than Timothy. His message is one we should all take to heart."

SOMETIMES GOD JUST HANDS YA ONE

SCOTT CHALLIS

John Challis was a junior at Freedom High School in the western Pennsylvania town of Freedom when he was diagnosed with hepatocellular carcinoma (Stage 4 liver cancer) in June 2006. John lost his battle to cancer on Aug. 19, 2008. His story continues to inspire others and now the John Challis Courage for Life Foundation grants life encouraging sports experiences to high school athletes with life threatening illnesses. Here, Scott Challis tells the story of Joe Maddon's visit with, and remembrance of, his son.

One day in late June of 2008, the phone rang in our house, and it was a man calling from **MIAMI*** named Joe Maddon. Joe Maddon said, "I'm sitting in my hotel room in Miami. I just watched your son's story on ESPN's *Outside the Lines.* We're down here playing the Marlins. I manage the Tampa Bay Rays. I've got to meet your son. We're playing in Pittsburgh this weekend. If you and your family can make it, I'll get your press passes and everything else you need, including parking."

When Joe called us, I didn't know who Joe was at all. My son had never heard of Joe. He didn't know anything about the Tampa Bay Rays. He didn't know one single player. My son, John, said, "Dad, find out of the names of the players on the Devil Rays, the big stars, so I can find out who I want to meet."

> ***The MIAMI** Heat retired uniform No. 23 in honor of Michael Jordan. Go figure. The coach of the Miami Heat, Erik Spoelstra, is the grandson of famed Detroit sportswriter Watson Spoelstra. Watson Spoelstra is the man who started Baseball Chapel, a Sunday service that has spread to all other major sports..

Well, we found out they didn't really have any big stars. Anyway, the big day came only three days later on a Saturday. What happened that day is we were down at PNC Park. We went with a Pirates representative to the dugout. We were introduced to Joe. My son sat in the dugout for a good half hour just talking baseball, not about his sickness, with Joe Maddon. Joe was a great guy. Joe took him back into the locker room. From there, we watched the game from the box of Frank Coonelly, the president of the Pirates.

The Rays gave John all kinds of paraphernalia like jackets and jerseys. It was unbelievable. A Pirates player, Adam LaRoche, saw John and recognized him from local stories and said, "John, you've turned traitor on us!"

My son had this saying: Courage + Believe = Life. This is something that my son had written on his baseball hat under the visor. Joe was quite taken with that. He thought it was a wonderful saying. To this day, Joe writes on his line-up card: C + B = L. He does that on every single line-up card.

Also during Cub games now, Joe wears three bands on his left wrist. Even though it's eight years later, if you look at his wrist, you'll see the three bands. He has a purple one, a light pink one and a red one. The red one is my son's band. It's so washed away, it looks light pink. That is my son's also. Joe Maddon said, "That will never come off my arm."

I saw Joe in Chicago last year. He said, "Look at it. Still good as gold." He still wears it every day. On that band is: "John Challis, Courage + Believe = Life." You can see more if you go to my son's website, which is courageforlifefoundation.org. After all these years, Joe still wears that armband. It is such a tribute to my son.

He called me when he won the Chuck Tanner Manager of the Year Award in 2008. It was October after his Rays played in the World Series. Joe Maddon said, "Mr. Challis, this is Joe

Maddon. Would you do me the honor and accept the Chuck Tanner Manager of the Year Award for me in Pittsburgh?"

I said, "Absolutely. I'd be honored."

He was getting married at the time and was calling from Italy. That was a great honor because Chuck Tanner is from my hometown of New Castle, Pa.

The day we met on June 28, 2008, John said, "I want to thank the Devil Rays for doing all these wonderful things for me." Joe turned around and said, "John, you're fined a dollar." He fined my son a dollar for calling them the Devil Rays. They changed the team name. They weren't the Devil Rays any more. They were the Rays. Somebody came out and gave John a dollar to pay the fine. John paid Joe the dollar. Joe gave him the dollar back and said, "John, sign it for me." John did. I never thought anything more about it.

When we were down in the dugout on the day we met Joe Maddon, I got a couple of baseballs. When we were up in Frank Coonelly's box later that day, I said, "John, why don't you sign a baseball for Mr. Maddon and for John Russell?" John Russell was the manager for the Pirates at the time. John didn't want to. He said, "Why would they want an autographed ball from me?"

John's baseball coach was there, and I said, "Talk John into this." It was something I wanted to do. John did it, and Frank Coonelly sent Neal Huntington, the Pirates general manager, down with the baseballs to give to the managers.

About **THREE*** years later, I got a phone call from one of my buddies. He said, "Your son was just on ESPN." "What are you talking about?" He said, "ESPN did a story on Joe Maddon. They did a tour of his whole office, and over the couch,

*In Johnny Lujack's first game with the Chicago Bears, he intercepted **THREE** passes. It's a team record that stood for more than a half century for most passes intercepted in one game.

Joe Maddon had in a frame that dollar bill your son signed that day in box of the president of the Pirates plus the baseball that Neal Huntington took down to the dugout. Joe Maddon also has your son's game jersey over his couch in a big shadow box." Wow.

I knew that Joe was really impressed with John's courage, his saying of "Courage + Believe = Life." That was very, very important to Joe. If you go to the MLB website and run a search of my son's and Joe Maddon's names, Joe talks about what that saying did for him. It hit him right where he believes. Joe does believe that Courage + Believe = Life. Joe was overwhelmed by that.

I rooted for the Pirates my whole life, but when the Cubs play the Pirates, I root for the Cubs now. We talk to Joe Maddon about once a year. We don't spend a lot of time together because he's so busy. We don't meet before or after the game. Normally, he'll come out of the dugout and meet me at the railing just to say hello. He was just touched by my son's story. In one of those ESPN videos, it shows me going out to Johnny's grave. He didn't have his tombstone up, yet. He just had a little marker. I put a Tampa Bay Rays hat on John's marker. I'll be darned if somehow or other Joe Maddon didn't get a picture of that, and he hung it in the Rays locker room.

I cannot tell you how much Joe Maddon meant to my son's life in his final 52 days, and how much he's continued to mean to the Challis family.

JOE MADDON ON JOHN CHALLIS:

C + B = L

"Those three letters are on the top of every line-up card I make out as manager of the Tampa Bay Rays. It's been that way since June 28, 2008. That was the day I met John Challis.

"The week before, we were in South Florida to play the Marlins, and I was in my hotel room killing time and watching ESPN when a story came on that hit close to home. While the tumor in his liver had reduced John to little more than a skeleton and snuffed out a varsity career before it began, he held tight to a dream: to get just one at bat for his Freedom High School team [and] to face a fastball one last time in his life, no matter how much pain it might bring.

"The single still photograph of that moment captured it all perfectly, freezing the ball leaving John's bat as it headed into right field for a clean single. It was witnessed by only a handful of people on a gray April day on a field with more dirt than grass, against a backdrop of trees not yet recovered from a cold Pennsylvania winter. That stark and colorless scene presented a powerful imagine, and for me, an eerily familiar one. I spent many days on fields just like it while growing up on the other side of the state. The magnitude of the moment, a young man achieving success in his first and only chance, under impossible circumstances, was overwhelming to me. That photo will stay with me forever.

"I knew I needed to meet this remarkable young hero. As fortune would have it, our next stop was an interleague series in Pittsburgh, about 20 minutes from the Challis home.

"We met in the first base dugout at PNC Park, and I was immediately impressed by his presence and how he conducted himself, knowing what was going on inside him.

"As we spoke, John slipped and called us the Devil Rays. Our franchise had just changed its name from Devil Rays to Rays, and to help enforce the name change we imposed a dollar fine on anyone who referred to us by our former name.

"I immediately told him that he owed me a buck. He didn't think it was fair and didn't want to pay it. But I insisted. 'You're no different than anyone else,' I gently scolded him.

"He eventually produced a bill, and I asked him to sign it. He did and then scrawled something else of his own making, his formula for living:

Courage + Believe = Life

"He nailed it with that thought, totally nailed it. The way any of us wish we could, I was completely in awe of this kid who was forced to mature so rapidly in the face of this terrible disease. He processed it the way I would think a grown man would have.

"A little less than two months later, John died. I still have the bill he signed and a ball. His uniform is framed in my office. And the red wristband I never remove is for the John Challis Courage for Life Foundation.

"The three letters at the top of my line-up card are also permanent. When things go too fast, or I get upset about something during the game, that message brings it back for me. Nothing gives me proper perspective than those three letters. Thank you, John. I will always be grateful."

Joe Maddon with the Challis family.

IF LIFE WERE FAIR THERE WOULD BE NO WHEELCHAIRS

PARKER LENTINI

At the age of 8, Parker Lentini of Tampa, Fla., was diagnosed with systemic juvenile onset arthritis. Now, years later, Parker has been able to endure many operations and much pain, thanks to his fondness for baseball in general and the Tampa Bay Rays in particular. His favorite player is Ben Zobrist, and his favorite manager is Joe Maddon. Little did he know that Lisa Andrews and her staff at the wonderful Make-A-Wish Foundation of Central and Northern Florida allowed him to meet his two heroes and much more. Now with Zobrist and Maddon at the Cubs, he's both a Rays and a Cubs fan.

I have something called systemic juvenile onset arthritis. It all started when I was 8-years-old. I used to be a very athletic kid who played a lot of sports. Slowly, I wasn't able to do that anymore because I was in pain. All the doctors said, "Oh, it's just growing pains. You're at that age."

When I was 10-years-old, I finally got diagnosed with juvenile rheumatoid arthritis. We thought, oh, arthritis. We can handle that. That's simple. Boy, were we wrong. We thought that arthritis was just in your joints. Well, I got diagnosed with the type of arthritis that affects my internal organs. On top of all of my joints and muscles hurting, my internal organs, like my lungs and heart, also get affected.

When I was 14, I had something called pericardial effusion, which is the swelling of my heart. If it were to swell more than it was, they would have had to drain the fluid of my heart. Luckily, we didn't get to that point. That's the moment when we finally realized that this disease isn't just joints. It affects all of my internal organs.

The juvenile arthritis was the start of it. Then I started getting overlapping syndromes like vasculitis and immune deficiency. It's called hypogammagloblinemia. Then I had an obstruction and restriction in my lungs, which made it hard to breathe, especially at night when I was sleeping. All these other diseases got tacked on to what was going on.

That got us to a point where we didn't know what to do. None of my medicine was working. We decided to do a study. In order to do that, we needed to stop all of my current medications. In doing so, man, I was in a lot of pain. In this study, you get either a placebo or you get the real drug for four weeks. Then, after that, you get the real drug guaranteed.

Unfortunately, I got the placebo. I went through some of the worst pain in my life. I went into something called MAS, which is Macrophage Activation Syndrome. It was bad. My doctor even came to me in tears. She said, "You can stop this. You don't need to continue the study. We can stop and go back on all of your meds and try to make things better." I looked at her, and I looked at my mom. I told them that there's no way I'm stopping this. Even if this makes me feel bad now, it will help other kids in the future, and that's what really matters.

I finished that study. That study was the best thing I ever did. Usually, I'm on a med for not even a year, and it stops working. That med lasted three years, which is the longest ever for me. I am so thankful that I went through that because I didn't know if it was going to help me at the time, but even if it didn't, to think that me going through this could help the other kids with arthritis in the future, that's what really mattered to me. I hate that I have to go through this, but I hate even more when I see some of my friends that are like 2-years-old going through this.

I had a life. I got to go through all those fun things that kids get to do. I got to play sports. Some of my friends were born with this. They'll never get to experience those things. Doing that study was my way of giving back.

I was always a big baseball fan and wanted to meet the players on my favorite team, the Tampa Bay Rays. That was my dream. I always told my mom about it. We didn't think I qualified for a Make-A-Wish, so we never really pushed for it. Out of nowhere, my mom decided to try. We were watching the Rays on TV when the doorbell rang. Two wonderful women came in. They told me that they were from Make-A-Wish, and they were going to be my wish granters. They had a bucket full of memorabilia from the Rays. They told me that I would get to meet Joe Maddon and Ben Zobrist of the Rays. They said that they would make it happen. They gave me a Rays hat, a Rays shirt, baseballs and Rays cowbells.

On the big day, the Rays put us up at the historic and beautiful Loews Don CeSar Hotel. They had a limo pick us up at the hotel to drive us to the Rays' stadium, Tropicana Field. We stopped at Subway first because I needed lunch. We took the limo to Subway, which was really different and fun. Then we rode to the stadium to meet the whole team, mainly Joe Maddon and Ben Zobrist because that was my big wish.

We got there, and there was a film crew plus paparazzi everywhere. It was so weird. I felt like a movie star. They were interviewing me. Can you believe that? We finally got into the stadium after 30 minutes of people wanting to talk to me and my family. When we got in, we met a woman named Jen Funk. She had a lot to do with putting my wish together. She gave me all sorts of more memorabilia. This was personalized memorabilia. I got a Rays jersey that had my last name on it. I got a baseball bat that had my name engraved in it with the Rays logo. And a bunch of baseballs for the Rays to sign.

Parker Lentini orders Joe Maddon to clean up his act or he'll
ship him off to Chicago.

We went down into the seating area of the stadium. At first, they walked us out onto the field because I always wanted to pretend I was at bat on the field. I had the bat they gave me. I was on the field, and my dad was pretending to pitch, and I was swinging. All of a sudden, I heard somebody say, "You've got good form."

It was Ben Zobrist. I was speechless. I didn't really know what to say. I knew that this was the moment that I was waiting for. I just sat there and talked to him and listened. Then I remembered that I had a couple of gifts for him and his family. I knew at the time that he had just had a newborn. He had his first child, and then he had a newborn. We got him baby toys, including a Tervis tumbler for him that was customized. It had Ben Zobrist printed on it.

After that, I went to the locker room. I thought my parents were following me the whole time, but apparently only I was allowed in the locker room. Ben gave me the whole grand tour. He gave me one of his baseball bats. He gave me a pair of his shoes. He gave me his batting gloves. He gave me a jersey that he wore in a game. He gave me all this stuff. I couldn't believe it.

After the tour, I got to meet a bunch of players inside the locker room, plus Joe Maddon. He was busy doing all of his pregame routine. I finally came out of the locker room, and I realized my parents weren't there. We went and ate lunch in the stadium with Ben and Joe. There's a VIP section that they have right next to the bullpen where we ate.

Then we sat near the dugout on the field, and Ben was giving me a bunch of his baseball cards that hadn't been released yet. They were for the next season. He had a couple of promo ones that he was supposed to keep. He gave me four of them that I could keep and give to my family, and he autographed them, all four.

Then, all of a sudden, Ben handed me a glove and a ball and asked if I wanted to play catch. That was my dream. My dream for this wish was to play catch on the field with Ben Zobrist, and that was happening. We played catch for awhile.

Then all the players had to get ready for pregame and do all of their stretches. The Rays had a little square on the field sectioned off for me and my family to stay in so we didn't get hit by any stray baseballs.

As they were doing their stretches, Joe Maddon came over and asked if I wanted to do the pregame interview with him. At the time, I thought he figured I would just stand there, but I had a couple of things I wanted to say. We were talking to the media and they asked me what I thought. At the time, we—the Rays—were trying out a six-man pitching rotation. They asked me my opinion on the six-man rotation, and I said I didn't like it. I said there should be a more stable line-up. Joe Maddon looked at me. He was like, this kid just came for my pregame interview, and now he's talking about my six-man rotation? You could tell he was thinking, is this really happening?

I gave my opinion. Then I went back to my little square and the first baseman, Casey Kotchman, was there. He looked at me and said, "Did you just talk about the six-man rotation?" I said, "Yeah. I told them I didn't like it." He said, "Oh, thank God. All of the players don't like it, and we didn't want to tell Joe. You just did it for us. That's great."

Throughout the day, I got to meet all of the players. They came by, and they kept telling me, "Thank you for that." I guess word got around that I said I didn't like the six-man rotation. All these players were coming around telling me that I did a great job, and I was just in awe.

I was getting autographs on all sorts of things, a little baseball bat, baseball cards that I brought, and a Tervis tumbler that I had just the inside of. Later, we got it made into a custom Tervis tumbler that has all of the autographs on it.

Ben Zobrist is my favorite player. When I was really little, I had a Ben Zobrist baseball card. I liked his card best because he was wearing sunglasses in the photograph. Not a lot of players were wearing sunglasses. One day I was sitting there watching baseball with my dad, and we were talking about it. It was right when Ben got brought up from the minor leagues. I was talking about how I liked him because I had his baseball card. About a month later, he was back in the minor leagues. I was sitting with my grandma watching baseball, and she was talking how she did not like the shortstop that we had then. She liked the guy from the minor leagues that they brought up and sent back down better.

I said, "Oh, you mean Ben Zobrist."

She said, "Yeah, that's the guy."

I felt special that I knew a player that my grandma didn't know because my grandma is also really into baseball. From that point on, I really liked him. I liked everything that he did. I thought it was really cool that he was able to play all these different positions. I don't know, a combination of all that made him my favorite player. He still is to this day.

I was heartbroken when Joe Maddon and Ben Zobrist left the Rays. I was so sad. I remember when Ben went to the World Series with Kansas City. I was rooting for him like crazy. I just kept saying, "Oh, I want the Royals to win." When he finally won, I was super excited, and I was cheering. Then, in the off-season, he went to the Cubs. I didn't know much about the Cubs, but my best friend and his family are huge, huge Cubs fans. In that way, I was a Cubs fan because I like to watch Cubs games with him. There are not many baseball teams that I like. I liked the Cubs just because my friend liked them.

I found out Ben went there, and that made me really excited. Of course, I knew Joe Maddon also was there. So that was really cool. Then I heard a couple of other Rays players were there. So, I slowly became a Cubs fan. I don't keep up with them nearly as much as the Rays. They're probably one of the other teams that I root for. I would love for them to go to the World Series, if not the Rays.

I liked Joe Maddon when he was managing the Rays. I thought he was a great manager. There were some things that he did that I questioned, but in the end, he got it done. He got them to the World Series. He got them to the playoffs a lot. There's nothing really bad I could say. I guess I talked him out of the six-man rotation with the Rays, but rumor has it he's going to start it soon to save the Cubs' arms. I just liked that he had a great personality in the interviews. A lot of the managers just sit there and talk in a monotone, but Maddon had all these quirks that were great. That whole 9=8, something crazy that he talked about that I just thought was funny. He had a personality to him, and I just loved that because a lot of the managers just sit there and do nothing. He made the best of the interviews and tried to make them fun.

When I met him, he was a lot nicer than I thought he'd be. I was expecting the manager to be super busy. He actually wanted to talk to me, which I didn't expect at all. That was really cool. Then a bunch of the players kept telling me that I looked like his son. I had the same style glasses. At the time, I dyed my hair blond. I looked just like him. That was also pretty funny.

When we did the pregame interview, there were a bunch of people asking questions, but it was just me and Joe Maddon answering. It wasn't filmed. It was for the newspapers. The main thing that he asked me to talk about was the six-man rotation. Otherwise, I just sat there and listened.

I was sad when Joe left the Rays and went to Chicago. He had been with us so long, and he had gotten us so far. When I heard he went to Chicago, I was happy for him. My friend was a big Chicago Cubs fan, so I was, too. I was like, it's not the worst team he could have gone to.

Typical Joe Maddon, having a good time while helping
other people.

I had my wish in 2011. I email Ben Zobrist once in a while or tweet him on Twitter. Ben and his whole family came to my arthritis walk, a walk to raise money for arthritis research. He came, did the walk with us, and hung out for the day, which was like really cool. That's the big arthritis event where my whole family and friends, everybody comes. It was cool because I got to see Ben again, but it was also cool because there were a lot of film crews there. It brought awareness to the whole walk to cure arthritis. The walk itself is only 30 minutes, but it's a whole day event. It's about four hours at a park, and we all just hang out and have fun.

I've thought about being a sportswriter or a sportscaster. For a while, I wanted to be the person who talks over the game on TV, the color analyst. I don't know. It all depends on what happens in life.

Currently, I'm not in school. I'm looking to get my GED this fall, and I'm going to start college in the winter or spring. I'm going to go to community college until I get my AA, and then I'll think about going to the University of South Florida or the University of Florida.

We're still friends with Jen Funk. She's working with the Pediatric Cancer Foundation in Chicago. She's really someone special. I was in the hospital for quite some time. When I came home from one of my many hospital stays, she had this huge basket for me from all the Rays. She's great. She still communicates with us via Facebook, email. She keeps up with our family.

Joe Maddon has done so much for Tampa. He was very active, always giving back. He would go in and make a whole Thanksgiving feast for the downtrodden. He was the chef. He's incredible, a really great guy.

On my Make-A-Wish day, I went into that stadium in my wheelchair. I was having a hard time walking. This past year I had reconstructive surgery on my feet, ankles and tibia. Once

I got into the stadium and met Ben, I stood up and did not sit back down the whole time we were there.

It was the excitement. I don't like being in my wheelchair. I don't want people to treat me differently. I wanted to stand up. Whenever I meet someone new, I like to make my first impression out of the chair, so they don't treat me differently. It was a combination of the excitement and adrenaline and all that just mushed together. I didn't want to sit down. I was so excited. It was the best day of my life.

Joe Maddon spent so much time with me. It was like a big whirlwind, but he must have been with me for nearly an hour. He had all the local radio and TV guys and the newspaper guys doing the pregame work. They talked quite a bit. I sat there probably a good five minutes listening. Then I started answering the questions. Then they started directing more questions toward me, which was pretty cool. Joe was very, very nice. He came over to the entire family. My brother was there, too. Joe made it a point to sit and talk to my brother for a couple of minutes, which was nice.

I will remember that day until my last day on earth, thanks to Ben Zobrist and Joe Maddon.

THERE WERE NO ST. LOUIS CARDINALS FANS HARMED DURING THE MAKING OF THIS BOOK.

The first of many curves
in the bleacher area

Cubs fans' view of a Sammy Sosa home run ball

Cardinals fans' view of a Sammy Sosa home run ball

Other Books by Rich Wolfe

I Remember Harry Caray
Ron Santo, A Perfect 10
For Cubs Fans Only
For Cubs Fans Only—Volume II
Da Coach (Mike Ditka)
Take This Job and Love It! (Jim Harbaugh)
Tim Russert, We Heartily Knew Ya
Oh, What a Knight (Bob Knight)
There's No Expiration Date on Dreams (Tom Brady)
He Graduated Life with Honors and No Regrets (Pat Tillman)
Take This Job and Love It (Jon Gruden)
Been There, Shoulda Done That (John Daly)
Jeremy Lin, The Asian Sensation
And the Last Shall Be First (Kurt Warner)
He Left His Heart in San Diego (Tony Gwynn)
I Saw It On the Radio (Vin Scully)
The Real McCoy (Al McCoy, Phoenix Suns announcer)
I Love It, I Love It, I Love It (with Jim Zabel, Iowa announcer)
Personal Foul (with Tim Donaghy, former NBA referee)
The Least Likely to Succeed (Food Network Founder)
Remembering Jack Buck
Remembering Harry Kalas
Remembering Dale Earnhardt
Sports Fans Who Made Headlines
Fandemonium
For Notre Dame Fans Only—The New Saturday Bible
For Cardinals Fans Only—Volume I
For Yankee Fans Only
For Yankee Fans Only—Volume II
For Red Sox Fans Only
For Browns Fans Only
For Mets Fans Only
For Bronco Fans Only
For Michigan Fans Only
For Milwaukee Braves Fans Only
For Nebraska Fans Only
For Buckeye Fans Only
For Georgia Bulldog Fans Only
For South Carolina Fans Only
For Clemson Fans Only
For Oklahoma Fans Only
For Mizzou Fans Only
For Kansas City Chiefs Fans Only

For K-State Fans Only
For KU Fans Only (Kansas)
For Phillies Fans Only
For Packers Fans Only
For Hawkeye Fans Only

All books are the same size, format and price.
Questions or to order? Contact the author directly at (602) 738-5889 or at rjwolfe52@gmail.com.

IF YOU LIKED THIS YEAR, JUST WAIT 'TIL NEXT YEAR.